Counseling With Native American Indians and Alaska Natives

MULTICULTURAL ASPECTS OF COUNSELING SERIES

SERIES EDITOR

Paul Pedersen, Ph.D., *University of Alabama at Birmingham*

EDITORIAL BOARD

VOLUMES IN THIS SERIES

1. **Increasing Multicultural Understanding (2nd edition): A Comprehensive Model**
   by Don C. Locke

2. **Preventing Prejudice: A Guide for Counselors and Educators**
   by Joseph G. Ponterotto and Paul B. Pedersen

3. **Improving Intercultural Interactions: Modules for Cross-Cultural Training Programs**
   edited by Richard W. Brislin and Tomoko Yoshida

4. **Assessing and Treating Culturally Diverse Clients (2nd edition): A Practical Guide**
   by Freddy A. Paniagua

5. **Overcoming Unintentional Racism in Counseling and Therapy: A Practitioner's Guide to Intentional Intervention**
   by Charles R. Ridley

6. **Multicultural Counseling With Teenage Fathers: A Practical Guide**
   by Mark S. Kiselica

7. **Multicultural Counseling Competencies: Assessment, Education and Training, and Supervision**
   edited by Donald B. Pope-Davis and Hardin L. K. Coleman

8. **Improving Intercultural Interactions: Modules for Cross-Cultural Training Programs, Volume 2**
   edited by Kenneth Cushner and Richard W. Brislin

9. **Understanding Cultural Identity in Intervention and Assessment**
   by Richard H. Dana

10. **Psychological Testing of American Minorities (2nd edition)**
    by Ronald J. Samuda

11. **Multicultural Counseling Competencies: Individual and Organizational Development**
    by Derald Wing Sue et al.

12. **Counseling Multiracial Families**
    by Bea Wehrly, Kelley R. Kenney, and Mark E. Kenney

13. **Integrating Spirituality Into Multicultural Counseling**
    by Mary A. Fukuyama and Todd D. Sevig

14. **Counseling With Native American Indians and Alaska Natives: Strategies for Helping Professionals**
    by Roger D. Herring

Counseling With Native American Indians and Alaska Natives

Strategies for Helping Professionals

Roger D. Herring

Multicultural Aspects of Counseling Series 14

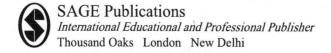

SAGE Publications
International Educational and Professional Publisher
Thousand Oaks   London   New Delhi

For information:

SAGE Publications, Inc.
2455 Teller Road
Thousand Oaks, California 91320
E-mail: order@sagepub.com

SAGE Publications Ltd.
6 Bonhill Street
London EC2A 4PU
United Kingdom

SAGE Publications India Pvt. Ltd.
M-32 Market
Greater Kailash I
New Delhi 110 048 India

Printed in the United States of America

Library of Congress Cataloging-in-Publication Data

Herring, Roger D.
    Counseling With Native American Indians and Alaska Natives:
Strategies for helping professionals / by Roger D. Herring.
      p. cm.—(Multicultural aspects of counseling series; v. 14)
    Includes bibliographical references and index.
    ISBN 0-7619-1386-6 (cloth: alk. paper)
    ISBN 0-7619-1387-4 (pbk.: alk. paper)
    1. Indians of North America—Services for. 2. Indians of North America—
Counseling of. 3. Indians of North America—Mental health services.
4. Social work with Indians—North America. I. Title. II. Series.
E98.S46 H47   1999
362.2′04256′08997—dc21   99-6396

This book is printed on acid-free paper.

99 00 01 02 03 04 05 7 6 5 4 3 2 1

Acquiring Editor:	Kassie Gavrilis
Editorial Assistant:	Heidi Van Middlesworth
Production Editor:	Wendy Westgate
Production Assistant:	Patricia Zeman
Typesetter:	Lynn Miyata
Cover Designer:	Candice Harman

Contents

Preface   ix

Overview   xi

Acknowledgments   xiii

Series Editor's Introduction   xv
    Paul Pedersen

1. Terminology and Demographic Distinctions   1
    Terminology Distinctions Regarding Groups   2
    Demographic Distinctions of Groups   4
    Summary   18
    Experiential Activities   19

2. Assessing Native Populations   20
    Concerns Pertaining to Assessment With Native Populations   21
    Issues to Consider in the Assessment Process   26
    Intellectual and Personality Assessment   35
    Value of Synergetic Assessment   43
    Summary   47
    Experiential Activities   48

3. Counseling Native American Indian/Alaska Native Youth ... 49
   Native Culture: The Key to Counseling Practice ... 50
   Effective Counseling With Native Youth ... 54
   Summary ... 66
   Experiential Activities ... 67

4. Counseling Native Adults ... 68
   Historical Overview ... 68
   Contemporary Demographics and Diversity ... 69
   Native Culture: The Key to Counseling Practice ... 71
   Conducting the Counseling Session ... 75
   Additional Implications for Interventions ... 76
   Summary ... 82

5. Career Development and Counseling With Native Populations ... 84
   Definitions, Demographics, and Theories ... 85
   Sociocultural Factors ... 88
   Major Psychosocial Factors ... 92
   Standardized Career Assessment ... 94
   Career Counseling With Native Youth ... 95
   Summary ... 102
   Experiential Activities ... 103

6. Using the Creative Arts in Counseling Native Populations ... 104
   Creative Art Mediums and Their Implications
     for Counseling ... 104
   Advantages and Limitations of the Use of
     Creative Arts in Counseling ... 119
   Summary ... 120
   Experiential Activities ... 121

7. Implications for Training, Practice, and Research ... 122
   Expanding the Political Agenda ... 123
   Implications for Training ... 124
   Implications for Practice ... 126
   Implications for Research ... 129
   Summary ... 136
   Experiential Activities ... 136

Appendix: Additional Resources ... 137
   Reproducible Resources ... 137
   Films and Videos ... 138
   Reservations ... 138

Literature   139
Music   144
Education   144
Selected Native Organizations   145

References   147

Author Index   169

Subject Index   177

About the Author   183

Preface

The five major ethnic groups of the United States are African Americans, Native American Indians/Alaska Natives, Asian Americans, Hispanic Americans, and European Americans. The mental health literature in many disciplines (e.g., psychology, psychiatry, social work, family therapy, counseling) is replete with assessment and treatment modalities for each of these ethnic groups, with the exception of Native American Indian and Alaska Native populations. One purpose of this book is to add to the sparse materials available relative to this population.

The code of ethics of the American Psychological Association (1992) states that helping professionals "must be aware of cultural, individual, and role differences, including those due to age, gender, race, ethnicity, national origin, religion . . . language, and socioeconomic status" (pp. 3-4). A second purpose of this book is to provide ethnic-specific information to avoid any principle that would be considered a case of "unfair discriminatory practices" (p. 3) and to eliminate such practices.

Early Spanish explorers first gave one name, "Indios," to all the indigenous peoples living in the new world, rather than seeing them as individual groups (Berkhoffer, 1978). When the Europeans first sailed to this land, at least "two thousand cultures and more societies practiced a multiplicity of customs and lifestyles, held an enormous variety of values and beliefs, spoke numerous languages mutually unintelligible to the many speakers, and did not conceive of themselves as a single people—if they knew about each other at all" (Berkhoffer, 1978, p. 3).

Since the time of Columbus, the dominant culture's concept of Native peoples has been characterized by inaccurate and conflicting images. They were romanticized as innocent savages living in a primitive paradise or reviled as heathens and bloodthirsty demons. Explorers, settlers, missionaries, and political leaders all exploited these images for their own purposes. In essence, Native cultures have been viewed as inferior to European beliefs and values. In retrospect, the "humanistic" policies of advocates for Native peoples (e.g., 18th-century reforms to "educate the Indian out of the Indian") have been almost as devastating as the U.S. Army's genocidal policies (Berkhoffer, 1978).

Such is the history of the population that will be discussed in the subsequent chapters. I hope the story will be told accurately and appropriately. In the words of Mary Catherine Bateson (1994), "What would it be like to have not only color vision but culture vision, the ability to see the multiple worlds of others" (p. 53).

Overview

Descriptions of Native American Indian and Alaska Native cultural variables reflect generalizations across nations, tribes, and clans. The diversity and within-group differentiations of this population are too complex to be addressed in a brief volume. There are differences across the subgroups of this population in terms of primary language, residence (i.e., rural, urban, reservation), degree of acculturation (i.e., pantraditional, traditional, transitional, bicultural, assimilated), and socioeconomic status (Herring, 1997a). Nevertheless, shared cultural variables do exist and are relevant to the assessment and intervention of this population. This sharing of cultural variables might be termed "cultural commonalities" (Chung, 1992).

Many helping professionals will have only limited opportunities to work with Native peoples or to conduct research with Native populations. Some will believe, therefore, that they need not attempt to become effective helping professionals for Native individuals. Others will concede that attempts to become effective with Native peoples are important, but will state that such attempts should be left to Native professionals. The reality is that the number of Native professionals is so small that Native clients are most likely to be treated by non-Native helping professionals. With this is mind, information is presented in this text that is useful for professionals who become involved in the helping process with Native peoples.

This book comprises seven chapters and addresses the status of Native American Indian and Alaska Natives in contemporary society. Chapter 1 focuses on terminology and demographics. Chapter 2 discusses the applicability of assessment instruments to this population. Chapter 3 highlights youth, and Chapter 4 addresses adult clients. Chapter 5 discusses career development and counseling issues. Chapter 6 presents the importance of the creative arts as counseling and guidance techniques. Chapter 7 stresses implications for training, practice, and research with Native American Indian and Alaska Natives. The Appendix presents additional resources for the reader's attention.

This book is not intended to elaborate on Native American Indian and Alaska Native teachings or ceremonies. Those readers wanting more in-depth discussions on that topic are directed to find an individual teacher or to study more narrowly focused literature. This book is designed as a tool to help the reader eliminate inappropriate content and process concerns and replace them with appropriate ones in the delivery of mental health services to indigenous populations.

Acknowledgments

I am indebted to many individuals whose support and advice greatly determined the completion of this book. I want to thank Timothy C. Thomason for his initial review of the prospectus for this project.

I thank Paul Pedersen, Series Editor, who was instrumental in the final preparation of this book for publication. It was he who first suggested that I undertake this project. In addition, I thank Don C. Locke, Action Editor, for his valuable comments and suggestions.

I also want to thank the staff at Sage Publications for their time and effort in the preparation of the book. I particularly thank Jim Nageotte, Editor, and Tracy Tomakin, Contract Administrator, for their commitment to this book. And last, but most assuredly not least, my thanks to Kate W. Harris, copy editor, for her invaluable skills.

Appreciation is also offered to the administration of the University of Arkansas-Little Rock, who supported my request for a sabbatical to complete this book. And a special thanks goes to my graduate assistant, Angela Thompson.

Series Editor's Introduction

The construct "synergetic" is defined as "working with . . . cooperating . . . or working together," which makes it an excellent descriptor for the strategies in Herring's book about Native American Indians. The objective of this book is not just to demonstrate how the very diversified Native American Indian tribes and peoples have learned to work together but also how we non-Native Americans can also cooperate as helping professionals. The book has a very positive and upbeat tone throughout that will help the reader learn at three levels. First, the reader will learn something about the diverse Native American Indian communities, which are similar and different at the same time. Second, the reader will learn something about him or herself as viewed from the perspective of the Native American Indian communities. Third, and perhaps most important, the reader will learn something about the future. With demographic trends moving toward a multicultural future, many minority groups are increasing in size proportionate to the white, middle-class dominant culture groups. Many of these rapidly growing populations tend to be more collectivist and less individualist, coming from Hispanic, Asian, or African American backgrounds where cooperation was both a necessity and a historical reality. Many of those values for working with . . . cooperating . . . and working together are reflected in the Native American Indian communities described in Herring's book. These may well be a preview of the "new rules" that will govern the lives of our children and our children's children.

The books in this **Multicultural Aspects of Counseling** series have emphasized practical strategies, an inclusive definition of culture, and a concise and economical perspective of problems confronting the helping professional in our multicultural society. This book fits well with this pattern. Herring includes case examples so that his statements are grounded not just in citations but also in narrative descriptions of reality. He provides experiential exercises so that teachers using this book can involve themselves and their students as active, not passive, participants in the learning process. He cites extensive references for those who want to go beyond this book in their learning about counseling across the Native American Indian communities. He provides definitions of often ambiguous or undefined terms to prevent confusion. Each chapter is summarized so readers can determine how well they understood what was said. Herring relates the experiences of Native American Indians to those of other ethnic minorities by connecting multicultural models to the Native American Indian communities. Herring also puts a lot of himself into this obviously very personal declaration of his own ideas and beliefs.

The **Multicultural Aspects of Counseling** series has emphasized the generic importance of culture to the counselor process. Herring tells us stories about what culture means to others and to ourselves. This book builds on that series by giving readers an "insider's view" of the values and beliefs of peoples living throughout the lower 48 states and in the vastness of Alaska. Readers are given the opportunity to "see" many different peoples and the helping professionals among them. If readers look very closely, they will see themselves.

Paul Pedersen
University of Alabama at Birmingham

1

Terminology and
Demographic Distinctions

This chapter will assist helping professionals in developing basic skills for proactive counseling interventions with Native American Indian and Alaska Native peoples. For purposes of clarity, this text will address the mental health conditions of only those indigenous peoples who are Native American Indians and Alaska Natives. Hawaiians, natives of Guam (Chamorro), Samoans, and Puerto Ricans, who are also indigenous peoples, are not indigenous to the North American continent and will be excluded from this discussion. In addition, the adjective "Native" will be used as a referent rather than overusing the terms "Native American Indian" and "Alaska Native" when referring to both groups. Ethnic-specific referents will be employed when the discussion or example warrants such specificity.

A major obstacle to providing effective and appropriate helping services for Native peoples is the lack of acknowledgment of within-group differences. Historically, the development and consequences of issues such as cultural mistrust, ethnic identity, and self-esteem for various Native groups in the United States have been inadequately examined. Moreover, the limited literature that does exist tends to emphasize between-group rather than within-group differences. Such research efforts have resulted in an impression of a homogeneous, monolithic Native population. Thus, continuing edicts call for more systematic examination of Native within-group variation (e.g., Atkinson & Thompson, 1992). The examination of within-group variation appears particularly relevant for Native peoples because of their varied histories, multifaceted influences, and diverse circumstances.

Another major obstacle to providing successful helping practices for indigenous peoples is reflected in the ambiguous, and often erroneous, terminology assigned to these populations. For example, a common myth about Native American Indian and Alaska Native groups is that they are all alike, which, of course, is not true. The diversity within these groups requires recognition of and differentiation among the various terms and labels associated with them. Hunkpapa and Lakota individuals are very different, even though they are both members of the Sioux Nation. Such is also the case with Aleuts and Inuits, both being Alaska Natives. This chapter will begin with a discussion of these two aspects of Native populations.

Terminology Distinctions
Regarding Groups

As Herring (1991, 1997a, 1997b) noted, a generic term for the indigenous peoples of the United States is nonexistent. *American Indian* is one label that has been used to refer to all indigenous peoples of North America, "including Indians, Alaska Natives, Aleuts, Eskimos, and Metis, or mixed bloods" (LaFromboise & Graff Low, 1998, p. 115), and to Mexican Indians, Indians of Central America, and Brazilian Indians. The use of multiple definitions, however, compounds the ethnic self-identification issue for these peoples. Other commonly used designations include: Native American, First or Original American, Alaska Native, Amerindian, or Amerind. However, negative and resented aspects are imbedded in each of these designations. For example, although the term "American Indian" is preferred by most Native nations and federal organizations, a valid objection to its use exists. At best, it is "a generalized gloss that was first foisted upon the Arawak, a now-extinct tribe once indigenous to islands off the southeastern coast of the United States, by a wayward Italian sailor who thought he had reached India" (Trimble, Fleming, Beauvais, & Jumper-Thurman, 1996). For many contemporary indigenous individuals, the continued use of that term perpetuates this misconception. The term "Native American Indian" will be used in this book as the referent to persons indigenous to the lower 48 states; "Alaska Native" will identify indigenous peoples of Alaska. The reader will note that several Native American Indian groups do reside in Alaska and will be subsumed under the term "Alaska Native."

Ideally, nation affiliation is the appropriate choice of identification for these populations, rather than a generic label. Most Native entities have historically considered themselves as the First Nations, and early writings and documents have used that referent. In addition, relationships between Native groups and the federal government have always been based on individual Indian sovereignties rather than on individual states of the union. Native American Indian and Alaska Native people tend to identify as members of a nation first, a tribe second, and then as Native American Indians or Alaska Natives.

"Tribe" generally refers to a kin-based society (Winthrop, 1991) or "a group which possesses social institutions but not political ones" (Seymour-Smith, 1986). A "nation" has political organization and a differentiated administrative structure (Winthrop, 1991). Although kin-based social units are common in most Native communities, Native societies today are nations that have been organized around democratic authority and political institutions: council government, chief executive officer, and judiciary. Using appropriate designations for nation and tribe recognizes the diversity of these people and may enhance pride in self and community, especially for children and adolescents.

Adding to the problem of terminology is a definitional problem related to the question of who is a Native American Indian or an Alaska Native. The Indian Law Center at the University of New Mexico has documented 52 different definitions or sets of criteria used in law to define an "Indian" (American Indian Education Handbook Committee, 1982). The Bureau of Indian Affairs (BIA), once under the Department of War and now under the Department of the Interior, defines a Native American Indian as a person whose blood quantum (i.e., degree of Native blood) is at least one fourth. Any less than one fourth and the individual is not eligible for BIA services (LaFromboise & Graff Low, 1998).

The Department of Education's definition, however, includes these criteria: tribal recognition (some do not require one fourth blood quantum), a descendant in the first or second degree of someone who is a tribal member (child or grandchild), someone who is considered to be an "Indian" by the Secretary of the Interior for any purpose, and an Eskimo (Inuit), Aleut, or Alaskan Native (Indian Fellowship Program, 1989). The choice of definition ultimately depends on the legal application of the term.

Similar to the term Native American Indian, Alaska Native subsumes the uniqueness of the many native peoples of Alaska, with its implication of a singular ethnic group. Many indigenous peoples (of the Athabascan linguistic group) make up the Alaska population including the North/West/South Inuit (Eskimo), Aleuts, Ingalik, Tanana, Tanaina, Ahtena, Eyak, and Koyukon. Another similarity to the Native American Indian of the lower states can be observed in the application of ethnic stereotypes. Whereas many people stereotype the Native American Indian as being represented by the characteristics of the Plains Sioux, the same can be said about Alaska Natives being characterized by the Inuit (Eskimo) peoples.

In addition to multiple designations, some individuals advocate that if a person is not full-blooded, then that person is not a true Native person. Differences in blood quantum and "Indianness" are based in "legalistic genetics," imposed largely from the outside and rooted in a European American paradigm (Wax, Wax, & Dumont, 1989). Also, as Peregoy (1993) emphasized, ethnic self-identity is "not only a blood quantum or lineage relationship, but more specifically, a relationship of sociocultural affiliation, embedded in reciprocal recognition" (p. 166). Finally, a person of mixed descent is no less than full-blood if the person's heart and soul are intertwined with the ethnic community (Wilson, 1992) as many "breeds" are often much more "native oriented" than many so-called "pure" Indians (Trimble et al., 1996).

Ambiguous terminology can have a particularly profound impact on traditional Native youth. Already confused about their ethnic identity due to their historical legacy, the additional burden of being mislabeled further hinders the development of a positive self-concept among many Native children and adolescents (Herring, 1991).

Such ambiguity affects not only how Native peoples view themselves, but also how ethnic-dissimilar individuals perceive them. One of the most significant of these misperceptions is that Native peoples represent one people with one set of needs. Such narrow perceptions tend to limit Native youths' vision of themselves, their potentialities, and their futures (Schafer, 1990). On the positive side, however, after more than 500 years of contact with European Americans, Native peoples have survived with both a distinct identity and a commitment to their people, regardless of the pain and consequence endured (Peregoy, 1993, 1999).

Demographic Distinctions of Groups

In addition to the ambiguity found in terminology, misinformation and myths are also inherent in demographic data concerning Native peoples. Native populations are culturally heterogeneous, geographically dispersed, and remarkably young. This discussion of demographic distinctions looks first at data relevant to Alaska Natives.

The Alaska Native

No Eskimo (Inuit) group has been studied more than the small group of Polar Eskimos of northwestern Greenland, the most northern native inhabitants of the world. They have been described by explorers, examined by anthropologists, idealized by novelists, and lionized by journalists since their

---

Testimony 1.1

Anonymous, Eskimo (Inuit)

We're not just Eskimos anymore. That's what my grandmother told me. At first I didn't know what she meant, but now I do. She meant what she said! She said that in this family we have Alaska's last and its first Eskimos. She was lying down, and I thought she was going to fall asleep after she told me that, but she didn't. She sat up, all of a sudden. She said that she was one of "the last." She said I'm one of "the first." She said I'd be lucky if I even remember when I'm older what it used to be like in our village. She said she's the child and I'm the grown-up, only she won't live long enough for me to teach her what I know.

I thought she was talking in her sleep. I didn't understand her at all! But she helped me out. She put her head down on the bed again. She stared at the ceiling, and started describing what she did when she was my age. Then she told me what my mother did at my age—the same thing her mother did.

But it's different for me, I know. I learned in school from the teachers how planes fly. They told us! I told my grandmother, and my mother. They laughed. They said that's for me to know. I've never seen a whale. I don't like fish. My mother says I'm the first Eskimo she's met who doesn't like fish. I told her she may be the last one in our family to like it so much!

---

displacement from their favored fjord in 1953 by U.S. military personnel (Harper, 1986). Their stories have been told, analyzed, and retold by numerous adventurers and academics whose international reputations received initial boosts from their work among the Polar Eskimos. Across the continent are other indigenous peoples who have a common historical and contemporary bond—the Alaska Native peoples. A brief background discussion about the two predominant Alaska Native groups will illustrate this kinship.

Inuit (Eskimo). Historically, the local peoples referred to themselves as simply *Inuit*—"The People." The name *Eskimo*, meaning "raw flesh eaters," was bestowed on them by Algonquian Indians and adopted by the world at large (Maxwell, 1990). Although cognizant of the fact that some Inuits prefer to be known as Eskimos today, I will nonetheless use the term *Inuit* when appropriate, to be consistent in avoiding a demeaning stereotypical label.

In many ways the Inuits are the most remarkable of all the Native peoples of North America. They inhabit the harshest natural environment on the earth—the desolate lands of the Arctic Ocean. Never exceeding 90,000 in number, their existence was historically dependent solely on the meager resources of snow and stone, animal skin and bone. Yet they have survived centuries of migratory travelings (see Testimony 1.1).

Historically, Inuits shared a deep-rooted belief in the supernatural, and their daily lives were directed by concerns about human and animal souls, good and evil spirits, ghosts, monsters, and deities. They believed in numerous taboos, which, if broken, could evoke the wrath of the spirit world. All Inuits relied on shamans, half priests and half sorcerers, to protect them and the community against the unpredictable whims of the supernatural world.

By the 1920s, Inuit traditional life was all but extinct. The white man's culture permeated their very existence. Anthropologist Diamond Jenness described its impact (Maxwell, 1990):

> We replaced their stone knives with knives of steel, their bows and arrows with rifles and shotguns, their garments of caribou fur with clothes of factory-woven cotton and wool, their homemade boats with motorboats, their log cabins and snow huts warmed by lamps burning animal fat with frame houses heated with wood-burning and oil-burning stoves; and for the ancient songs and dances which relieved the tedium of their long winter nights we substituted Christian hymns. They may speak the Eskimo language still; they may still roam the hunting grounds of their forefathers; but most of them are Eskimos no longer. (p. 390)

The Aleuts. The Aleutian archipelago of nearly 100 treeless islands, located some 1,000 miles southwest of Alaska's southwest coast, is characterized as fog bound, cold, and damp. These islands have been home to the Aleuts for several thousand years. They speak a language related to that of the Inuits, with whom they share numerous characteristics.

The Aleuts traditionally derived much of their sustenance from the sea, but supplemented their sea mammal diet with birds, fish, shellfish, roots, and berries. They developed an expertise in deriving maximum benefit from the meager natural resources available to them. For example, waterproof parkas were fashioned from seal intestines. In addition, tools and weapons were fashioned from stones and bones.

Villages were generally situated along the coast and contained large communal houses called *barabaras*. They were partially underground and roofed with sod-covered driftwood or whale bones. Kinship was normally accounted in matrilineal terms, and boys were trained by maternal uncles. When a young man married, the couple lived for at least two years with the wife's parents.

Aleutian social organization more closely resembled Northwest Coast Indian societies than that of the Inuits. They existed within an extremely rank-conscious society, with each island and village having chiefs, the *toyons*, persons of wealth and social standing. The chiefs consulted with "honorables," the local nobility, and together they ruled over the commoners and slaves (usually orphans or captives from inter-island raids). Slaves, dentalium shells, amber, and decorated clothing were all signs of wealth and power.

In the 1740s, the traditional Aleutian life was destroyed with the occupation of the islands by Russian sea otter traders. The people adopted—or were forced to accept—a variety of foreign customs. They learned the Russian language, wore Russian clothes, gradually abandoned their semi-subterranean homes for box-like Russian-style houses, and even took Russian names— which most Aleutian islanders retain today. Thousands died from brutalities or "white man" diseases during the century-long occupation. By the time the United States took over the islands in 1867, the native population had dropped from more than 15,000 to 2,500. Currently, there are about 3,300 Aleutians, but only about half remain on the islands.

Current Conditions for Alaska Natives. Contemporary Alaska Natives are experiencing socioeconomic and political improvements very similar to those of the Native American Indians of the lower 48 states. Tribal autonomy and financial settlements have considerably enhanced the lives of these people, yet conditions continue to be deplorable for many. Both the state and federal governments are endeavoring to ensure equitable and appropriate educational opportunities.

Many of the cultural values and belief structures of Alaska Natives are analogous with those of the Native American Indians of the lower states. Similarly, many of the counseling endeavors and strategies discussed in this book may be adapted to address the mental health and development concerns of both groups.

The Native American Indian

Actual counts of the numbers of Natives residing in North America at the time of Columbus's alleged discovery vary. Estimates range from as few as 800,000 to as many as 9,000,000. Josephy (1968) noted that Native American Indians were speaking no less than 2,200 different languages and dialects, and some 200 languages were mutually unintelligible. In appearance there were and are some similarities: hair and eye color, dental patterns, amount of body and facial hair, and skin tone. However, in a sub-band of the Mandan-Hidatsa, blue eyes, blond and brown hair, and a light skin tone were prevalent. In today's context, largely because of intermarriage, the physical characteristics of Native American Indians have changed dramatically.

Native American Indian groups have been involved for nearly 500 years in a defensive war to retain their traditional rights: freedom from governmental tyranny, ownership of their ancestral lands, traditional tribal organizations, traditions and beliefs, historical way of life, and, in fact, their very existence (Herring, 1997a). Their numbers have been decimated by wars with European Americans (declared and undeclared) and through diseases brought by the early colonizers. After initial European contact in 1492, the native population was reduced considerably, to about 250,000 in 1850. People talked then about the "vanishing American" and the complete submission of the rebellious "savage" (Trimble et al., 1996). By 1900, the Native American Indian population had reached its lowest point. This was followed by a slow increase to approximately 650,000 in 1960. Atkinson, Morten, and Sue (1998) observed that although "the population increased by 21.6% in the 1980s (now at 2.2 million—less than 1% of the U.S. population), this cultural genocide continues to exist" (p. 133).

Oklahoma has the largest Native American Indian population (252,000), followed by California (244,000) and Arizona (204,000) (U.S. Bureau of the Census, 1996). Members of the Cherokee Nation, who reside in several southern and southwestern states, make up what appears to be the largest tribe, with more than 369,000 members. However, if one considers only one Nation in one geographical location, the Navajo are the largest Nation. Numerous tribes (i.e., bands) have as few as five members, and some may have only one remaining survivor.

Two of the least acknowledged characteristics of these peoples are their diversity and their current conditions of life. Brief discussions of these aspects will be presented to enhance the reader's understanding of these factors.

Diversity. The 1990 census reported the Native American Indian population as approximately 1.96 million (U.S. Bureau of the Census, 1993b). Although Native American Indians account for only about 1% of the total U.S. population, they have been described as comprising "fifty percent of the diversity" in the United States (Hodgkinson, 1990). This relatively high percentage is derived from the hundreds of different nations and tribes with diverse languages, customs, and socioeconomic conditions. That census also verified a lessening of the trend toward increased urbanization for subsistence and for gainful employment, which occurred among Native American Indians in the 1970s and 1980s (Snipp, 1996). In 1990, at least 63% of all Native American Indians lived off reservations, an increase from 50% in 1980, with large enclaves in urban areas; moreover, 22% lived on reservations, 10% lived in tribal jurisdiction statistical areas (the historically Native American Indian areas of Oklahoma), 2% lived in Alaska Native villages, and 3% lived in tribal designated statistical areas (Herring, 1997a; Snipp, 1996; U.S. Bureau of the Census, 1990). A major result of this shift is seen in the increase of intertribal and interethnic marriages. Today, over 60% of

Native American Indians are of mixed ancestry, resulting from marriages and couplings with African Americans, European Americans, Hispanics, and dissimilar tribal individuals (Herring, 1994).

Nearly 39% of Native American Indians are under 20 years of age (U.S. Bureau of the Census, 1990). Moreover, the median age of Native American Indians (26.7 years) is significantly younger than the median age of the U.S. population in general (33 years). Recent projections suggest that the Native American Indian population is likely to double within the next 15 years, proportionately the fastest growing ethnic group in the United States (Herring, 1992, 1997c). However, this prediction is considered controversial in that many individuals claim Native American Indian heritage. In addition, the increase in marriages and couplings with non-Native American Indians will decrease the actual number of Native American Indians with traditional lifestyles, which include tribal language and tribal rituals.

Diversity is also noted in the existence of the 547 federally recognized Native entities (226 in Alaska, 321 in the lower states), 365 state recognized tribes, and 52 tribes without official recognition—not to mention that more than 200 tribal languages are still spoken (Bureau of Indian Affairs, 1993; Herring, 1997b). These figures change frequently as more and more Native entities petition for federal and state recognition.

This diversity can also be seen in varying degrees of cultural commitment among members of a given tribe based on variances in value orientation (LaFromboise, Trimble, & Mohatt, 1990). This trend is especially apparent in varying family patterns and styles of parenting.

The preceding demographic discussion illustrates that the contemporary Native American Indian is not isolated on a reservation but is often a member of the general community (Peregoy, 1991, 1999). The discussion also supports the view that Native American Indian populations are culturally heterogeneous, geographically dispersed, and remarkably young, giving credibility to the need for increased attention to helping services within educational settings (LaFromboise, 1998).

Regardless of the immense diversity and varying demographics reflected in the Native American Indian population, common threads are woven throughout this population. For example, a prevailing sense of "Indianness" based on a common worldview appears to bind Native American Indians together as a "people of many peoples" (Garrett & Garrett, 1994).

Current Conditions. Historical and contemporary discriminatory policies and practices have devastated the standard of living of Native American Indians and created major cultural conflicts. As summarized by Atkinson, Morten, and Sue (1998), the current plight of Native American Indians is tremendous: (a) death from alcoholism is six times greater and terminal liver cirrhosis is 14 times greater than in the general population; (b) suicide rates are twice the national average; (c) average income is 75% less than that of European Americans; (d) unemployment is 10 times the national average; (e) dropout rates are higher and educational attainment is the lowest of any ethnic group; (f) infant mortality after the first three months of life is three times the national average; and (g) delinquency and mental illness far surpass most other groups (p. 133).

In addition, Native American Indian peoples have been further affected by recent national economic cycles. Between 1980 and 1990 their unemployment rate increased 12.6%. This rate hovers at about 46% and ranges from a high of over 80% on some reservations to a low of 0% in the case of more prosperous tribes (Kaufman & Joseph-Fox, 1996; U.S. Bureau of the Census, 1993a).

By almost all economic indicators of poverty, Native American Indians can be classified as the "poorest of the poor" in this nation. Poverty and prolonged unemployment have combined with substandard housing, malnutrition, inadequate health care, shortened life expectancy, and high suicide rates to affect and limit opportunities for educational attainment (LaFromboise, 1998). To further complicate matters, some Native American Indians feel that they have no choice or control in their lives. The following quote from Warrior (1967, p. 72, as cited in Atkinson et al., 1998) illustrates the anger and frustration of these peoples:

> We are not free. We do not make choices. Our choices are made for us; we are the poor. For those of us who live on reservations these choices are made by federal administrators, bureaucrats, and their "yes men," euphemistically called tribal governments. Those of us who live in non-reservation areas have our lives controlled by local white power elites. We have many rulers. They are called social workers, "cops," school teachers, churches, etc. (p. 133)

The reader should note that Native American Indian peoples do experience many social, economic, and health problems. However, these problems are not insurmountable nor are Native American Indians only victims, incapable of improving their lives. In reality, thousands of Native American Indians have overcome their personal plights.

Ambiguous Cultural Terminology

This text does not emphasize any single tribe or nation but rather all the people who currently constitute the Native population of the United States. The emerging trend of viewing "within-group" differences among individuals from the same ethnic and cultural heritage (e.g., Oglala Sioux) is a central focus of this book, rather than viewing a generic group (e.g., the Sioux Nation).

To appreciate fully the differences within Native cultures, distinctions in terminology are necessary. The following discussion is intended to clarify misconceptions and establish terminological uniqueness. The more knowledgeable reader may perceive some of the material as tangential to the overall subject of this text. The discussion is included for the edification of the less knowledgeable reader. Whereas the material is not specific to Native individuals, its cogent value is beneficial. Helping professionals are alerted to the erroneous assumptions of these terms and are encouraged to use them in the proper context (Johnson, 1990).

Culture

There is considerable confusion in the general public and the helping professions about the terms *culture, race,* and *ethnicity.* The myriad of confusing definitions of culture can be clarified with the most succinct and useful one offered by Linton (1968), who defined culture as "the configuration of learned behavior and results of behavior whose components and elements are shared and transmitted by the members of a particular society" (p. 32). Every society that shares and transmits behaviors to its members has a culture (Atkinson et al., 1998).

Whitfield, McGrath, and Coleman (1992) identified 11 elements that can be used in understanding specific cultural patterns. Each element can be defined for any culture and can include how members in each culture tend to:

- Define their sense of self
- Communicate and use language
- Dress and value appearances
- Embrace certain values and mores
- Embrace specific beliefs and attitudes
- Use time and space
- Relate to family and significant others
- Eat and use food in their customs
- Play and make use of leisure time
- Work and apply themselves
- Learn and use knowledge

Emic, Etic, and Idioemic. Culture can also be seen from different perspectives. The terms *emic* and *etic* are frequently used to describe phenomena that have culture-specific (culturally localized) or universal (culturally generalized) application (Atkinson et al., 1998). These terms reflect contrasting perspectives in analyzing and describing cultural phenomena. The emic-etic dichotomy describes a way of viewing a culture either from the inside or from the outside. Whereas emic examines a given culture, rather than making an external comparison of cultures, etic focuses on similarities and dissimilarities of the cultures being examined (Draguns, 1996). Viewing a culture as represented by individuals could be described as taking an *idioemic* perspective (i.e., examining a particular manifestation of the emic). Thus, emic, etic, and idioemic are categorically related, as they are all classes of context, and none replicates the other exactly (Johnson, 1990).

Culturally Deprived Versus Culturally Disadvantaged. The discussion of culture cannot come to a conclusion without dismissing two terms, *culturally deprived* and *culturally disadvantaged.* Both of these labels have been applied to Native peoples. The term culturally deprived implies the absence of culture, a (perhaps hypothetical) situation that has no relationship to Native peoples. The term culturally disadvantaged suggests that the person to whom it is applied is at a disadvantage, lacking the cultural background formed by the controlling social structure. The use of "disadvantaged" rather than "deprived" is intended to recognize that the individual possesses a cultural heritage, but also implies it is not the *right* culture.

Even the more accepted terms, culturally different and culturally distinct, can have negative connotations when they are used to imply that a person's culture is at variance (out of step) with the dominant (accepted) culture (Atkinson et al., 1998). Taken literally, it is grammatically and conceptually correct to refer to a majority client or counselee as culturally different or culturally distinct from the helping professional if the helping professional is from an ethnic or cultural minority (Herring, 1997c).

Race

Whereas the concept of culture has been based on such characteristics as shared personality traits, values, belief systems, and life patterns, "race" has been defined in two ways: a biological classification and a biological social classification.

Biological Basis. The first definition is based solely on physical or biological characteristics. "To the biologist, a race, or subspecies, is an inbreeding, geographically isolated population that differs in distinguishable physical traits from other members of the species" (Zuckerman, 1990, p. 1297). To the social scientist, race is defined as "a geographical variety or subdivision of a species characterized by a more or less distinct combination of traits (morphological, behavioral, physiological) that are heritable" (Rushton, 1995, p. 40). Fundamental to a biological definition of race is the view that humans can be divided into a set number of genetic groups on the basis of physical characteristics (e.g., skin pigmentation, facial features, body hair type).

Race as a biological concept can be questioned on several grounds. When we look beneath the superficial characteristics used to categorize racial types, we find there are more similarities between groups than differences, and more differences within racial groups than between them (Littlefield, Lieberman, & Reynolds, 1982). Also, as Schaefer (1988) noted, "Given frequent migration, exploration, and invasions, pure gene frequencies have not existed for some time, if they ever did" (p. 12).

In addition, no biological explanation exists for why some physical features (e.g., skin color) have been selected to determine race while others (e.g., eye color) have not (Atkinson et al., 1998). "Many of the features are not correlated and none by themselves could furnish an indisputable guide to the anthropologists' definitions of racial groups" (Zuckerman, 1990, p. 1298). Moreover, scientists cannot agree on how many races there are, with estimates ranging from 3 to 200 (Schaefer, 1988). These concerns have spurred many social scientists to either redefine race or refrain from using the term in the literature (Allen & Adams, 1992; Dole, 1995; Yee, Fairchild, Weizmann, & Wyatt, 1993).

Biological Social Basis. A second definition of race combines biological and social components. Cox (1948) was among the first to define race from a social perspective, as "any people who are distinguished or consider themselves distinguished, in social relations with other peoples, by their physical characteristics" (p. 402). The social component is dependent on group identity, either evolving within the group or assigned by those outside the group (Atkinson et al., 1998). This definition is reinforced by Morris (1980) who defined race as "any group of people united or classified together on the basis of common history, nationality, or geographical distribution" (p. 1075). Regardless of its biological validity, the concept of race has taken on important social meaning in how outsiders view members of a racial group and how individuals within the racial group view themselves, members of their group, and members of other racial groups (Atkinson et al., 1998).

Conclusions. Similar to the biological perspective on race, the biological social perspective has not demonstrated much applicability. Ascribed and self-reported racial designations have not been shown to be effective in making meaningful distinctions between groups or adequate in amplifying within-group comparisons (Parham & Helms, 1982). The reality is that racial classifications draw attention to group characteristics, ignore or submerge the individual, and contribute to the perpetuation and maintenance of destructive racial stereotypes (Johnson, 1990).

Ethnicity

The term "ethnicity" also has two different perspectives, one broad and one narrow (Feagin, 1989). Bernal (1990) defined an ethnic group as "a group of individuals who interact, maintain themselves, have some social structure and system of governing norms and values, are biological and cultural descendants of a cultural group, and identify as members of the group" (p. 261). Similarly, "ethnicity refers to differences of language, religion, color, ancestry, and/or culture to which social meanings are attributed and around which identity and group formation occurs" (Nagel, 1995, p. 443).

A more narrow definition of ethnicity distinguishes groups on the basis of nationality or cultural characteristics, with physical characteristics not necessarily a part of ethnic differences. This definition is based on the Greek root word *ethos*, originally meaning "nation" (Feagin, 1989). Thus, an ethnic group may be defined as a group in which the members share a unique social and cultural heritage passed from one generation to the next, or as a group "set apart from others because of their national origin or distinctive cultural patterns" (Schaefer, 1988, p. 9).

In short, various *ethnic* groups within *racial* categories have their own unique *cultures* (Johnson, 1990). Therefore, the tribes of the Sioux Nation, who share religious and perhaps similar ancestral characteristics, may be considered an ethnic group but may not share the same culture; similarly, Native American Indians may be considered a race by some but may not share the same culture or be of the same ethnic group.

Degree of Culturation

Helping professionals need to be aware of the degree of culturation inherent in their Native clients or counselees. Native peoples represent a range of orientation from fully traditional to fully acculturated. English or Spanish is a second language for many, but proficiency in English *and* the tribal dialect is also prevalent. Culturation (whether enculturation or acculturation) is a major and complex construct (Domino & Acosta, 1987). The concept describes "the changes in behaviors and values made by members of one culture as a result of contact with another culture" (Burnam, Telles, Hough, & Escobar, 1987, p. 106). The *ac* or *en* prefixes denote the voluntariness (acculturation) or coerciveness (enculturation) of that action. The following discussion serves as an encouragement for helping professionals to research further the complexities of this concept.

Acculturation. Gordon (1964) has identified acculturation as one of seven different types of assimilation. Acculturation refers to cultural assimilation or the acquisition of the cultural patterns (e.g., values, norms, language, behavior) of the dominant society (Atkinson et al., 1998). Although originally proposed as a group phenomenon, acculturation is also considered to be an individual phenomenon—*psychological acculturation.* At the individual level, psychological acculturation describes changes in an individual whose cultural group is collectively experiencing acculturation (Graves, 1967). Individuals who experience acculturation must deal with their new circumstance by adjustment, reaction, or withdrawal (Berry, Kim, & Boski, 1988).

Enculturation. The history of Native peoples in the United States is replete with examples of coerced culturation, or *enculturation.* It is paradoxical that, as more European immigrants came to the mainland of North America, the founding principles of the Declaration of Independence and the Bill of Rights seem to have been interpreted as the rights of only the European American ethnic majority (Wehrly, 1995). These immigrants, who had come to the New World for a better life and to escape tyranny and injustice. frequently looked the other way when tyranny and injustice were meted out to the non-European American population.

Assimilation. The concept of assimilation implies more than the adoption of the dominant culture. In addition, it requires that structural assimilation be achieved, or that "members of the two groups interact with one another as friends and equals and that they select marriage partners without regard to ethnic or racial identities" (McLemore, 1983, p. 35). For a time, it was thought that the United States would become a "melting pot" (i.e., an idealized national culture) of all the cultures brought by immigrants and those held by indigenous peoples. However, as immigrants began to arrive from places other than Europe, the European American men in power became concerned about the different values and behaviors brought by these immigrants, and so the norm was changed from the melting pot to that of assimilation. Cultural assimilation, as practiced in the United States, is the expectation by the people in power that all immigrants and all people outside the dominant group will give up their ethnic and cultural values and will adopt the values and norms of the dominant society—male European American (Wehrly, 1995).

The United States has been (and continues to be) a nation of immigrants and indigenous peoples whose value systems differ. However, a major theme of European American individualistic psychology seems to have been that of assimilation (Wehrly, 1995). In principle, the "melting pot" notion of creating one idealized national culture prevailed until well past the midpoint of the 19th century. In practice, however, many immigrants retain their cultural values in the ethnic enclaves in which they live. In addition, even though some immigrants (and their descendants) may wish to become acculturated and may make every effort to adopt the culture of the dominant society, total assimilation may be beyond their grasp because it requires acceptance by members of that society. Therefore, for some individuals, assimilation may be a desired but unachievable goal (Atkinson et al., 1998).

Cultural Pluralism. For many ethnic and cultural minority individuals, assimilation may not be a desired goal. They find the cultural assimilation philosophy objectionable because it calls for relinquishing their traditional racial or ethnic values and norms in favor of those of the dominant culture. With the civil rights movement of the 1960s and 1970s came a growing interest in *cultural pluralism.* According to the theory of cultural pluralism, individual racial or ethnic groups maintain their cultural uniqueness while sharing common elements of the so-called "American" culture (Kallen, 1956).

Cultural pluralism is often compared to a cultural stew: the various ingredients are mixed together, but rather than melting into a single mass, the components remain intact and distinguishable while contributing to a whole that is richer than the parts (Atkinson et al., 1998). The analogy of a "mosaic" is also frequently used.

Cultural pluralism enjoyed some popularity during the 1970s as evidenced by the passage of the Ethnic Heritage Studies Bill by Congress in 1973 and the implementation of bilingual and bicultural education in many school districts. However, the 1990s witnessed a polarization of public sentiment regarding bilingual education. Bilingual education is exploding into one of the nation's most divisive political issues, fueled on one hand by a backlash against immigration and affirmative action and, on the other, by the failures and ideological strictures of some existing bilingual programs (Hornblower, 1995). For example, Beard-Williams (1994) asserted, "At what point do we hold non-English-speaking persons accountable for their disinterest (sic) in learning the language of this country . . ." (p. 12A). In addition, Turbak (1994) wrote about "the erosion of English" (p. 178) and claimed that "LEP [limited-English-proficient] children often remain in native-language classes for several years, and some never learn English" (p. 178).

Reports such as these motivate proposals to protect the English language in the United States, including a proposal to make English the official language. In reality, however, non-English-speaking individuals, both children and adults, are not at all reluctant to use English, and are doing an incredible job of acquiring it. In fact, it is the home languages that are eroding (Krashen, 1996).

Implications of Degree of Culturation. Berry, Trimble, and Olmedo (1986) emphasized that individuals vary in their degree of culturation and that "not only will groups and individuals vary in their participation and response to acculturative influences, [but] some domains of culture and behavior may become altered without comparable changes in other domains" (p. 297). Considering the sociocultural diversity of Native peoples, the tendency to underuse mental health services, client reactions to counseling styles, and the existence of a variety of tribal-specific approaches to mental health problems, how can a conventionally trained helping professional expect to know if intervention will be appropriate and effective? Helping professionals can increase their effectiveness (preferably during the initial intake session) by learning about a Native client's or counselee's acculturative level.

Several studies have provided consistent evidence that the degree of culturation is related to how Native individuals, especially Native youth, perceive and respond to helping services (e.g., Atkinson, Thompson, & Grant, 1993; Johnson & Lashley, 1989). These studies suggest that less culturated Native individuals are more likely to trust and express a preference for, and a willingness to see, an ethnically similar helping professional. In addition, less culturated Native individuals have expectations for nurturance and expect techniques to facilitate the session. Specific suggestions regarding helping strategies and helper attributes will be presented in subsequent chapters.

Social Class

An individual's *social class* may cut across a common ethnic, cultural, or racial heritage. Even though individuals may share similar heritages, they may have little in common with one another because of differences in social class (Neukrug, 1994). For example, a poor, reservation Native American Indian may find little in common with a wealthy, urban Native American Indian. In reality, social class may be a "missing dimension" in understanding diversity (Hannon, Ritchie, & Rye, 1992).

Through centuries of conquest, cultural extermination, genocide, and coercive assimilation, the Native American Indian has experienced the most pervasive physical, economic, political, and cultural discrimination in the history of the United States. The best way to keep people down is to deny them the means to improve and achieve and to cut them off from equal opportunities. Racism in the United States began for economic reasons that spread into societal aspects of colonial America. For slavery to exist and to continue as a source of free labor, a concerted effort had to take place to dehumanize Native peoples and African Americans (Pewewardy, 1997). The fact that the perpetrators of slavery went to great lengths to disprove Native humanity with false scientific facts, religious teaching, media, gross misconceptions and illustrations, and rumors establishes the point.

Contemporary society in this nation continues to reflect such discrimination against Native peoples. As has been previously established, the "poorest of the poor" continually face economic and educational barriers to improving their conditions, on reservations or off. The powerful influences of classism continue to mitigate the plight of this population.

Power Differentials

Neukrug (1994) warned helping professionals that, in the rapidly changing culture of the United States, power differentials may represent greater disparities between people than culture, ethnicity, race, or social class. The Native American Indian businessman or businesswoman who holds an upper-level management position (e.g., in a casino or bingo parlor) may be disliked because of his or her power over lower-level employees. Or the Native American Indian female tribal leader may be disliked by a male Native American Indian tribal member because of her position in the tribal hierarchy.

Summary

This chapter has surveyed the influences of ambiguous terminology and of demographics on the development of Native peoples. A primary emphasis was placed on the importance of helping professionals understanding distinctions in terminology and assessing the degree of culturation among Native peoples, especially Native youth. In addition, discussions emphasized how culture, race, ethnicity, degree of culturation, social class, and power differentials influence the lives of Native peoples.

This chapter illustrates the confusion and miseducation surrounding terminology and demographics. For the reader's edification, I prefer the term *ethnicity* to *race* when referring to groups of people who are distinguished by their ancestry, culture, or both. Race assumes a unique, isolated gene pool that clearly does not apply to many individuals who identify as Native

American Indian or Alaska Native. Moreover, the abundant within-group differences speak to the inappropriateness of race as a legitimate referent. The importance of culture for this population is vital.

Experiential Activities

1. Make an attempt to visit a traditional Native family or group. Describe the context and any insights you may gain.
2. Visit a popular meeting place (e.g., a mall or recreational area). Observe social class and power differential discrimination or prejudice. Give a report on your experiences.
3. Demonstrate how you, as a helping professional, can incorporate the information presented in this chapter into a helping situation.
4. Hold a debate on various perspectives on the term *race* and whether the concept is germane to today's multicultural society.

2

Assessing Native Populations

The term *assessment* refers to a process through which a clinician obtains information regarding a client. Suzuki and Kugler (1995) stated that the assessment process "includes both quantitative information (e.g., test information) and qualitative information (e.g., information yielded in a clinical interview) that can be put together to provide a more comprehensive picture of the total functioning of a client" (p. 493). The reader is alerted to the fact that "any person who can read and memorize instructions can administer a particular instrument, [but an individual's] professional judgment is needed to integrate the information into a comprehensive and appropriate client conceptualization" (p. 493).

Assessment is an integral part of the learning-teaching process. The process should be designed to fulfill two general objectives: (a) to determine student progress toward learning objectives and (b) to assist teachers and other educational personnel in determining student progress (Marsh & Horns-Marsh, 1998). Assessment is perhaps the most controversial aspect of the educative experience. Teachers find it time-consuming and a source of conflict with students. Students find it threatening and often an important determinant in their academic and career progress. Parents often question the end results.

The complexities of the assessment process are obvious because of the essential need to integrate information obtained from various sources. There may be cultural differences in the client, the clinician, the norm group on which the test is based, culture-specific constructs being assessed, and related issues, which may influence the assessment process and the interpretation of results (Suzuki & Kugler, 1995).

This chapter emphasizes issues to be recognized in counseling assessments with Native students and adults. Helping professionals may not have the luxury of referrals when working with Native individuals, because of the shortage of Native professionals (0.2% of mental health professionals [Russo, Olmedo, Stapp, & Fulcher, 1981]). The numbers have increased during the past decade but not sufficiently. In this chapter, selected instruments will be briefly discussed in the context of educational and clinical environments. Career development and assessment are presented in Chapter 5. The reader is encouraged to seek more in-depth discussion in other sources (e.g., Dana, 1993a; Paniagua, 1994; Samuda, 1998; Samuda & Associates, 1998).

Concerns Pertaining to Assessment With Native Populations

The issue of bias in psychological testing has been a source of intense and recurring social controversy throughout the history of mental measurement (Reynolds, Lowe, & Saenz, 1999). Many questions have been raised by clinicians and researchers regarding the use of standardized intellectual and personality instruments and their application to various ethnic groups. Discussions of test bias are frequently accompanied by polemic debate, decrying the use of mental tests with any ethnic minority members because ethnic minorities have not been exposed to the cultural and environmental circumstances and values of the so-called European American middle class (Reynolds et al., 1999). Some of the most common biases will be briefly presented in the following discussions.

Cultural Variables That May Affect Assessment

Systematic group differences on standardized intelligence and aptitude tests occur as a function of socioeconomic level, race or ethnic background, and other demographic variables (Reynolds et al., 1999). However, whether one considers race, ethnicity, gender, or socioeconomic status (SES), there is always more within-group than between-group variability in performance on psychological tests. Chapter 1 alluded to the effects of historical events and environmental issues on the delivery of mental health and educative services to Native populations. Other cultural variables include familialism, sharing and the concept of time, cooperation, nonverbal communication, and within-group differences. Space constraints prevent further discussion of these variables. The reader is encouraged to consult the references for additional in-depth information.

Authentic Indian?

As introduced in Chapter 1, Native American Indians who want to be considered for assistance from federal Native American Indian programs must prove that they are Native American Indian according to the definition established by the federal government (Trimble & Fleming, 1989; Wise & Miller, 1983). This definition states that the client must have at least one quarter "Indian blood" and proof of tribal status (Harjo, 1993). However, the federal government does not have the final word in that definition, as it must also recognize the sovereign status of each tribal definition of "Indian" (O'Brien, 1989). Absent this verification, Native American Indian individuals cannot avail themselves of mental health services funded by the federal government.

Use of Folklore

A thorough knowledge of the oral literature of Native peoples can enhance the helping professional's understanding of a client's verbal and nonverbal communications. Oral literature, such as folklore, reflects the client's culture and can help with a glimpse of the types of problems faced by the client as well as the available problem-solving skills.

The folklore of Native American Indians communicates their appreciation of and relationship to the earth and its animals. They believe that the earth is a member of the family and should be respected and cherished, not controlled (Bruchac, 1991; Caduto & Bruchac, 1991). Caduto and Bruchac (1991) wrote that "to the native people of North America, what was done to a frog or a deer, to a tree, a rock or a river, was done to a brother or sister" (p. xviii). These beliefs are passed down from one generation to the next through experience and storytelling. Native American Indian folktales are meant to teach as well as to entertain. Bruchac (1991) wrote that if a child misbehaves, he or she will be told a story rather than punished because "striking a child breaks that child's spirit, serves as a bad example and seldom teaches the right lesson, but a story goes into a person and remains there" (p. i).

Boyer (1979) described the manner in which the Chiricahua and Mescalero Apache use their folklore. These tribes use folklore as a group-supported means of expressing and transiently resolving unresolved, repressed infantile conflicts. Apache people also use their folklore as a complement to the defensive and adoptive functions of individual dreams, fantasies, and daydreams. Traditional lore projectively reflects personality configurations and socialization experiences (Boyer, 1979).

Use of Culturally Biased Instruments

Inaccuracies in the assessment and diagnosis of Native students can have three consequences: overdiagnosis, underdiagnosis, and misdiagnosis. Biases in testing are generally considered determinant factors in such inaccuracies. Many attempts have been made to eliminate or control biases in the assessment and diagnosis of cultural groups, including the translation of tests into the language of the group being tested and the development of culturally appropriate norms (e.g., Westermeyer, 1993). Despite these attempts, the overall sense among researchers and clinicians is that biases in cross-cultural testing still exist (e.g., Dana, 1993b).

Flaherty et al. (1988) emphasized that culture-free tests (i.e., a test that is not biased against specific culturally diverse groups) must meet five validity criteria, as cited in Paniagua (1994):

1. *Content equivalence:* Are items relevant for the culture being tested?
2. *Semantic equivalence:* Is the meaning of each item the same in each culture?
3. *Technical equivalence:* Is the method of assessment comparable across cultures?
4. *Criterion equivalence:* Would the interpretation of variables remain the same when compared with the norm for each culture studied?
5. *Conceptual equivalence:* Is the test measuring the same theoretical construct across cultures? (p. 105)

Currently, researchers and clinicians lack a test or assessment of any kind that could fulfill these criteria (Escobar, 1993). Escobar's conclusion suggests that culture-free tests are not yet available for assessment of major ethnic minority groups (Paniagua, 1994). However, the literature reveals many guidelines that school counselors may use to minimize bias during the assessment and diagnosis of Native students (e.g., Dana, 1993a, 1993b).

The Indian Child Welfare Act (Public Law 95-608)

Helping professionals involved in the assessment and treatment of Native American Indian children need "extensive knowledge of the [Native American] Indian Child Welfare Act (ICWA) [passed by the U.S. Congress in 1978] and its implications for the client system" (Goodluck, 1993, p. 222). This act "acknowledged the tribe as the best agency to determine custody issues for [Native American] Indian children. The act reaffirmed that tribes possessed jurisdiction over child-custody proceedings for all [Native American] Indian children living on the reservation" (O'Brien, 1989, p. 212).

In addition, the ICWA states that if a Native American Indian child resides off-reservation or in a Public Law 280 state (a state with the authority to use its civil and criminal laws on reservations), the state court must transfer jurisdiction to the tribal court unless the parents object to this requirement (O'Brien, 1989). A helping professional should not handle court actions involving child abuse, foster care, and adoption among Native American Indian families in the absence of extensive knowledge and applicability of the ICWA (Paniagua, 1994). The basic elements of this act are (Goodluck, 1993):

- Child custody proceedings (e.g., procedures for defining a child or Native American Indian, tribal court jurisdiction, placement standards, and returning the child to tribal jurisdiction)
- Native American Indian child and family program development (provides information for tribes interested in developing service programs for Native American Indian children)
- Record keeping and information (procedures for disclosure of information, Native American Indian rights, and benefits)

Cultural-Bound Syndromes

Culture-specific disorders are known as *cultural-bound syndromes* in the literature. Simons and Hughes (1993) proposed the term *cultural-related syndromes* because many of these syndrome have been observed across different cultures. Examples of cultural-related syndromes that helping professionals are most likely to find in their practices with Native American Indians include the following (Simons & Hughes, 1993):

- *Ghost sickness* (weakness, dizziness resulting from the action of witches and evil forces)
- *Wacinko* (feeling of anger, withdrawal, mutism, suicide resulting from reaction to disappointment and interpersonal problems)

Native individuals of the Southwest may also display cultural-related syndromes that are associated with Mexican Americans. The long history of interactions with Mexicans and Mexican Americans has had considerable influence on Native cultures in that region. These syndromes include the following (Simons & Hughes, 1993):

- *Ataque de nervios* (out-of-consciousness state resulting from evil spirits)
- *Mal puesto* hex, root-work, voodoo death (unnatural diseases and death resulting from the power of people who use evil spirits)
- *Wind/cold* illness (a fear of the cold and the wind; feeling weakness and susceptibility to illness resulting from the belief that natural and supernatural elements are not balanced)

It is important to consider the impact of cultural-related syndromes on the assessment of Native clients. In reality, though, such syndromes are not considered by helping professionals in their practices. Two reasons account for this omission (Paniagua, 1994):

1. Current standard clinical ratings and diagnostic instruments do not include criteria for the assessment of such syndromes. They do not require nor include an assessment of cultural-related syndromes to distinguish between these syndromes and true psychopathology.
2. Reimbursement for clinical practices regarding cultural-related syndromes is not a practice among major private insurers, Medicaid, and Medicare. (pp. 113-114)

Helping professionals should have some familiarity with cultural-related syndromes shared by Native clients. For example, if a Native American Indian client reports that, "I believe that my weakness, loss of appetite, and fainting are the result of the action of witches and evil supernatural forces," this would be an example of schizophrenia to a helping professional unfamiliar with the effect of ghost sickness among Native American Indians. If the client's belief is not shared by family members or peers, this belief is probably not culturally supported (Westermeyer, 1993).

Shamanic Healing

Native healing practices cannot be separated from Native religious beliefs (Hultkrantz, 1992). That is, for Native healers spirituality is a necessary aspect of medicinal and out-of-balance treatments. In addition, Native ethnobotany (the study of plant use) includes the medicinal uses of plants. Both of these Native aspects are used extensively by Native shamans such as *Anqakoq* (plural *Angakut*), the widespread term for shaman used by the inland North Alaskan Inuit groups.

Unfortunately, many contemporary scholars or physicians who have never set foot on a reservation, let alone ever attended an authentic shamanic healing, will be quick to say that shamanism is mere trickery and deception. Ample evidence exists to the contrary. For example, Lyon's (1996a) fieldwork over two decades has documented several cases in which Native shamanic treatments succeeded after Western medicine had failed.

Recently, anthropologists have reversed their skeptical treatment of shamanism, causing the professional study of shamanism to come into vogue (Lyon, 1996a). These studies have been generally limited to psychological studies of shamans per se. That is, interest is focused mainly on the shaman's altered states of consciousness, the various techniques used for inducing trances, the general nature of shamanic trances, EEG readings of shamans, and other such psychophysiological aspects of shamanism. Blatantly absent are theories, hypotheses, and research regarding the actual physics of shamanism. The interplay between psychology and the physical theories now emerging from the fields of special relativity, general relativity, quantum theory, and quantum field theory need to be explored (Lyon, 1996a). The first noteworthy attempt to this end was made only recently by the physicist Fred Alan Wolf (1991). He set forth nine hypotheses that attempt to interrelate the laws of modern physics with the known psychology of shamanism.

The shamanic state of consciousness is the particular state of consciousness that a shaman must attain to be able to communicate with his or any spirits. "The shamanic state of consciousness is the very essence of shamanism, and critical to the premise that the shaman is the past and present master of the imagination as healer" (Achterberg, 1987, p. 108).

Among European scholars, there is a tendency to differentiate between a shaman and a medicine man: A shaman uses ecstatic trance (i.e., an altered state of consciousness, and a medicine man does not (Lyon, 1996b). Thus, the word "medicine," as used in Europe, is closer to the Latin meaning of the word, "physician's art," whereas in North America it is used to mean "supernatural power" (Lyon, 1996a). Some scholars object to the use of this term, opting to define shamanic abilities or activities as the products of several different levels or states of consciousness. For example, some shamans remember their trance possessions, while others do not.

Issues to Consider in the
Assessment Process

At the national level, the American Psychological Association's Board of Ethnic Minority Affairs published guidelines in 1993, which address several major areas of concern, primarily related to ethical issues in dealing with other cultures or ethnic groups (American Psychological Association, 1993). These areas, as synthesized by Lonner and Ibrahim (1996), include (a) providing cultural knowledge through research and practice; (b) lessening any biases that providers of services might have by encouraging the awareness of oneself and one's culture; (c) encouraging understanding of and respect for diverse values, beliefs, worldviews, and other factors affecting psychosocial functioning and distress; (d) communicating, whenever possible, by using the client's preferred language; (e) coming to terms with the overall impact that specific interventions might have in a given cultural environment; and (f) taking an advocacy stance when issues of racism and discrimination might affect the client's welfare. Several specific, and in some ways unique, issues must be considered in the assessment process with Native individuals.

Authentic or Performance Assessment

There has long been debate over the most efficacious method to assess student ability. Parents demand assessments that accurately reflect the essential capabilities their children need to become successful adults. Educators, on the other hand, mandate assessments that serve as an integrated component of the instructional process (i.e., assessments should model high quality instruction and promote student learning).

Approximately 90% of classroom testing is regurgitation (Simmons, 1998). Researchers discourage such low-level examinations (e.g., multiple choice tests), because they leave the impression that memorization is the sole aim of education. Whether a test is standardized or written by a teacher, its purpose should be diagnostic (Simmons, 1998). The most important aspect of standardized testing is not public reporting; rather, it is making use of the results to improve student achievement and instructional programs. Assessment should serve as an instructional tool for meeting student needs (Stiggins, 1997).

Educational psychologists are concerned with ethnic-appropriate assessment and the concept of multiple intelligences. They have begun experimenting with assessment models that expand the simple measurement of learning. The most notable example of these new approaches concerns *authentic* or *performance assessment,* defined simply as "an evaluation of how well individuals can do something, as opposed to determining what they know about doing something" (Educational Testing Service, 1995, p. 6).

Supporters of this assessment approach view it as a major policy initiative for education reform. However, performance assessment faces some controversy. For example, performance assessment is reminiscent of the time-consuming, subjective assessment techniques that were rejected long ago in favor of more objective, less expensive alternatives. Other detractors challenge the practical and psychometric problems of performance testing. Something to Consider 2.1 illustrates the use of performance-based assessments with Native students.

Something to Consider 2.1

Using Performance-Based Assessments
With Native Students

The following seven steps provide a basic outline to initiate performance-based instruction and assessment with Native students.

Start with objectives. Communicate objectives in a manner students can understand or demonstrate the skills yourself. (For example, create a description of a person, place, or event in Native history, or investigate Native art, music, literature, and artifacts, and involve Native resource people.)

Provide models and examples of the expected performance. Instead of telling students about something, they are invited to participate, examine, critique, and analyze efforts and models already present.

Identify ways to exhibit, display, or perform student learning. "Portfolios require students to be active learners. Instead of instruction being something 'done to' students, they assume control of the learning process. Passivity produces nothing" (Grady, 1992, p. 14). Other ways include bulletin boards, productions, reviews, demonstrations, presentations, journals, writing logs, and special events.

Engage students in their work. The role of the teacher is that of a coach when describing a "thinking" classroom. Students not engaged see little meaning in their work.

Performance-based learning is both product and process. When reviewing students' works, consider both the process—how it was accomplished—and the product—how well it was done. A Native potter, for example, is skillful in how he or she creates a piece, including the steps involved.

Establish meaningful assessment criteria or rubrics to measure performance. When evaluating portfolios, for example, criteria might include degree of personal selection, organization, reflection and analysis, clarity and achievement of goal, and display and demonstration quality.

Use a graduated scale for assessments. A differentiated scale allows for judgments among inadequate, initial, adequate, completion, or mastery demonstration.

SOURCE: Adapted from Educational Testing Service (1995).

Those arguing for changing achievement testing believe that one short test cannot adequately measure an individual's abilities. They suggest that multiple measures gathered over a period of time provide a more authentic assessment of the individual's achievement level or ability to perform.

Table 2.1 Minimum Competencies of Test Administrators Necessary for Proper Test Use

---

1. Avoid errors in scoring and recording.
2. Do not label Native students with personally derogatory terms (e.g., dishonest) on the basis of test scores that lack perfect validity.
3. Keep scoring keys and test materials secure.
4. Ensure that each examinee follows directions so that test scores are accurate.
5. Use environments for testing that allow for optimal performance by examinees (e.g., adequate personal space).
6. Do not coach or train examinees on test items; this can result in misrepresentation of the examinee's abilities and competencies.
7. Give interpretation and guidance to examinees in counseling/guidance situations.
8. Do not photocopy copyrighted materials.
9. Do not use homemade answer sheets that do not align properly with scoring keys.
10. Establish rapport with examinees.
11. Do not answer questions from examinees in greater detail than the test manual permits.
12. Do not assume that a norm for one ethnic group or gender automatically applies to other groups.

Therefore, a move toward portfolio assessment is increasingly popular. In this assessment, teachers systematically collect multiple indicators of performance. The evaluation then focuses on the total evaluation of the products in the portfolio. The rationale is that, through the evidence of multiple performance tasks, better evaluation of the student's strengths and limitations can occur (Gronlund, 1998). Authentic or performance assessment, however, is not simple to implement, and appropriate implementation requires a substantial time commitment. Linn and Burton (1994) suggested that at least two independent judges are needed to evaluate portfolios. Evaluating portfolios is more complicated than scoring multiple choice tests, and well-defined scoring rubrics are needed to perform fair and sound evaluations. The entire area of achievement testing is being influenced by performance based and authentic assessments. However, standardized testing continues to be the more frequently implemented type of assessment. Table 2.1 offers some guidelines for appropriate test use.

Training programs must, at the least, expose their students to the increasing support for authentic methods of assessment (i.e., performance). The educational, policy, and assessment communities must unite to determine the appropriate balance of assessment tools that will facilitate their shared goal: improved learning for all students (Educational Testing Service, 1995). School counselor training programs must become active participants in this endeavor.

Ethnic Identity and Degree of Acculturation

The helping professional must be able to determine the degree of acculturation prior to the assessment process. Within-group variances of Native individuals and families were briefly discussed in Chapter 1. The familial patterns of pantraditional, traditional, transitional, bicultural, and assimilated reflect different degrees of acculturation. Knowledge of these different family patterns is paramount for appropriate and unbiased assessment. Paniagua (1994) stated this complexity in this manner:

> For example, when [Native] American Indians living in Arizona, New Mexico, or other states with a large number of reservations move from their reservation to cities, they experience the impact of a societal lifestyle quite different from the lifestyle they experienced on the reservation. Competition and individualism are two values with little relevance to [Native] American Indians who reside on reservations. These values, however, are extremely important for anyone who resides outside a reservation. In this example, the group simply moves from one area to another within the United States; and the assimilation of new values and lifestyles in the new area is a function of the process of internal acculturation. The impact of the internal process of acculturation would be minimal if [a Native] American Indian were to move from one reservation to another reservation in the United States. (pp. 8-9)

As a result of these varying degrees of acculturation, the ethnic identity of many Native individuals may need to be addressed. In particular, individuals from transitional and bicultural families may be experiencing ethnic identity confusion. Individuals from assimilated families will identify with the majority ethnic group. Helping professionals can assist in the process of developing a positive ethnic identity for those Native individuals who are confused about their ethnic identity.

Instruments for assessing the level of acculturation among Native American Indians have often been developed using instruments for other minority groups as models. For example, Garrett (1996) adapted the Acculturation Rating Scale for Mexican Americans (Cuellar, Harris, & Jasso, 1980) and the Suinn-Lew Asian Self-Identity Acculturation Scale (Suinn, Ahuna, & Koo, 1992) into a Native American Acculturation Scale (NAAS). The NAAS is a 20-item questionnaire with a ninth-grade reading level. Scores range from 1.00, suggesting low acculturation, to 5.00, suggesting a high level of acculturation. A pilot study determined a score of 3.08 to be the cutoff point between those who identified as Native American Indian and those who were more acculturated. Another scale is the Rosebud Personal Opinion Survey (Hoffmann, Dana, & Bolton, 1985).

In addition, researchers at the National Center for American Indian and Alaska Native Mental Health have recently described a sophisticated measure of ethnic identification validated on over 2,000 Native adolescents (Moran, Fleming, Somervell, & Manson, 1995). In cases of ambiguous identity, with or without tribal enrollment, helping professionals need to avail themselves of appropriate ethnic identity measures when working with Native individuals presenting ambiguous and undeveloped ethnic identities.

Biases in Reporting the Epidemiology of Mental Health

Two issues affect the nature of psychiatric epidemiological data: lack of a uniform definition of mental disorders and lack of cultural validity. Collected data are translated into prevalence and incidence scores. When these scores are reported, biases may occur. Practitioners must determine whether errors exist in the reporting of data. Paniagua (1994) offered three guidelines (modified for this subject) for a quick screening of epidemiological data collected with Native groups:

1. Identify the sample (number of Native individuals) from which the data were collected.
2. Determine the population (i.e., how many people in the entire population) from which the sample was selected to reach conclusions regarding the representativeness of the sample (e.g., Is the sample of Native individuals representative of the population of Native peoples in this country?).
3. Carefully read the conclusions of the study, which summarize major findings in words rather than in complex statistical procedures. (p. 101)

An example of bias in the collection of mental health epidemiological data is provided by Thompson, Walker, and Silk-Walker (1993). Data from the Indian Health Service (IHS) "are widely quoted as being representative of all Indians" (p. 199). A major bias in the reporting of such data is that the IHS recognizes as Native individuals only those living on 32 reservations, which means that Native persons from other reservations and those living in urban areas are not included in IHS statistics. Thompson and associates also emphasized that "some tribes are not recognized by the federal government and, therefore, are not included in most statistics" (p. 199). If the sample (which includes only those Native individuals recognized by the federal government) is not representative of the majority of Native peoples in the United States, a certain degree of bias can be inferred in the report of such data (Paniagua, 1994).

Use of Translated Measures

The dangers of using translated versions of tests or including translators or interpreters during the assessment procedure are clearly evident. Direct translations are often not possible, as psychological constructs may have relevance in one culture but not another. As Butcher and Pancheri (1976) reported, "As soon as a test is published, it is translated, often without validation in the target population and in some instances in the population of origin" (p. 28). Reynolds, Lowe, and Saenz (1999) noted the following:

> It is inappropriate to simply translate a test and apply it in a different linguistic culture. A test basically must be redeveloped from scratch before any such application would be appropriate. New items, new normative data, and new scaling would all be required. This has been known since the early days of psychological assessment and testing. (p. 584)

Determining whether to use a translated measure in the assessment process involves consideration of the following questions (Butcher & Pancheri, 1976):

1. Do the constructs of interest exist in the culture of the client?
2. Is the format of the test (tasks presented) meaningful in the client's culture? For example, traditional Native peoples may find a true-false format completely foreign to them.
3. Is the test valid in the client's culture?
4. Has the test followed appropriate translation procedures?
5. Have the test translators and publishers kept the response format the same so that the scores can be interpreted accurately?

The reader should note that no specific monitoring body or code of ethics exists regarding test translation.

Language Dominance

Challenges become apparent when assessing individuals whose primary language may not be Standard English. This is especially clear for helping professionals testing traditional Native students in schools, who may be identified as limited-English-proficient (LEP), that is, students who speak a language other than English in addition to demonstrating some English language skills. LEP students' proficiency and competency in speaking their native language and English ranges from a mastery over both languages, to mastery over one and limited fluency in the other, to mastery over neither language (Vance, 1998). LEP students frequently come from home environments in which a primary language other than English is spoken and in which the use of English varies considerably.

It is an established fact that intelligence tests, with the exception of the so-called performance or nonverbal tests, are heavily loaded verbally and that, therefore, familiarity with the language of the test becomes paramount (Samuda, 1998; Samuda & Associates, 1998). Many studies investigating the effects of bilingualism on intelligence test performance have demonstrated its adverse effects on test results (Anastasi & Cordova, 1953; Klineberg, 1935). It is often recommended that bilingual individuals be evaluated in both languages, given legal and ethical guidelines regarding appropriate assessment procedures (Rogers, 1993a). Scales are available to assist professionals in determining proficiency and dominance in various languages. It should be noted that individuals may demonstrate a lack of proficiency in standard English for a variety of reasons, such as a limited exposure to it.

Language issues must be addressed. Colleagues have shared tragic stories of students classified as learning disabled because they could not communicate effectively in English (Suzuki & Kugler, 1995). Mercer (1987) reported that individuals in the process of learning a new language may experience difficulty with academic concepts and language, given their abstract nature. Children who are in the process of learning English score consistently lower than those who have already mastered the language (Anastasi & Cordova, 1953; Klineberg, 1935). In addition, communication patterns of second-language learners may appear similar to language disorders because of dysfluencies common in the process of learning a new language (Suzuki & Kugler, 1995).

Klineberg (1935) illustrated the fact that speech, upon which the large majority of tests depend in more or less pronounced degrees, is basically a culturally oriented concept. He found "that the injunction to 'do this as quickly as you can' seemed to make no impression whatsoever on the [Native] American Indian children on the Yakima reservation in the state of Washington" (p. 159).

Klineberg (1935) gave several accounts of how different modes and ways of living can affect test results. He cited his experiences with the Dakota Sioux Indians, whose custom it is not to answer a question in the presence of someone who does not know the answer. An individual Dakota Sioux may answer only when absolutely certain of the response.

Bernstein's (1961/1967) findings on the verbal behavior of socially different groups have been considered valid for the lower and middle classes of the United States. Generally, it is agreed that what differentiates a lower-class home from a middle-class home is paucity of verbal stimulation and interaction (Samuda, 1998; Samuda & Associates, 1998). Unlike privileged children, who learn by feedback by being heard, corrected, and modified (John & Goldstein, 1967), poor children's early vocalizations are rarely, if at all, reinforced, and the corrective feedback they receive, if any, tends to be very poor and faulty (Samuda, 1998; Samuda & Associates, 1998). Lower-class parents and lower-class mothers, in particular, have been judged to be very poor linguistic models for their young children. Hunt (1967), for example, stated that "the variety of linguistic patterns available for imitation in the models provided by lower class adults is both highly limited and wrong for the standard of later schooling" (p. 203).

Interestingly, Porter (1998) reported on a study of 112 schools in Pulaski County, Arkansas, which focused on schools where students scored surprisingly well on standardized tests. One key finding is that school principals are vital in implementing priorities in schools. The report concluded that standardized test scores are related to income levels. However, three of the targeted schools did much better than the income levels of their students' families would predict. One school, with 85% participation in its free and reduced-price lunch program for children from low-income families, significantly outperformed its predicted average Stanford Achievement Test (SAT) score. The unexpected increase in SAT scores is attributed to good communication among teachers, parents, and principals; high expectations for students, regardless of their socioeconomic backgrounds; and principals with good organizational skills.

Attrition

Attrition is generally defined as a client's failure to return to therapy. An appropriate approach to prevent attrition would be an emphasis on a client's cultural variables and the effect of those variables on attrition. Table 2.2 presents general guidelines for the prevention of attrition.

Legal Considerations

To a large extent, considerations regarding how best to assess and educate Native and other ethnic minority children are guided by federal, state, and local legislation, and by litigation outcomes (Vance, 1998). By becoming aware of these legal influences and changes, helping professionals will be better equipped to provide assessment services within the prescribed legal parameters. For a description of some of the most important court cases and legislative acts pertinent to culturally and linguistically diverse youth, readers are referred to Fischer and Sorenson (1996) and Rogers (1993b).

Table 2.2 Prevention of Attrition of Native Clients and Counselees

---

The helping professional must establish trust and provide Native clients and counselees with an accommodating environment. In addition, the following guidelines will help ensure the chance of subsequent sessions. These guidelines must be effected during the initial session.

1. The helping professional must emphasize listening to the Native individual rather than dominating the session by talking to the Native individual.
2. Time is not a traditional Native value. The session should be flexible and not limited to a structured time schedule.
3. The helping professional should use therapies that emphasize cooperation rather than individualism and competition.
4. The helping professional should avoid the use of statements that imply a degree of pseudosecrecy.
5. The helping professional should avoid the use of medicine to reinforce therapy, especially during the initial session.
6. The helping professional should avoid therapies that emphasize control and power.
7. The helping professional should concentrate on how to handle the problem rather than how to control the problem.
8. The helping professional should avoid personalizing the client's or counselee's problem.

Specifically, the evaluation of Native youth must be based on (Vance, 1998) the following:

1. multidisciplinary assessments involving information gathered from a variety of sources and methods,
2. assessments conducted in the child's native language as well as English,
3. assessments that protect children from selection and administration practices that are ethnically and culturally discriminatory,
4. clearly specified procedures for assessing linguistically diverse children, and
5. informed parental consent and notification of rights to due process. (p. 357)

Intellectual and Personality Assessment

Intellectual and personality assessments of Native individuals have the greatest potential for bias. These two areas of assessment represent double-edged swords. On one hand, they can facilitate the understanding of problems and concerns. On the other hand, they can inflict great harm if they result in misdiagnosis and biased instruments. The following discussions will serve to elucidate these areas of assessment, relative to Native individuals.

Intellectual Assessment

Samuda and associates (1998) contended that classic intelligence tests and traditional standardized tests of cognitive ability are only appropriate for middle-class mainstream individuals, not for those of different cultural backgrounds. For those who grow up in deficient "environmental backgrounds" (inadequate rearing, serious economic stress), the traditional objective standardized tests are neither valid nor reliable in measuring intelligence. Numerous scholars have introduced alternative approaches to assessing cognitive ability in persons from such backgrounds, including treating individuals on an individual basis.

With the above qualification, helping professionals need to be careful not to generalize Native American Indians' performance on intelligence tests, in view of the multitude of distinct tribes within this general population. Traditions and values differ tribally, and performance on aspects of intelligence tests also tends to vary. A general finding is that Native American Indian children seem to score lower on the verbal scales than on the performance scales (Neisser et al., 1996). In addition to cultural differences, McShane and Plas (1984) suggested that Native American Indian children are plagued by chronic middle ear infections that can negatively affect their verbal development. Native American Indians may also be misperceived by test examiners, as they tend to be deferential to a European American test examiner and appear to lack motivation. Something to Consider 2.2 presents an outline of the suggested format for the initial assessment session.

Kaufman Assessment Battery for Children

The Kaufman Assessment Battery for Children (K-ABC; Kaufman & Kaufman, 1983) is a test of intelligence and achievement designed for use with children between the ages of 2 years, 5 months and 12 years, 5 months. The scale contains 10 mental processing subtests and 6 supplementary achievement subtests, yielding a total Mental Processing Composite (MPC) score with a mean of 100 and a standard deviation of 15. In application with ethnic minority populations, the K-ABC has several attractive and distinctive features (Vance, 1998):

1. The K-ABC contains many tasks that do not require expressive language skills.
2. A Spanish version of the scale is available, which was normed on a Spanish-speaking sample.
3. Test items were analyzed during test development both by a panel of ethnic minority experts and by statistical procedures to identify biased items.
4. Each of the mental processing subtests is preceded by an unscored sample item.
5. The first two scored items are designated as teaching items to help familiarize children with task demands and provide experience in test taking.

Something to Consider 2.2

The First Assessment Session

1. *Recognize the limited understanding of Native peoples' culture and the positive feeling of being a Native individual.* Non-Native helping professionals should begin with a clear statement regarding their limited knowledge of values, religions, and traditions.

2. *Avoid pseudosecrecy statements and do not ask questions unrelated to the core clinical problem.* Avoid statements such as "Why don't Native people want to assimilate into mainstream society?"

3. *Do not discuss medication.* Synthetic medicine is not preferred by traditional Native individuals. They have their natural herbal and spiritual "medicines."

4. *Accept relatives, friends, a Medicine Man or Woman, and tribal leaders.* The elders in the tribe (particularly the principal chief) and traditional medicine men and women have a special place in the family; they are seen as an integral part of the extended family (Dana, 1993a; Ho, 1992) and would be included in the extended family tree of Native American Indian clients.

5. *Avoid taking many notes.* Doing anything other than listening is considered a sign of disrespect.

6. *Listen rather than talking.* Native clients come to talk to, not listen to, the professional.

7. *Confidentiality versus resistance.* Traditional Native clients may not answer personal questions, which may be interpreted as resistance by the helping professional. Relatives or friends may work in the setting and clients may fear that their answers will be recorded and become public (Thompson et al., 1993). The appropriate approach is not to label the client's behavior as resistance but to consider it a sign indicating that issues of confidentiality have not been resolved (Paniagua, 1994).

8. *Explore important potential problems.* The helping professional should screen for symptoms of alcoholism and depression. Alcoholism is not only the primary concern among Native groups, but is also considered the main cause of suicide and violence in this group (O'Brien, 1989; Walker & LaDue, 1986). Native women should also be screened for symptoms of alcoholism to prevent fetal alcohol syndrome. Feelings of inadequacy and low self-esteem are indicators of depression in Native individuals (Walker & LaDue, 1986).

---

6. The mean MPC yielded by the scale for ethnic minority groups comes closer to the mean MPC for European Americans than do the full scale quotients of other similarly developed intelligence instruments.

7. The manual provides sociocultural norms by SES and ethnicity for those interested in comparing the test taker's performance with other children from similar ethnic and SES groups.

The largest discrepancy on the K-ABC occurs between African American and European American school-age children (mean MPC = 93.7 and 100, respectively), followed by Navajo Indians (mean MPC = 94.2), and Hispanics (mean MPC = 97.5). A mean MPC reported for a small sample of Sioux Indians (100.6) most closely approximates the European American sample (Vance, 1998, p. 373).

The K-ABC also has a number of shortcomings in its applications with ethnic minorities (Vance, 1998):

1. Although the norm group approximated the 1980 U.S. census data in terms of ethnicity, the sample underrepresented Hispanics and African Americans at the lower-SES level and overrepresented both groups at the upper-SES level.

2. No evidence is found that the Spanish instructions or interpreters were part of the test development or standardization process.

3. LEP and/or bilingual children were not included in the norm groups.

4. The Nonverbal scale is promoted as an alternative for use with non-English-speaking children age 4 years to 12 years, 5 months; but, since the norms did not include LEP children, comparisons with this population would be of limited usefulness. (pp. 373-374)

Therefore, caution should be used in employing the English version of the K-ABC with non-English-speaking children.

Stanford-Binet Intelligence Scale-Fourth Edition

The Stanford-Binet Intelligence Scale-Fourth Edition (SB-IV; Thorndike, Hagen, & Sattler, 1986) is the latest revision in the long history of Binet intelligence scales. It is used with children, adolescents, and young adults between the ages of 2 and 23. This revision contains 15 subtests, 6 new and 9 retained from the previous version. Several steps were taken during the development and standardization of the scale to respond to the special characteristics of ethnic minority children (e.g., pictures representing ethnically diverse people, removal of biased items).

Nevertheless, six major concerns have been expressed about the psychometric qualities of the scale (Vance, 1998):

1. The accuracy of the norms has been questioned.

2. The upper-SES level was oversampled and weighting procedures were needed to adjust for the effects, resulting in inaccurate norms (Cronbach, 1989).

3. The reliability of the scale has yet to be determined using large and representative samples of ethnic minority populations (Vance, 1998).

4. The construct validity of the scale and, specifically, the stability of the factor structure across ethnic minority groups has not yet been demonstrated (Vance, 1998).

5. The SB-IV requires verbal skills on at least half of its subtests (Vance, 1998).

6. To date, a Spanish version of the scale has not been developed and marketed (Vance, 1998).

The Wechsler Scales

The Wechsler Adult Intelligence Scale-Revised (WAIS-R; Wechsler, 1981), the Wechsler Intelligence Scale for Children-III (WISC-III; Wechsler, 1991), and the Wechsler Primary Preschool Scale of Intelligence-Revised (WPPSI-R; Wechsler, 1989) are some of the most frequently used individual intelligence measures in the United States, especially in the assessment of exceptional children. The tests are divided into two scales, Verbal and Performance, and yield an overall Full Scale IQ (FSIQ).

Numerous studies have been conducted addressing the reliability and validity of the Wechsler scales in relation to various ethnic groups. In general, the Wechsler scales have been found to be valid and reliable (e.g., Kaufman, 1990; Sattler, 1988). Concerns still need to be raised regarding discrepancies in FSIQ between ethnic groups, especially in determining educational placement (Suzuki & Kugler, 1995). The standardization sample of the WISC-III reflects the 1988 U.S. census, and representative numbers of the Native population were included. Helms (1992) recommended that the procedures used to develop the WISC-III be employed as a model for redevelopment of intellectual measures, with particular consideration of sociocultural experiences of ethnic groups.

Reschly (1978) concluded that the usual interpretation of the WISC-R FSIQ as a measure of overall intellectual ability appears to be equally appropriate for European Americans, African Americans, Mexican Americans, and Native American Indians (Papagos). He also concluded that the Verbal-Performance distinction on the WISC-R is equally appropriate across ethnicity, and that there is strong evidence for the integrity of the WISC-R's construct validity for a variety of populations.

Reschly and Sabers (1979) evaluated the validity of WISC-R FSIQs in the prediction of Metropolitan Achievement Test (MAT) scores. They found evidence of bias in the predictor of the various achievement scores. The bias produced generally significant underprediction of European American performance when a common regression equation was applied. Achievement test performance of the Native American Indian (Papago) group showed the greatest amount of overprediction of all non-European American groups.

On the negative side, only English-speaking children were represented in the standardization group of the WISC-III (Vance, 1998). The test does not contain a parallel form or alternate Spanish version nor does it provide administration instructions and normative data for use with students for whom English is a second language. In addition, no evidence is found that LEP children were included in the standardization sample of the WPPSI-R, and a Spanish version of the scale is not available. Evidence for internal, interrater, and test-retest reliability of the scale suggests that the highest reliabilities are for the full scale (Vance, 1998). All of the Wechsler scales require frequent use of verbal skills. Evaluators concerned about testing individuals who do not speak standard English will need to pay attention to the test taker's verbal responses to reduce the likelihood of scoring errors.

The Minnesota-Percepto-Diagnostic Test-Revised (MPDT-R). The MPDT-R is a clinical and educational instrument designed to assess visual perception and visual-motor abilities in children and adults. It consists of six Gestalt designs, which the subject copies. The scores have been adjusted for both IQ and age. The MPDT-R provides a rapid and objective source of evidence for differential diagnosis that can be used in conjunction with other information about a client or counselee. It provides scores that (a) classify learning disabilities as visual, auditory, or mixed; (b) divide behavioral problems of children into normal, emotionally disturbed, schizophrenic, and organic groups; and (c) distinguish among adults who are normal, brain damaged, or have personality disturbances (Vance, 1998).

Fuller and Vance (1995) compared the performance on the MPDT-R of members of three Native American Indian groups (40 Navajo, 40 Papago, and 40 Hopi) and 40 European American children. One-way analysis of variance and an analysis of covariance (age covaried) were computed along with a Scheffe test. The results indicated significant differences among the four groups on the MPDT-R rotation score and on two of the three configuration scores. When age was controlled for, significant differences were obtained on the MPDT-R scores. The European American children performed significantly better than did the Papago and Hopi children on rotation. They also had significantly lower Separation of Circle-Diamond scores than the Navajo and significantly lower Distortion of Circle-Diamond scores than the Hopi children. Many of the Native American Indian children obtained MPDT-R scores above the range for normal perception. The clinician is cautioned to be careful in determining whether differences in scores on cross-cultural validity studies are a true clinical sign or a culturally different reaction or interpretation in visual-motor perception (Vance, 1998).

Personality Assessment

Personality assessment is of particular importance because of the lifetime consequences of a potential misdiagnosis. To ensure appropriate and accurate diagnosis, helping professionals must always be aware of that possibility. The most commonly used assessment measures will be briefly discussed as they relate to Native individuals.

Minnesota Multiphasic Personality Inventory (MMPI). The MMPI has been cited as the most "useful psychological test available in clinical and counseling settings for assessing the degree and nature of emotional upset" (Walsh & Betz, 1990, p. 117). It is also one of the most well-researched instruments currently in use (Suzuki & Kugler, 1995).

Development of the MMPI-2 incorporated a representative sample of Native American Indians. Examination of scores and MMPI-2 profiles indicates no substantial mean differences between Native American Indians and the general normative sample on the MMPI-2 validity and standard scales (Butcher & Williams, 1992). However, Graham (1987) and Dana (1988) have cautioned professionals in using the test with ethnic minority individuals.

Suzuki and Kugler (1995) cautioned professionals who use computer-generated reports on the MMPI: "In order to be sensitive to the complexities of the multicultural assessment process, it is imperative not to rely upon a computer report, which cannot possibly integrate all of the relevant cultural information" (p. 503).

California Personality Inventory (CPI). The CPI (Gough, 1987) is an inventory that measures folk concepts—"concepts that arise from and are linked to the ineluctable processes of interpersonal life, and that are found everywhere that humans congregate into groups and establish societal functions" (p. 1). Some of these concepts include responsibility, tolerance, sociability, empathy, and sense of well-being. The CPI was developed to assess overall well-adjusted individuals in relation to social, educational, vocational, and family issues (Walsh & Betz, 1990).

Dana (1993b) reported that currently "cross-cultural invariance is neither apparent nor believed to be necessary by CPI proponents" (p. 184). His review of the cross-cultural usage of the CPI indicated the presence of item differences between ethnic groups. For example, Davis, Hoffman, and Nelson (1990) found that differences exist in CPI response patterns between Native American Indian and European American samples equated on age, occupation, and education. They also noted scaled score differences related to an interaction between gender and ethnic group membership. The authors concluded that ethnic background should be considered in use of the CPI as a screening device.

Projective Techniques. Projective techniques present ambiguous stimuli to an individual in an effort to obtain a response reflecting the individual's inner needs. Examples include pictures (e.g., Thematic Apperception Test), ink-blots (e.g., Rorschach), sentence completion exercises and drawings (e.g., House-Tree-Person). As Aiken (1989) stated, "It is assumed that whatever structure is imposed on the stimulus material represents a projection of the observer's own individual perceptions on the world. It is also maintained that the more unstructured the task, the more likely the responses are to reveal important facets of personality" (p. 306).

Projective techniques have been used frequently in cross-cultural studies. However, they have been criticized by those who state that projectives can be subject to "loose" interpretations, given their ambiguity (Suzuki & Kugler, 1995).

The Rorschach. The Rorschach (Rorschach, 1921) is reputed to be the "pinnacle of the psychodiagnosis methods known as projective techniques" (Aiken, 1989, p. 329). However, there are no special norms for different cultural groups in the United States on the Exner Comprehensive Rorschach (Exner, 1990), currently the primary scoring system (Dana, 1993a). DeVos and Boyer (1989) noted that the Rorschach can be used with Native American Indians; however, they stressed the importance of understanding a "culture's normative percepts and patternings" (p. 55). What may be "normative" in one culture could be considered "aberrant" in another.

Thematic Apperception Test. The second most popular projective method is the Thematic Apperception Test (TAT) (Murray, 1943). It consists of 30 picture cards and one blank card. The client is presented with a card and asked to tell a story about the picture. Native clients would respond more readily to pictures of Native characters rather than to the European American characters depicted in the original TAT.

Children's Apperception Test (CAT). The CAT (Bellak & Bellak, 1949) has also been used in cross-cultural counseling. It uses pictures of animals rather than humans and administration is similar to the TAT. French (1993) noted that the animals depicted in the cards may insult or mislead Native American Indian children, whose culture places value on animal clans and fetishes.

Q-Sorts. Manson (1994) described the creative use of Q-sort methodology to help understand depressive symptomatology among a group of Native

American Indian patients. Using a similar methodology, Berry and Bennett (1989) used multidimensional sealing creatively to help understand the idea of cognitive competence from a Cree perspective. Once disorders of affect are understood properly in *culturally isomorphic* terms, the selection of better and more appropriate treatment methods may be possible (Lonner & Ibrahim, 1996).

Value of Synergetic Assessment

Synergetic assessment is the integrating of multiple approaches into an organized paradigm of delivering appraisal services successfully to Native youth and adults (Herring, 1997a, 1997b). Integrative theorizing is currently becoming more common and influential. Theoretical approaches involving cognitive behavioral theory and developmental counseling have brought diverse theories together in a coherent fashion. For example, Attneave's (1969, 1982) network therapy involves extensive multiple interventions and assessments with individuals, families, and the community to produce and maintain change, especially with Native students and adults.

The synergetic approach to assessment is a road less traveled, but surely worth taking. To be effective with Native students and clients, helping professionals and training programs must broaden their base of cultural knowledge and be willing to develop new structures, policies, and strategies that are more responsive to the uniquenesses of Native students and clients. This approach is important not only because of humanistic reasons, but also because within the next 20 years, most credible demographers project ethnic minority groups will become a numerical majority, and European Americans the minority. At its best, synergetic assessment can be a creative synthesis and a selective blending of the unique contributions of diverse assessment techniques. This model presents a dynamic integration of the concepts and techniques that fit the helping professional's individual personality and style. In addition, the cultural and environmental worldview of the Native student is recognized and respected. Finally, synergetic assessment perspectives represent an opportunity to help professional training programs reflect a pluralistic society.

According to Ivey, Ivey, and Simek-Morgan (1993), synergetic assessment does not

> dismiss traditional methods but rather recognizes their value, as long as they are employed in a culturally meaningful and culturally sensitive fashion. . . .
> Rather than to impose a theory on the client, these approaches seek to find how the client constructs and makes meaning in the world and stress an

egalitarian, non-hierarchical therapist/client relationship. They suggest that counselor and client together draw from other theories in an integrated fashion to meet individual, family, and cultural needs. . . . In effect, self-in-relation becomes the focus rather than individually oriented self-actualization. (p. 361)

Native Children and Adolescents

In most educational settings, the school counselor uses a variety of assessments to assess students' characteristics and behaviors. In these assessments, school counselors administer standardized tests, interest inventories, behavior rating scales, and nonstandardized procedures to individual students and to groups (Herring, 1997b). A culturally responsive school counselor needs to have the ability to consider the dynamics of culture and ethnicity when interpreting data from standardized tests and other assessment tools (Lee, 1995). The school counselor also needs to be able to recognize potential cultural bias in assessment instruments and to bear this in mind when making educational decisions about Native students.

A most important assessment coordinated by the school counselor involves the influence of environment on students' development and learning. The question posed is, "What therapy activities are most appropriate for what type of problem, by which therapist, for what kind of ethnic minority student?" (see Herring, 1997b; Lazarus & Beutler, 1993). It is critical to be aware of how Native students' cultural backgrounds contribute to their perceptions of their problems. Although it is unwise to stereotype Native students because of their heritage, it is useful to assess how the cultural context interacts with Native students' concerns. Some techniques are contraindicated because of Native students' unique socialization experiences. Thus, the Native student's responsiveness (or lack of it) to certain techniques is a critical barometer in judging the effectiveness of these methods (Herring, 1997b).

Consequently, the school counselor's task becomes one of assessing the influences of environmental factors on the Native student. To obtain a complete and accurate description of Native students, the school counselor will assess factors such as the school atmosphere, classroom environment, peer groups, and family and home environments.

The value of synergetic assessment is the integrating of multiple approaches into an organized paradigm of delivering assessment services successfully to Native students, depending largely on the school counselor's primary theoretical orientation (Herring, 1997a, 1997b). Several models illustrate synergetic school counseling. For example, Lazarus's (1981) multimodal therapy reflects a major effort to organize primarily behavioral tenets into his "BASIC-ID" paradigm (Behavior, Affective response, Sensations, Images, Cognition, Interpersonal relationships, and Drugs). His paradigm created a holistic approach and was one of the first to move eclecticism to an organized, or synergetic, format.

Dana's Assessment Model and Native Adult Clients

Dana (1993a, 1993b) provided an assessment model that clinicians may use in an overall approach to minimizing biases during the assessment of Native clients. Dana recommended five steps in the application of his model:

1. Conduct an assessment of acculturation.
2. Provide a culture-specific service delivery style.
3. Use the client's native language (or preferred language).
4. Select assessment measures appropriate for the cultural orientation and client preferences.
5. Use a culture-specific strategy when informing the client about findings derived from the assessment process.

For example, a Native American Indian client may be told, "This finding suggests that you have low self-esteem, are reserved and timid, lack interest in activities, and that you are a shy person. My understanding is that among Native American Indians these behaviors are culturally accepted in their tribes. So, we probably need to talk more about these behaviors to ensure that they are not part of the clinical diagnosis of the mental problem you reported earlier to me" (Paniagua, 1994, p. 122).

In addition, a review of the literature suggests an order concerning the degree of bias across assessment strategies (Dana, 1993a). In summarizing that degree of bias, the order (from less to more bias as the number increases) would be:

1. Physiological assessment (e.g., the use of electrodermal activity in the assessment of psychopathology; Boucsein, 1992)
2. Direct behavioral observations (e.g., intervals during which Native children display attention to task materials; Dana, 1993a)
3. Self-monitoring (e.g., clients record their own overt or covert behaviors, such as obsessive thoughts and number of tasks completed, respectively)
4. Behavioral self-report rating scales (e.g., Fear Survey Schedule; Wolpe & Lang, 1964)
5. Clinical interview (which includes the mental status examination)
6. Trait measures (e.g., California Psychological Inventory; Dana, 1993a)

7. Self-report of psychopathology (e.g., MMPI, Beck Depression Inventory; Dana, 1993a)

8. Projective tests with structured stimuli (e.g., Tell-Me-A-Story or TEMAS; Constantino, Malgady, & Rogler, 1988; Malgady, Constantino, & Rogler, 1984)

9. Projective tests with ambiguous stimuli (e.g., Rorschach test; Dana, 1993a)

Similar concerns involve developing greater sensitivities in formal psychometric assessment. For example, the International Test Commission recently sponsored a series of meetings that revolved around the adaptation and use of educational and psychological tests in both intracultural and cross-cultural research. Looking into these matters is a 13-member commission representing a number of international organizations (Hambleton, 1993). The commission has prepared drafts of guidelines for adapting educational and psychological tests. These guidelines are organized into four categories: context, instrument development and adaptation, administration, and documentation/score interpretation. Final details of these efforts are welcome additions to the literature on cross-cultural assessment, and further enhance synergetic assessment practices.

All assessment strategies listed above have some degree of bias (Dana, 1993a; Jenkins & Ramsey, 1991). The important guideline to remember is to emphasize assessment techniques in which interpretations and speculations are minimized (Paniagua, 1994). The helping professional should make an effort to select measures with evidence of cross-cultural validity.

Table 2.3 presents a list of assessments that have been used effectively with ethnic and cultural minority individuals. The reader should note that assessments that have been designed to provide complex demographic corrections to IQs obtained by ethnic minorities have the effect of equating these groups' IQ mean scores. One system, known as the System of Multicultural Pluralistic Intelligence Assessment (SOMPA; Mercer & Lewis, 1978), was quite popular for several years but is rarely used today because of its conceptual and psychometric inadequacies (Reynolds et al., 1999). In addition, the validity of many projective techniques has been challenged by many scholars unless the cultural environment of the test taker has been included in the technique. For example, the Tell-Me-A-Story Test (TEMAS; Constantino et al., 1988) should not be interpreted from mainstream society's perspectives.

One alternative to traditional assessment measures is reflected in the use of narratives (Lieblich & Josselson, 1997; Lieblich, Tuval-Mashiach, & Zilber, 1998). The use of language in counseling is often referred to as the narrative approach. Stories or narratives represent a mechanism for human knowing, in that individuals "construct their identities from the symbols or

Table 2.3 Tests Recommended With Culturally Diverse Groups

Name	Area	Reference
Center for Epidemiologic Studies Depressives Scale (CES-D)	Depression	Radloff (1977)
Culture Fair Intelligence Test	Intelligence	Anastasi (1988)
Draw-A-Person Test (DAP)	Projective	French (1993)
Eysenck Personality Questionnaire (EPQ)	Personality	Eysenck & Eysenck (1975)
Holtzman Inkblot Technique (HIT)	Projective	Holtzman (1988)
Kaufman Assessment Battery for Children (K-ABC)	Intelligence	Kaufman, Kamphaus, & Kaufman (1985)
Leiter International Performance Scale	Intelligence	Anastasi (1988)
Progressive Matrices	Intelligence	Anastasi (1988)
Schedule for Affected Disorders and Schizophrenia (SADS)	Most Disorders	Spitzer & Endicott (1978)
System of Multicultural Pluralistic Assessment (SOMPA)	Intelligence	Mercer & Lewis (1978)
Tell-Me-A-Story Test (TEMAS)	Personality/Cognition	Constantino et al. (1988)
Information Test: C-4	Attitudinal	S. W. Cook (1990)

meanings on offer within their culture" (McLeod, 1996, p. 178). It is assumed that an individual's need to seek counseling is brought about by life stories or self-stories that are "incomplete, confused, or have negative or tragic outcomes" (p. 178). In addition, a narrative approach may enable individuals to tell stories that have been silenced (Patton & McMahon, 1999). This approach is compatible with the traditional oral history of Native cultures. Also, storytelling is prevalent among Native peoples as a means to teach and preserve their history and culture.

Summary

This chapter has attempted to address potential assessment problems and complexities in helping Native populations. A review of the literature suggested that assessment of Native populations can pose various areas of bias. To appreciate why Native groups may have difficulties with the components of assessment and why such difficulties could increase bias in the assessment of these groups, try to picture yourself in the place of one of these groups and attempt to deal with the elements of the exam. For example, could you name the location and the building you are in after you have experienced a panic or shock attack in an unfamiliar city? Such is the case of an Alaska Inuit or Hunkpapa Sioux student who is transported from his or her natural surroundings to a modern, urban setting for assessment processing. Such is the case of a traditional Cherokee or Lummie adult, with limited standard English proficiency, who is interviewed by a European American psychologist for presenting problems of ghost sickness.

The central purpose of this chapter is to alert helping professionals who engage in intellectual and personality assessments to the uniqueness of the Native peoples, especially those who remain pantraditional or traditional. This alertness is mandatory if appropriate and ethnic-specific diagnoses are to be rendered. If these ethnic-specific parameters are overlooked or not accounted for, misdiagnosis and mislabeling will continue.

Experiential Activities

1. Visit the library and research the availability and authenticity of the so-called "culture free" tests.
2. Locate a Native individual and obtain his or her perspective on formal assessment versus "the Native way."
3. Visit a school setting that includes Native students. Interview the school counselor relative to any assessment accommodations provided for these students.
4. Conduct a survey in your area relative to the attrition rates of Native clients and counselees. In particular, obtain the rationales for individual attrition.

3

Counseling Native American Indian/ Alaska Native Youth

By 2030 only 50% of children in the United States under age 18 will be European American, as will 59% of adults aged 18 to 64, and 73% of the elderly. Thus, in the 21st century, children are more likely than the elderly to belong to ethnic minority groups, and the elderly will be more dependent on ethnic minority group working adults for their economic support (Johnson-Powell & Yamamoto, 1997). Furthermore, in 1900, the dependent child population was 91% of the general population; by 2050, children will be 53% of the population (U.S. Department of Health & Human Services [U.S. DHHS], 1996).

Over 625,000 Native American Indians, representing 32% of the total Native American Indian population, are 15 years of age or younger; 41% are 20 years of age or younger (U.S. Department of Commerce, 1992). This number reflects an increase of nearly 36% from the 1980 census. Projections indicate that Native American Indian populations will likely double within the next 15 years, making them proportionately the fastest growing ethnic group in the United States (Herring, 1992).

Many Native youth exist as both Natives and as non-Natives—attempting to retain their traditional values but seeking as well to live in the dominant culture (Herring, 1997c). This dualistic life increases the developmental stress and strain on these young people. To further complicate counseling efforts, within-group differences prevent treating these ethnic young people homogeneously. The most efficacious manner of addressing this young population lies in the understanding of Native cultures and their inherent within-group variances.

Native Culture: The Key to Counseling Practice

Helping professionals, especially school guidance counselors, are confronted with major tasks in promoting the career, academic, social, and personal development of Native youth. Before examining counseling practices with Native children and adolescents, however, two important issues need to be considered: (a) the importance of adopting a proactive approach to counseling Native school age youth and (b) the need to assess each student's level of acculturation (Herring, 1992, 1997a, 1997b, 1997c).

The Promise of a Proactive Perspective

Effective counseling with Native children and adolescents is predicated on adopting a proactive developmental perspective (Herring, 1991). This perspective would include gaining a thorough knowledge of past and current Native culture and history. It would also entail having an expanded understanding of Native young people.

For example, many Native individuals' trust increases as the helping professional becomes more involved in their lives and shows more interest in them. Making home visits and getting to know the family can significantly improve the chances of obtaining relevant information. Native peoples tend not to make decisions quickly (Woodside & McClam, 1998). This slow process could influence how soon the client or counselee is willing to share information or make judgments. Native cultures sometimes incorporate a fatalistic element—a belief that events are predetermined (Woodside & McClam, 1998). During the initial stages of the process, the client or counselee may not understand how his or her responses and actions can influence the course of service delivery.

Counseling professionals need to develop strategies to modify the effects of political and socioeconomic forces on Native youth. They may also need to become systemic change agents, intervening in environments that impede the development of Native youth (Eberhard, 1989). In the school setting, for example, counselors can encourage the revision of curricula to include the impact of the cultural environment on the behavior of Native youth (Trimble, LaFromboise, Mackey, & France, 1982). School counselors can also encourage Native tribes and groups to assume a more active role in providing mental health services.

Level of Acculturation

Effective counseling with Native youth requires the school counselor or helping professional to recognize a minimum of two within-group variances: cultural commitment and view of seeking mental health services. (For purposes of inclusiveness, the term "helping professional" will be used in this chapter as the referent for those individuals who work to improve the mental, emotional, and cognitive aspects of Native peoples.)

Cultural Commitment. The historical idea of cultural assimilation as a solution to the so-called "Indian problem" remains untenable (Ford, 1983; Herring, 1989). "In general, Indian people do not wish to be assimilated into the 'dominant culture' and to recognize this is important," summarized one contemporary Navajo man (Rehab Brief, 1986). A Chippewa described it in this way:

> We view this place [North America] as being given to us by the Creator to take care of and to pass onto our future generations. We believe all other people are visitors, and when they leave, we'll still be here to pick up the pieces, no matter what shape it's in. (Mulhern, 1988, p. 1)

Fifty percent of Native American Indians have lived off reservations for over a decade (U.S. Bureau of the Census, 1981). This physical separation from reservation culture has resulted in a varied degree of commitment to tribal customs and traditional values. Native American Indians are a people of many peoples whose diversity is played out in a variety of customs, languages, and family types (Garrett & Garrett, 1994). This diversity exists not only between members of different tribes but also among members within a single tribe.

Helping professionals must be careful not to make assumptions regarding the cultural orientation of Native students. As discussed in Chapter 2, the continuum of acculturation found in Native families can be generally described as comprising the following five patterns—pantraditional, traditional, transitional, bicultural, and assimilated (Garrett & Garrett, 1994; Herring, 1989, 1997a; LaFromboise et al., 1990; Valle, 1986). The reader should consult the references for additional discussions. Each of these familial types reflect a different level of acculturation and cultural commitment, and that commitment determines the counseling process.

View of Seeking Mental Health Services. Effective helping with Native youth must recognize their varied orientations to mental health professionals and school counseling. Research indicates that traditional Native adults seldom look to the mental health services of the dominant culture as a means of improving their chosen way of life (LaFromboise, 1988). In addition, many traditional Native adults recognize the need for professional aid only when community-based helping networks are unavailable or undesirable (Weinbach & Kuehner, 1985). Such reluctance to use professional counseling may also be attributable to older Native adults' memories of frequent negative and tragic interactions with non-Native people. Furthermore, many traditional Native individuals believe that mental illness is a justifiable outcome of human weakness or the result of avoiding the discipline necessary to maintain cultural values and community respect (Harras, 1987). Native youth are socialized to these traditional beliefs and values.

Native individuals who do avail themselves of mental health services often express concern about how conventional Western psychology superimposes biases onto their problems and molds their behavior in a direction that conflicts with Native cultural lifestyle orientations (LaFromboise, 1988). This incompatibility between conventional counseling approaches and indigenous approaches constitutes a cultural variance that may hinder effective counseling by the unknowing helping professional.

Biethnic Native Youth

The 1990 census estimated that at least 63% of all Native American Indians live off reservations, an increase from 50% in 1980. One result of this shift from reservation life to life in urban and rural areas is reflected in the increase of intertribal and interethnic marriages. Tucker and Mitchell-Kernan (1990) reported that interethnic marriage of Native American Indian women is practically normative, with 53.7% of Native American Indian females in interracial marriages. Over 60% of Native American Indians today are of mixed ancestry, resulting from intermarriages and intercouplings with dissimilar ethnic populations (Trimble & Fleming, 1989).

As a direct result of these interethnic interactions, the number of mixed ancestry youth is increasing, and this is reflected in school populations. The helping professional must be prepared to assess and accept this dualistic identity. In many situations, the presenting problem may be one of confused ethnic identity, and the need for support may be apparent.

Testimony 3.1

Anonymous, Biracial

One thing I can't get over is the way many Indians talk about Whites. I am particularly sensitive to it because I am part White. I realize that some Indians, having had discriminatory experiences with Whites, may have reason to feel anger; still this does not justify reverse discrimination. But the real hypocrisy is with those who are partially White themselves (most Indians, even those on the reservations, have some White blood, as their French, Spanish, and German names may indicate).

Recently I heard a guy who is half Indian sneer at "White ways." Today the dominant society has great influence upon Indians. Many Indians, even those who are pure bloods, have adopted White ways. They drive cars, work at factories, worship at White churches, adhere to White morals, and dress as Whites. Most Indian customs are just remnants. The true Indian (one who knows his religion, customs and their meanings, practices Indian crafts and can survive in the wilderness) is rare.

What is Indian? I don't know. Perhaps that is because I have been raised in White society. My mother was raised on the reservation so perhaps I should know what Indian is. People say, "It doesn't matter how much Indian you are if you feel Indian." I don't "feel" Indian. I accept my mother as I do myself without pinpointing what is Indian. Perhaps this feeling of Indian is feeling kinship for people with Indian blood.

I am defensive because I do not feel truly Indian. People talk about White ways and I fear being called an Apple [red outside, white inside]. I wonder how many people feel the same way and thus knock Whites.

I search for something to validate myself as an Indian. I can make general statements about Indians such as: they are sharing and giving people, they lack materialism and live close to nature. But these apply only to Indians of the past who have lived close to the old culture. The true Indians are all but gone.

Within myself I feel rejected or feel the threat of rejection. My mother married a White man. Her family wanted her to marry an Indian. My aunt excludes my father from the address on her letters. As the offspring of such a marriage I am in a precarious position. I feel like an outsider.

When I was growing up I feared being rejected for my dark skin. I saw drunkenness and poverty when I visited the reservation during the summer. I wanted to be accepted in White society with Donna Reed mothers and modern homes. I was ashamed of being Indian. My White relatives talked about "Dagoes" in reference to Latin Americans and Italians. They are dark and so again I felt defensive about my skin color. As a half-breed, I was not fully accepted by either set of relatives.

In the TV commercial society, where Whites reign, any different skin color was inferior. I set out to prove that I was White. I believed in good grades, popularity, etc. Now I am tired of that, although these expectations still haunt me. Unfortunately many traditionalists are turning to these new same shallow values. Where are the Indians who still have an answer and are willing to share their wisdom with those who listen sincerely? Probably most Indians will adopt materialistic values. But an alternative should be available for those who want it.

McFee (1968) believed that those individuals who are comfortable being half in the Native world and half in the non-Native world possess a third dimension stemming from biculturality that renders them 150% men and women. Whether his conclusion is valid or not, it gives pause to reflect. As a reader of this text, how would you interpret this statement?

Effective Counseling With Native Youth

Because of relatively few Native counselors, most Native students will likely be counseled by dissimilar ethnic helping professionals. The non-Native helping professional planning interventions with Native youth should consider the following questions: What unique Native cultural and developmental characteristics are important to know? How can the counselor develop trust, rapport, and genuine respect for Native youth? Will individual, family, or group therapy be most effective? (Baruth & Manning, 1999).

In addition, Trimble and Fleming (1989) suggested that a helping professional can be effective if he or she can communicate and exhibit behaviors that characterize traditional helpers such as shamans, spirit healers, and medicine people. They describe a traditional healer's qualities as exemplifying "empathy, genuineness, availability, respect, warmth, congruence, and concreteness. . . . Effective counseling with Indians begins when a counselor carefully attends to these basic characteristics" (p. 185).

Also, Tafoya (1989) used a traditional Sahaptin legend to serve as a paradigm "for the way many Native American Indians conceptualize relationships, responsibilities, learning, and teaching, . . . [the aspects Tafoya sees as] core elements in family therapy" (p. 72). Tafoya discussed traditional healing approaches in Native cultures, cross-cultural concerns, concerns related to spouse interactions, and family therapy issues. He discussed the importance of the circle as a sacred symbol and model for relationships and asked helping professionals: "How can you assist your clients and patients to creatively complete their circles?" (p. 97).

A review of the literature on counseling Native young people (Thompson & Rudolph, 1988) highlighted several aspects of the Native culture that are important for helping professionals to remember (depending on the level of acculturation):

- Young people are respected to the same degree as adults.
- Cooperation and harmony are valued.
- Generosity and sharing are important, and individuals are judged on their contributions.

- Competition may be encouraged as long as it does not hurt anyone.
- The Native individual lives in the present, with little concern for planning for tomorrow.
- Native students may consider some behaviors strange or rude (e.g., loud talking, reprimands).
- Ancient legends and cultural traditions are important.
- Peace and politeness are essential; confrontation is rude.

Directions for Synergetic Counseling

Successful counseling often hinges on understanding traditional cultural attitudes, beliefs, and values, and being able to incorporate them into the helping intervention. Helping professionals may need to become familiar with both content and process concerns when working with Native youth as well (Herring, 1990b). Content concerns might include worldview differences between counselor and counselee, or the special needs and unique problems of Native youth, whereas process concerns might include varied levels of acculturation or differences in socioeconomic status. Inherent in process and content concerns, helping professionals might heed the following cautions and recommendations relative to the helping environment and atmosphere.

Create a Culturally Affirmative Environment. Zitzow and Estes (1981) called the degree to which people identify with their ethnic heritage "heritage consistency." Despite pressure from the dominant culture to conform to "majority" standards for behavior, and thereby subjugate their heritage, most Native individuals have learned to survive by becoming bicultural in a functional sense. This cultural fluency has implications for counseling in light of recommendations from some professionals that helping professionals "go Native" when counseling cross-culturally (Eldredge, 1993).

If a non-Native helping professional attempts to use Native practices (e.g., burning herbs during counseling, conducting rituals, wearing Native jewelry and clothing), the traditional Native student may be offended or alienated. They may view these pseudo-Native practices with distrust or disdain, which would be injurious to the counseling relationship (Eldredge, 1993).

Similar recommendations that helping professionals who are working with Native students dress informally and that women counselors use subtle makeup may also be negatively perceived by the student. Littrell and Littrell (1983) conducted a study of Native American Indian counselees, which included counselor dress as a variable in client perceptions of empathy, warmth, and genuineness. The results indicated that Native American Indians who are bicultural may perceive such "dressing down" in a negative way. Because of their ability to survive in two, or perhaps three, cultures, they are aware of the dominant culture's values of professional dress and may feel insult rather than comfort and rapport (Trimble & Fleming, 1989).

Arguments have been made for the superiority of Native helping professionals to non-Native counselors in working with Native students (e.g., Darou, 1992). Trustworthiness, however, has been identified as a more significant variable than ethnicity in the effectiveness of helping professionals (LaFromboise & Dixon, 1981; Lazarus, 1982).

The role of social influences in the counseling process as perceived by Native students also needs to be considered. For example, the underuse of mental health services and school counseling by Native students is often associated with the tension surrounding power differentials in helping relationships and perceived conflicting goals for acculturation between counselors and Native counselees (LaFromboise et al., 1990).

Some practical, synergetic recommendations, which may help create a culturally affirmative environment for Native students but which do not require helping professionals to deny their own culture, include the following:

1. *Address openly the issue of dissimilar ethnic relationships rather than pretending that no differences exist.* The student will perceive the helping professional as sensitive and aware of the tensions, as well as open to discussing them without defensiveness (Katz, 1981). Richardson (1981) encouraged school counselors to admit that they may say something offensive, albeit out of ignorance, and to enlist the student to help clarify and correct the error.

2. *Evaluate the degree of acculturation of the student.* The helping professional can use cues from dress, daily activities, family involvement, involvement with tribal functions, friendship patterns, body language, and eye contact. Evaluate the student's behaviors within the context of the predominant cultural identities.

3. *Schedule appointments to allow for flexibility in ending the session* (Katz, 1981). Frequently, traditional Native students prefer open-ended sessions to ensure complete closure to the presenting problem without time constraints. Do not be upset if the traditional Native student is late for appointments or insists on staying longer than the scheduled time.

4. *Be open to allowing the extended family to participate in the session.* In the case of absent family members, develop surrogate families. For example, the problem of child abuse has been addressed by creating surrogate

extended family networks in urban areas (Metcalf, 1979). At times it may be appropriate to hold the session in the family's home environment, in their house, on their property, or, when working on the reservation, perhaps in the counselor's car. Also, consultation with tribal healers and elders should be accepted, if desired by the student. And although it is not recommended that non-Native counselors attempt to direct traditional ceremonial activities, encouraging students to participate in certain rituals and healing arts may be beneficial (Kaplan & Johnson, 1964; Locust, 1985).

5. *Allow time for trust to develop before focusing on problems.* Locust (personal communication to N. M. Eldredge, September, 1991) suggested that, particularly during an initial session, the helping professional should allow a "warm-up" time by talking about common interests or other neutral topics, before focusing on counseling issues. The first session should be extended.

6. *Use strategies that elicit practical solutions to problems.* Although it is not advisable to be directive to the point of making suggestions and giving advice, the active role of "joining," in which the student and helping professional work together to solve a problem, would be appropriate (Pedersen, 1977). In addition, a nondirective approach may allow self-exploration and self-generated goals. A blend of techniques to fit each counselee is beneficial. Avoid intense and provocative confrontation. Also, helping professionals may want to consider using nontraditional methods of counseling that rely on myth-making and metaphor as an alternative to straight talk therapy.

7. *Establish eye contact.* Even if the Native student avoids eye contact (a culturally appropriate behavior), the helping professional may maintain eye contact (without staring) sufficient for appropriate conversation, especially with a Native student who is hearing challenged.

8. *Respect the uses of silence.* Silence may be the beginning of an important disclosure or may signify deep thought. Nonproductive silence, or "waiting out the client," is not recommended, however. During the session, paraphrasing is useful, as is summary, to show the student you have been listening carefully (Richardson, 1981).

9. *Demonstrate honor and respect for the student's culture(s).* Helping professionals should observe carefully and be very aware of their own values and their effect on the session. If the helping professional has a strong emotional response (either positive or negative) to the student or session content, the values of the helping professional are probably affecting the session. Helping professionals should carefully analyze the root of the emotional response.

For example, traditional Native students are socialized not to ventilate feelings. Among traditional Oglala Lakota, ventilation of feelings about death or dying is unacceptable (Broken Nose, 1992). To grieve for someone who is in the process of dying is viewed as hurrying the person on his or her way. And to talk about someone who has died is viewed as holding his or her spirit back from the spirit world. One can talk to the person during the wake period of four days and nights.

10. *Assist Native students in their ethnic identity issues.* To expand awareness of the effect of their ethnocultural and racial heritages on their thinking and behavior, Native students need to be encouraged to look beyond the broad category of Native American Indian or Alaska Native for self-identification (e.g., the Nation of Sioux). To expand Native students' knowledge of the historical background of Native peoples, including their history of oppression and their history of helping services, Native students need to summarize the history of their tribe or nation from the time of first contact with European immigrants, explaining how the immigrants treated their tribe or nation, and determine who performed the helping service needs for their group throughout its recorded history (Wehrly, 1995).

11. *Maintain the highest level of confidentiality.* Native communities are extremely close. A wrong word or questionable ethical practice can rapidly destroy credibility and trust. Honesty and genuineness are vital.

Conducting the Synergetic Session

The goal of synergetic counseling, as with most other paradigms, is to create a dialogue of growth with individual students, their families, their communities, and across mainstream cultures. Embedded in this goal is the recognition of cultural and environmental influences on the individual. To accomplish this task, the helping professional needs to develop an open-mindedness toward the Native student's worldview (Ibrahim, 1991; Pedersen, Fukuyama, & Heath, 1989).

Initial Session. The initial session or contact is vital to developing the counseling relationship with Native students. From the beginning of the encounter, Native students may be evaluating the total presentation of the school counselor (e.g., manner of greeting, physical appearance, ethnicity, nonverbal behavior and communication, and other subtle characteristics). The first few minutes of the session are very important to its success or failure. The helping professional has to demonstrate content knowledge of the culture to gain the respect of the counselee. For example, awareness of the tribal identity and familial pattern of the student may need to be acknowledged immediately. Such an acknowledgment will convey to the student the attitude and concern of the helping professional for Native culture.

Something to Consider 3.1

Common Presenting Problems for Native Children

A review of the literature reveals multiple presenting problems of Native children in school settings or mental health clinics. These problems include the following, depending on the level of acculturation:

- Failure to develop a strong ethnic identity and self-identity
- Adverse effects of misperceptions about Native peoples in general
- Adverse effects of discrimination and hatred toward Native peoples, both generally and specifically
- Distrust of European American school counselors and helping professionals based on historical and contemporary negative interactions
- Poor Standard English skills or limited use of English
- Nonverbal communication style conflicting with European American verbal expectations
- Inability to reconcile Native cultural values and mainstream values
- Lower academic achievements after the fourth grade
- Conflicts resulting from changing from an extended family-centered world to a peer-centered one
- Physical appearance, psychosocial, and possible intellectual differences (including learning style differentiations)

Something to Consider 3.2

Common Presenting Problems for Native Adolescents

A review of the literature reveals multiple presenting problems of Native adolescents in school settings or mental health clinics. These problems include the following, depending on the level of acculturation:

- Failure to develop a positive self and ethnic identity
- Reactions to stereotypical misperceptions of Native peoples
- Communication conflicts, such as ESL or a preference for nonverbal communication
- Conflicts between family loyalty and peer pressures
- Effects of misunderstandings and misperceptions of school personnel
- Poor academic achievement
- Substance use and abuse
- Adverse effects of discrimination and bias
- Generational conflicts resulting from varying degrees of acculturation

Within-Group Variances. Helping professionals working with Native youth must ascertain three important characteristics: cultural commitment (i.e., familial pattern), place of residence (reservation, rural, or urban setting), and tribal affiliation (Garrett & Garrett, 1994). Given the variance in family patterns, residences, and tribes, several ideas can be suggested to enhance effective counseling interventions with Native children and adolescents. First, most Native history and culture is characterized by an oral tradition of communication (Herring, 1990c). The helping professional must pay attention to and subtly match the Native student's tone of voice, pace of speech, and degree of eye contact (LaFromboise et al., 1990; Thomason, 1991). Assessments of cultural commitment and tribal structure, customs, and beliefs will provide useful information on how to proceed (Garrett & Garrett, 1994). But remember, every Native student should be approached as an individual first.

In counseling and guidance activities, this oral tradition can easily be integrated with the Native respect for elders. Community and tribal leaders can be effective resources in sharing customs and the "old way" through oral histories. Such oral communication can be an important adjunct to school guidance activities.

Second, helping professionals might consider using various media resources in their interventions. Media resources, however, must be authentic and bias-free. Videos and films are also available depicting Native art, crafts, and music. Appropriate media materials can be obtained by contacting tribal organizations, Bureau of Indian Affairs offices, federal and state offices of Indian education, and other such agencies. Such media examples can supplement non-Native perspectives, as well as expand Native views about different tribal characteristics. In addition, both Native youth and non-Native youth can benefit through vicarious exposures to "the Indian way." The helping professional, however, must always remember not to generalize a particular media presentation to all Native groups.

Establishment of Trust and Respect Via Linking Practices. Helping professionals must establish trustworthiness and respect to receive trust and respect. They need to be attentive and responsive to the Native student, giving structure and direction to the process, and displaying respect for culturally relevant values and beliefs (LaFromboise & Dixon, 1981). Showing respect could also mean being open to or suggesting the possibility of consultation with a traditional healer. In fact, "linking" services could prove to be very effective if services could be provided by traditional healers in conjunction with traditional counseling or therapy (Garrett & Garrett, 1994). Such linking would be a clear demonstration of respect for traditional ways while providing a more comprehensive service to Native students.

To illustrate linking counseling paradigms, Garrett (1991) described the unique system of health service practiced by the Cherokee Indian Hospital in North Carolina:

> Anybody in the hospital who wanted to go to a medicine man, or have a medicine man visit them, could do so, as long as the mode of treatment didn't interfere with the treatment modality used by the clinicians in the hospital. And if it did, then the patient could sign a waiver, or release themselves from the care of the hospital physicians. That way they could make a clear choice about which medicine pathway they wanted to follow. That was the whole idea. There was no judgment made about the way they were going. It gave the choice back to them, so that they could become a part of their own care. (p. 171)

Another way of demonstrating respect for the traditional way is to encourage extended family members to participate in the healing process. Working in the presence of a group, giving people a choice about the best way to proceed with the process, and encouraging the participation of family members and friends are all natural components of the traditional healing-way (Garrett & Garrett, 1994).

Practicality. Native students are influenced by several cultures and to rigidly classify them establishes yet another prejudicial system and contributes to a variation of oppression (Peregoy, 1991). Research studies have indicated that Native students seek someone who understands the practical aspects of tribal culture and conveys sound advice (Dauphinais, Dauphinais, & Rowe, 1981). Peregoy (1991, 1993) concluded that although cultural similarity of the helping professional was not necessary, Native students preferred a professional who possessed a general awareness of historical and current relationships between Natives and non-Natives, some specific tribal knowledge, an understanding of Native family relationships, and who was culturally sensitive.

Many traditional Native students may view the helping professional as an elder, expecting him or her to be less verbal than most helping professionals. Peregoy (1993, 1999) suggested that the counseling process and confidentiality of the relationship be briefly discussed and an example be given of a typical session. This format serves several purposes: (a) It provides Native students with an understanding of the counseling process; (b) It emphasizes the importance of confidentiality, which may enhance the Native student's trust in the relationship; and (c) It indicates to Native students what their expected role in therapy might be.

Most Native students will experience great discomfort in what is perceived as intrusive questioning or the demand for self-disclosure (Good Tracks,

1973). Early in the relationship the helping professional may make the Native student more comfortable by practicing or modeling some self-disclosure and indicating the desire for reciprocity (LaFromboise & Bigfoot, 1988). Thomason (1991) described the shared worldviews of the Native perspective of health as the need for balance in all domains of life—social and community, spiritual, and right living—as components of a whole that cannot be divided into its parts.

A traditional Native student who seeks assistance from an indigenous healer looks to the healer to identify the cause of the problem and work the cures (Peregoy, 1993, 1999). A helping professional must demonstrate patience, exemplified by not offering advice or interpretation without being invited to do so. At the same time, possibilities must be described and solutions suggested with the realization that no one knows as well as the client what course is best (Garrett & Garrett, 1994).

Communication Style. Helping professionals should also describe possibilities in a language that will be understood by the student—both verbally and nonverbally (Garrett & Garrett, 1994). Similarly, the Native student's verbal and nonverbal language should not be misinterpreted. Native adolescents, like adolescents of other cultures, need the security and psychological safety provided by a common language (Baruth & Manning, 1999). Some Native adolescents, however, speak only their Native language, some speak only standard English, and others are bilingual. The Native adolescent's ability to reach out to a wider world depends greatly on his or her ability to speak and understand the language of the majority and other cultures (Youngman & Sadongei, 1983).

Attending a school staffed with non-Native educators and facing problems associated with not being understood may affect the adolescent's perceived ability to cope successfully in a predominantly European American society (Baruth & Manning, 1999). Language problems might also contribute to the adolescent's tendency to decline in academic achievement, especially because lack of cognitive and academic skills do not appear to be major factors in this coping process (Sanders, 1987).

Another language problem results when adolescents must decide which language to speak. "Native youth respect their language as a part of their culture. This regard for their native language, however, conflicts with the European American opinion that English is the Native student's means to success (or, at least, the European definition of success) and should be the predominant language" (Baruth & Manning, 1999, p. 329).

Smolkin and Suina (1996) examined issues that extend beyond language and individual students and the losses experienced in Native communities. Specifically, these researchers explored issues related to Native children as

Native cultures lose their languages. These authors demonstrated how children become lost in language, how teachers and other helping professionals often experience difficulty understanding the importance of Native languages, how some schools prohibit Native language use in schools, and how some schools offer bilingual programs. For those lost in language, greater links between school and community can be forged so that teachers and other helping professionals can access knowledge about the nature of the Native language and its functions.

The methods of silence, restatement, and general lead tend to be most effective with Native students, because they are the least intrusive and allow plenty of room for clarification (Herring, 1990b; Richardson, 1981). Silence, for example, should be viewed in positive terms, rather than as a reflection of counselor inadequacy. Native students in the counseling situation may exhibit silence, a seeming lack of attentiveness, and passive noncompliance (LaFromboise et al., 1990; Trimble, 1981). Native children are taught from a very early age the importance of learning through observation. Modeling and role playing are justifiable and invaluable methods of counseling and guidance.

Dimensions of Life. Arredondo (1986) recommended a holistic counseling approach, which encompasses six dimensions of the Native student's life: the historical era, sociopolitical factors, sociocultural factors, individual variables, developmental tasks, and esteem and identity themes. The helping professional can combine these dimensions with social cognitive interventions. This synergetic framework is considered less culturally biased than other approaches because it recognizes the impact of personal and environmental variables. This approach also allows the Native student to define individually appropriate behaviors or targets for intervention. The approach is culturally sensitive in that it provides for differences across and within tribes (LaFromboise & Rowe, 1983).

Group Work. Group skills training with Native students has been an effective means for teaching new behaviors and skills, especially with social cognitive interventions (LaFromboise & Bigfoot, 1988). Social cognitive strategies reduce the emphasis on individual disclosure, which is difficult for some, and introduces collective responsibility, which responds to the collective approach characteristic of some tribes (LaFromboise & Graff Low, 1998).

LaFromboise and Graff Low (1998) pointed out that when working with Native students, the school counselor must be aware of the influence the dominant culture may have on the student's self-deprecating and irrational belief system. Beliefs that are irrational by standards of the dominant culture may be perfectly legitimate given the course of Native and non-Native relations or within the specific cultural context (LaFromboise et al., 1990). For example, mistrust of the educational system and even counseling may be rooted in historical mistrust resulting from assimilationist policy (Locust, 1988).

Guided Imagery. Another culturally appropriate technique is the use of guided imagery (Peregoy, 1993). For example, a Native female student comes to the school counselor's office with presenting concerns related to her self-concept. The school counselor may want to use guided imagery techniques to have the student visualize herself as she perceives herself to be, and then have her visualize how she would ideally like to be. Once this is done, the student then develops steps, with the assistance of the counselor, to work toward the goal of how she would like to perceive herself in the future.

Indigenous Methods. The vision quest can be creatively incorporated into individual treatment strategies or implemented within ongoing treatment programs (Heinrich, Corbine, & Thomas, 1990). Outward Bound Schools (and wilderness education programs) have used one- to three-day solo wilderness experiences in helping troubled adolescents to reduce depression, tension, and rage and to develop a more positive self-concept (e.g., Marsh, Richards, & Barnes, 1986). This solo experience is similar to the vision quest, without its cultural spiritualism.

If the counseling process is concerned with finding one's way and with the recovery of purpose and meaning, then the vision quest is an important, culturally relevant metaphor for helping professionals (Heinrich et al., 1990). In speaking of this rite, Brown (1964) stated:

> This sacred retreat is still practiced by a number of Plains Indian men and women who have the wisdom to know that without vision man loses his sense of relationship and harmony with the world around him; he is caught up in the darkness of his ego, and too easily forgets the purpose for which he was given the precious gift of life. (p. 21)

Manson (1986) reported that "many traditional Indian and Native healing practices are gradually being incorporated into contemporary approaches to mental health treatment" (p. 64). He described three such practices as (1) *four circles*—concentric circles of relationship between client and Creator, spouse, nuclear family, and extended family as a culturally based structural concept of self-understanding; (2) *talking circle*—a forum for expressing thoughts and feelings in an environment of total acceptance without time constraints, using sacred objects (e.g., feathers or stones), the pipe, and prayer; and (3) *sweat lodge*—a physical and spiritual self-purification ritual emphasizing the relationship of the human being to all of creation.

Hall (1986) reported that the sweat lodge ceremony was being used or encouraged in 22 of 44 Indian Health Service alcohol treatment programs surveyed. Broken Nose (1992) described this ceremony in these words:

> The sweat lodge is a dome-like structure, usually constructed from willow branches and covered with heavy cloth and canvas. (The construction materials may vary as long as steam is contained and light is kept out.) It serves as a sacred place of prayer. When the boys gathered there, the leader poured water over a pile of rocks in the middle of the circle, filling the lodge with steam. Each boy prayed aloud. Sometimes the boy received a sign from the spirits— lights around his head or the touch of an eagle feather. The spirits spoke to the leader about the prayers of each boy. The leader, in turn, passed along the spirits' suggestions and advice. (p. 383)

Hall concluded, "The possibility exists that, fostered by but not controlled by or restricted to alcohol treatment programs, the sweat lodge may have a major role in the prevention of alcohol abuse and in the creation of a new Indian identity" (p. 176).

Hayne (1993) compiled two catalogues describing programs, events, and activities designed to prevent the use of alcohol and other drugs by Native peoples, particularly adolescents and other young people. Together the catalogues include 61 descriptions of programs developed and implemented by the five agencies under the auspices of the Regional Centers for Drug-Free Schools and Communities Program (Portland, Oregon). Program strategies include comprehensive, ongoing prevention programs, as well as annual stand-alone events that may be school- or community-based. In addition to drug and alcohol education, many programs incorporate health education, training in coping and communication skills, group and individual therapeutic activities, counseling services, camping or other outdoor activities, recreation, and cultural events and activities. The catalogues contain information about contact persons, target group, special features of the program, program description, and an overview of activities, including program evaluation and staff training.

The work of healing is most effectively done with metaphors: "Traditional healing systems draw on metaphors resonant within the culture to construct the illness reality and then symbolically manipulate it to effect healing" (Good & Good, 1986, p. 18). Helping professionals must be able to identify what these metaphors are within the student's reality. "Now, if a patient believes in rituals and sacraments, I put down cedar. I use feathers and herbs. It isn't that I have any magic; it's the rituals and their sacramental quality—

they *are* healing" (Hammerschlag, 1988, p. 87). Familiarity with traditional healing practices can provide access to those metaphors.

Summary

This chapter has attempted to convey to future and current school counselors, and other helping professionals, ethnic-appropriate information relative to the delivery of mental health services to Native children and adolescents. A primary emphasis was placed on within-group differences and level of acculturation and how helping professionals can ascertain these differences within the counseling context. Garrett and Garrett (1994) offered a few basic recommendations for counseling with Native students:

- Ask permission whenever possible and always give thanks.
- Never interrupt—allow sufficient time for responding.
- Be patient.
- Use silence whenever appropriate.
- Use descriptive statements rather than questioning.
- Model self-disclosure through anecdotes or short stories.
- Make use of metaphors and imagery when appropriate.
- Try not to separate the person from the spirituality or from affiliation with the tribal group. Honor those sacred relationships.
- Recognize the relative nature of value judgments such as "right or wrong" and "good or bad." (p. 143)

If helping professionals will heed the content and process information presented in this chapter, the gaps between cultural worlds, and between harmony and disharmony, can be bridged. If Native American Indian and Alaska Native youth are expected to learn and practice mainstream culture, then school counselors and educators should also enter the counseling situation with a willingness to learn. As Garrett and Garrett (1994) concluded:

If counselors and educators come first as students, and second, as professionals, they might be surprised at how much growth would take place by members of both worlds. We all want to "walk the path of Good Medicine," and we can always use a little help. (p. 143)

Experiential Activities

The following case study illustrates some of the dilemmas of contemporary Native American Indian peoples. How has the sociocultural developmental process affected the individuals involved? What other factors can be inferred? How would you help the individuals in this vignette?

One woman tells the story of her son and her father. Her father was the medicine man of the tribe, and because his own sons were killed or had died, he looked forward to teaching and leaving to his grandson the ways of the medicine man. He would say to his grandson that one day, when he died, the grandson would be able to heal the people of the tribe and be held in great respect and esteem. The grandson had been raised in a missionary boarding school and felt that his grandfather was out of step with the 20th century. He would argue with his grandfather about the practical usefulness of his medicine and would look with disdain at the people who sought his grandfather's help, advice, and healing. The grandson would often feel disgusted and angry with his mother for making him visit his grandfather. His mother could not validate the grandfather's way of life because she, too, had gone away to school. Although she had not completed school, she had learned enough to know that some things were simply not discussed, like her father being a medicine man. She, herself, had some difficulty "fitting in" when she returned to the reservation. Even though it pained the mother greatly to see the widening gap between her father and her son, she felt powerless to do anything about it. She didn't understand her father's ways and could not really understand her son either. She became more and more depressed and began to drink heavily in response to the growing distance between the two. She blamed herself for not understanding her father's beliefs and for having sent her son to a missionary school. She felt totally disenfranchised by her family and her community, and wrestled constantly with trying to discover her own identity. (G. P. Sage, 1991, pp. 24-25. Reprinted with permission)

4

Counseling Native Adults

When questioned by an anthropologist on what Indians called America before the white man came, an Indian said simply, "Ours."

Deloria, 1988, p. 166

Over the past 20 years, the United States has witnessed many social, cultural, and demographic shifts that continue to mold our contemporary society, a population of diverse peoples (Herring, 1995). However, historical factors continue to exert a powerful influence on the experiences of many Native peoples. This chapter attempts to convey the influences of history and environment on the mental health needs of the adult Native population. As Baruth and Manning (1999) aptly concluded:

> Counseling Native adults requires an understanding of their culture's historical traditions, an appreciation of the effects of centuries of discrimination, and an awareness of such contemporary problems as high suicide rate, low educational level, and high alcoholism rate. (p. 357)

Historical Overview

Throughout U.S. history there have been deliberate attempts by mainstream communities (e.g., government agencies, schools, and churches) to destroy the Native institutions of family, clan and tribe, religious belief systems, customs, and traditional ways of life (Deloria, 1988; Heinrich et al.,

1990; Herring, 1989, 1997a; Locust, 1988; Reyhner & Eder, 1992). Concurrently, characterized by institutional discrimination, Native peoples have also experienced a history of misunderstanding of cultural values by the dominant culture (Deloria, 1988; Herring, 1997a; Locust, 1988). A cursory glimpse at this history provides the foundation for this chapter's discussion.

U.S. policies of enculturation (i.e., coercive assimilation) have had a pervasive impact on Native peoples and their way of life (Burnam, Telles, Hough, & Escobar, 1987; Domino & Acosta, 1987; Herring, 1989, 1997a; Locust, 1988). For example, the U.S. citizenship of Native peoples was not recognized until 1924 (Deloria, 1988). In addition, Native peoples' religious freedoms were not recognized until the American Indian Religious Freedom Act of 1978, which guaranteed Native peoples the constitutional right to practice traditional religion (Deloria, 1988).

These examples represent a few of the historical factors that have affected Native peoples psychologically, economically, and socially. Although the experiences of many Native peoples changed as circumstances and policies changed, historical factors and the processes of culturation are still powerful influences on the lives of a people faced with difficult decisions about who they are and how they want to live (Garrett, 1996; Herring, 1989, 1997a; Reyhner & Eder, 1992).

Contemporary Demographics and Diversity

Most non-Native people lack an adequate awareness of Native groups and their diversity. As presented in Chapter 1, the numerous nations, tribes, clans, and bands have some commonalities but also many differences. This diversity is also seen in varying degrees of cultural commitment among the members of a given tribe, based on variations in value orientation (Johnson & Lashley, 1989; LaFromboise et al., 1990).

Another example of diversity is found in the 1990 census estimate that at least 63% of Native peoples live off reservations, an increase from 50% in 1980. Urban Native peoples are more likely to be extremely migratory, from urban setting to urban setting or from reservation to urban setting and back (Sage, 1997). Some are searching for the "American dream," some are looking for economic opportunities and adequate housing, and others are seeking educational opportunity (Witt, 1980). Many are mixed-bloods and have limited, if any, relationship to the reservation of their parent or parents (Sage, 1997). One result of this shift from reservations to urban or rural areas is reflected in the increase of intertribal and interethnic marriages. Currently, over 60% of Native peoples are of mixed ancestry, resulting from intermarriages and intercouplings with other tribal and ethnic populations (Trimble et al., 1996).

Over 4% of Native adults have less than five years of formal education. Over 34% of Native adults have less than 12 years of schooling, compared with 22.1% for European Americans. In 1990, 2.1% of Native 18- to 24-year-olds had completed undergraduate degrees, compared with 8.6% of European Americans (Ward, 1995). From 1989 to 1991, the Native adult suicide rate was 16.5 per 100,000, compared with 11.5 per 100,000 for the rest of the U.S. population (Indian Health Service, 1994). Although the proportion of the population of Native adults between 18 and 64 years of age fluctuated between 55% and 63% between 1900 and 1990, this is expected to decrease to about 56% between 2030 and 2050 (U.S. DHHS, 1996).

These demographics, and others presented in previous and subsequent chapters, illustrate that the contemporary Native adult is not isolated on a reservation but is often a member of the general community (Peregoy, 1991, 1999). However, a prevailing sense of "Indianness" based on common worldview appears to bind Native peoples together as a "people of many peoples" (Garrett & Garrett, 1994).

Current socioeconomic, educational, and cultural challenges to the positive growth of Native adults can be attributed, in large measure, to the history of their people, a history characterized by military defeat, ethnic demoralization, and forced displacement. This conflict of cultural worldviews between Native and non-Native peoples continues to create negative influences. Many challenges associated with this conflict are apparent in contemporary Native life (Herring, 1994, 1997a, 1997b).

Some discussion is required regarding gender-specific problems among Native adults. A consensus statement on Native women's health care identified a number of physical and mental health problems from which Native women suffer in disproportionate numbers (Indian Health Service, 1991). Native women face incredible dilemmas that increase the risk of psychological disturbance (LaFromboise, Berman, & Sohi, 1994). Lifestyle-related clinical issues shed light on the complex and multifaceted problems of Native women. One clinical issue is depression, which, when coupled with ethnic discrimination from the surrounding community, seriously affects the mental well-being of Native women. Diagnosis of cyclothymic personality was more frequent among women than men when the American Indian Depression Schedule was used. Far fewer men (22%) than women (78%) were diagnosed as having experienced primary depression (Manson, Shore, Bloom, Keepers, & Neligh, 1987). Depression was found in 76% of women using Indian Health Service (IHS) mental health services (Indian Health Service, 1988).

Alcoholism and its multigenerational effects remains the most critical mental and physical health problem plaguing Native peoples today. The death rate of young Native women 15 to 24 years of age from alcohol or substance abuse exceeds that of Native men by 40% (Indian Health Service, 1991). Native women have a much higher alcoholism rate than women in the general population. In fact, one study indicated that alcoholism rates for Native women are the same as those for Native men (Manson, Shore, Baron, Ackerson, & Neligh, 1992). The rates of alcoholism do vary from tribe to tribe, and in some tribes only a small proportion of Native women have serious alcohol abuse problems (Hill, 1989). According to Ozer (1986), Native men are twice as likely as non-Native men to be in treatment for drug-related problems. A high rate of fetal alcohol syndrome (FAS) and fetal alcohol effect (FAE) is evident among the children of Native women. Finally, a majority of female substance abusers in Native substance abuse treatment programs are survivors of childhood sexual abuse (Dixon, 1989).

Prevention of alcohol and other drug abuse among Native peoples, especially women, is vital to the perpetuation of Native culture. Native American Indian culture places a high value on femininity, because many aspects of nature are seen as feminine (e.g., "Mother Nature"). The sky, wind, and mountains have both masculine and feminine elements. In these cultures, women's sexuality seems to be more respected than in machoistic societies (Quintero, 1995). In these cases, femininity is synonymous with the expression of the female principles of nurturance and life-giving receptivity. These principles are considered as strong as the male principles of dominance, achievement, and intrusiveness, and exist in balance and rhythm.

Native Culture: The Key to Counseling Practice

Helping professionals are confronted with major tasks in promoting the career, mental, and social development of Native adults. Before examining counseling practices for Native adults, however, four important issues need to be emphasized: (a) ambiguous terminology, (b) Native cultural perspectives, (c) effective counseling with Native adults, and (d) the importance of adopting a proactive approach to counseling Native adults (Herring, 1997b). Space constraints necessitate only a brief review of these issues.

Ambiguous Terminology

The reader may recall from Chapter 1 that there is no generic term for Native peoples (Herring, 1997a, 1997b). Using appropriate and truthful designations recognizes the diversity of Native people and may enhance Native adults' pride in self and community. For example, on the 1990 census, more people said they were Cherokee than could possibly have been the case; 1.8 million people said they were Native American Indian, but some claimed they were from "Arabic," "Polish," "Hispanic," or "Haitian" tribes (Roberts, 1995). The Southwest interior decorating and "Indian artifacts" fads of the 1990s have no doubt encouraged many individuals to seek their "roots."

Cultural Perspectives

To intervene effectively in the daily existence of Native adults, helping professionals must demonstrate a knowledge of the dynamics of Native culture. Although variations exist across tribes, Native values generally specify a harmony of the individual with the tribe, the tribe with the land, and the land with the Great Spirit (Garrett & Garrett, 1994). Central to this harmony is constancy—the timelessness and predictability of nature as the foundation of existence. Nature's cycle symbolizes eternity, and it transcends everything and gives respect to everything.

Generally, Native values consist of sharing, cooperation, noninterference, being, the tribe and extended family, harmony with nature, a present-time orientation (cyclical rather than linear), preference for explanation of natural phenomena according to the supernatural, and a deep respect for elders (Herring, 1990d, 1997b; Sue & Sue, 1990). By contrast, mainstream values emphasize saving, domination, competition, aggression, doing, individualism and the nuclear family, mastery over nature, a future-time orientation, a preference for scientific explanations of everything, "clock watching," "winning," and a reverence for youth (Herring, 1997b; Sue & Sue, 1990).

Many contemporary concerns are the products of this cultural clash. Native adults may experience conflict when they either have internalized, or attempt to internalize, the unfamiliar values of the dominant society, or have practiced, or seek to practice, the traditional roles necessary for the preservation of traditional values and practices (Herring, 1997b). The chasm between mainstream expectations and the cultural values of Native peoples can be referred to as *cultural discontinuity* (Garrett & Garrett, 1994, p. 135). This conflict leaves many Native adults "not knowing which way to go" (p. 136).

Frequently, this historical contrast has resulted in a resentment of European American authority figures (Trimble & Fleming, 1989). A long history of confusing messages from the federal government has created a double bind from which no escape is apparent. For example, the Indian Health Service—a governmental agency—provides mental health services, and although the government has given Native peoples no reason for trust, they must trust the agency to use these services (Sage, 1997).

Baruth and Manning (1999) described typical Native adult characteristics as including "passivity, shyness, a tendency to avoid assertiveness and aggressiveness, reverence for the person rather than possessions, respect for elders and the aged, adherence to fairly specific sex roles, noninterference with others, humility, an inclination to share, and a reluctance to criticize the Native American culture" (p. 358).

However, helping professionals must not generalize these characteristics to all Native groups or persons. For example, the Eastern Cherokee of North Carolina would not like being compared with the Catawba, the Mohawk, or the Chippewa, even though they have similar lifestyles, values, and problems. Another common mistake is to assume similar characteristics for all Native populations in a particular region (Attneave, 1982).

View of Health and Illness. Native peoples have their personal "medicine," or way of life, wherein they seek a balance of the Four Directions. The Medicine Wheel symbolizes the way of things as represented in the Four Directions, each of which stands for one aspect of living: east for spiritual, south for natural, west for physical, and north for mental. One's medicine is the way one balances self and the universe. Being in harmony implies being "in step with the universe"; being in disharmony means being "out of step with the universe" (Garrett & Garrett, 1994, p. 139).

Illness is traditionally viewed as an imbalance of various elements, with each tribe having its own understanding of equilibrium and balance within its oral history and religion; however, all describe conditions or behavior in terms of where it lies on a continuum of balance (Trimble, Manson, Dinges, & Medicine, 1984). The understandings and explanations for diseases of the mind and body (although not all tribes distinguish between the two) are based on the concept that a cure (restored balance) requires interwoven healing (Sage, 1997). Thus, if an individual is, for example, plagued by diabetes, healing benefits can be sought both from contemporary medical treatment and from traditional ceremonies and treatment. Balance is thus achieved or restored by using the total healing system (Sage, 1997).

Locust (1985) described the Native view of illness in the following manner:

> Native American Indians believe that each individual chooses to make himself well or to make himself unwell. If one stays in harmony, keeps all the tribal laws and all the sacred laws, one's spirit will be so strong that negativity will be unable to affect it. If one chooses to let anger or jealousy or self-pity control him, he has created disharmony for himself. Being in control of one's emo-

---

Something to Consider 4.1

Guidelines for Responding to Cultural Diversity

Giordano and Giordano (1995) suggested eight guidelines to respond to cultural diversity. They are adapted here for Native clients.

1. Assess the importance of ethnicity to Native clients and families. To what extent or degree of identification does the client reflect Native ethnicity?
2. Validate and strengthen the ethnic identity of Native clients. Be prepared for clients with low self-concepts.
3. Be aware of and use the Native client's natural support systems. The extended family is an extremely valuable resource.
4. Serve as a "culture broker" when addressing value conflicts. Emphasize positive aspects of all value systems.
5. Be aware of "cultural camouflage" as a defense against change. For example, "I'm late because I'm Native."
6. Know that there are advantages and disadvantages in being of the same ethnic group as your client (e.g., unresolved issues about one's own ethnicity).
7. Do not feel you have to "know everything" about all Native groups. Know as much as possible about the Native groups from which your clients may come.
8. To avoid polarization, always try to think in categories that allow for at least three possibilities. (p. 39)

---

tional responses is necessary if one is to remain in harmony. Once harmony is broken, however, the spiritual self is weakened and one becomes vulnerable to physical illness, mental and/or emotional upsets, and the disharmony projected by others. (p. 14)

**Implications for Effective Counseling
With Native Adults**

Most Native adults exist as dual citizens (i.e., as Natives and as non-Natives), retaining their traditional values but also seeking to live in mainstream society, at least materialistically. This dualistic lifestyle compounds the stress on these adults. To further complicate matters, within-group differences prevent the homogeneous treatment of this population.

Effective counseling with Native adults requires the helping professional to recognize within-group variances and level of acculturation. The helping professional will also need to employ strategies and interventions that are ethnically appropriate for this population. Examples of effective interventions with Native youth have been presented in the previous chapter and they are also congruent with adult populations. Something to Consider 4.1 presents some general guidelines for responding to cultural diversity.

A Proactive Perspective

Effective counseling with Native adults is predicated on adopting a proactive developmental perspective (Herring, 1997b). This perspective includes acquiring a thorough knowledge of Native history and past and present Native culture. It would also entail having an expanded understanding of Native adults.

Helping professionals will need to develop strategies and interventions that take into consideration the numerous effects of political and socioeconomic forces on Native adults. Initially, helping professionals should develop a battery of open-ended questions to obtain information in the areas of education, employment, urbanization, media influence, political participation, religion, language, daily life, and social relations (Trimble & Fleming, 1989). In addition, they may need to become systemic change agents, intervening in environments that impede the development of Native peoples. In particular, helping professionals will need to create a culturally affirmative environment in which to accomplish their helping goals. In Chapter 3, the following suggestions were offered to achieve this: (a) Address openly the issue of dissimilar ethnic relationships rather than pretending that no differences exist; (b) Evaluate the degree of acculturation of the client; (c) Schedule appointments to allow for flexibility in ending the session; (d) Be open to allowing other family members to participate in the counseling session; (e) Allow time for trust to develop before focusing on deeper feelings; (f) Use counseling strategies that elicit practical solutions to problems; (g) Maintain eye contact as appropriate; (h) Respect the uses of silence; (i) Demonstrate honor and respect for the client's culture; and (j) Maintain the highest level of confidentiality.

Conducting the Counseling Session

The goal of counseling is to create a dialogue of growth with individuals, their families, their communities, and across mainstream cultures. Embedded in this goal is the recognition of cultural and environmental influences on the individual. To accomplish this, the helping professional needs to develop an open-mindedness toward the client's worldview (Herring, 1997a). The helping professional needs to be cognizant of the suggestions in Chapter 3 relative to conducting the counseling session. The reader will recall that the importance of the initial session cannot be overemphasized. Other aspects previously discussed in Chapter 3, concerning Native youth, are also applicable to Native adults. Those aspects to be considered are within-group variances, establishment of trust and respect via linking practices, practicality, communication style, dimensions of life, group work, and guided imagery. The remaining discussions in this chapter will address some other aspects of counseling with Native adults whose presenting problems and concerns include the following:

- Difficulties stemming from overcoming myths and stereotypes that the Native culture is evil, savage, and inferior
- Negative effects of injustice, discrimination, hardship, and degradation
- Negative effects of poverty (e.g., high unemployment, low SES)
- Diverse cultural characteristics
- High suicide rate and low life expectancy
- Language difficulties and nonverbal communication misunderstandings
- Midlife crises
- Substance use and abuse
- Low self-concept and feelings of inferiority/rejection
- Low educational attainment

Additional Implications for Interventions

Interventions with Native clients present helping professionals with numerous challenges: intracultural diversity, lifestyle preferences that vary considerably from one client to another, communication differences, the reluctance of clients to disclose personal thoughts, and the shyness of some clients in helping situations (Trimble & Fleming, 1989). Native clients seek therapy for the same reasons as other people: marital problems, chemical dependency, and depression, for example (Sutton & Broken Nose, 1996). The goals of counseling will depend largely on the tribal heritage of the individual client and on the helping professional's assessment of the client's problems and degree of acculturation (Heinrich et al., 1990).

Although some interventions are effective for all cultures, Richardson (1981) recommended the following strategies to enhance the possibility of effective helping sessions with Native clients:

- *Admit your ignorance.* The helping professional may admit a lack of specific knowledge and may ask to be corrected if a cultural error is made.
- *See the positives.* The empathic helping professional recognizes the value and strengths of Native cultures.
- *Help by listening.* The helping professional must learn to listen to, not talk at, the Native client. Allow the client to teach and inform about his or her culture.

- *Make the client comfortable.* The helping professional should be flexible in the location of helping sessions. Rather than sitting side by side, some clients may prefer that the helping professional sit behind the desk (as a form of separation).
- *Settle back.* Helping professionals should not lean toward clients as if studying them. They may desire to take short notes and summarize at the end of the session to let the client know they have been listening.

Individual and Group Therapy

The decision to use individual or group therapy should be based on the individual client and his or her culture. Whichever is chosen, the fact that there is a 50% initial withdrawal rate of Native clients suggests that helping professionals should strive to make the first interview therapeutic, rather than simply using it to collect information and to make a diagnosis of the client's problems (Thomason, 1991). One important element for successful therapy with Native clients is to be aware of the impact of genocide.

It is worth being redundant to emphasize two important points. First, the Native client may be silent for long periods of time. To the Native client, nonverbal communication is as important as verbal communication. The non-Native helping professional may misinterpret Native individuals' tendency to look the other way in speaking and listening situations and to let conversation lapse for a few moments (Baruth & Manning, 1999). Silence may connote that the client is showing respect, is forming thoughts, or is waiting for signs that it is all right to speak. Native persons may be very indirect; for example, a Lakota woman may refer to her father-in-law as "he" rather than speak his name (Sutton & Broken Nose, 1996).

Second, restatement or summarization at the end of the session may enhance understanding. Taking lengthy notes maybe interpreted as not paying attention to what the Native client is saying. Similarly, receiving telephone calls may suggest that the caller is more important than the client.

Individual Therapy and Counseling. The helping professional must balance the need for establishing trust and the desire for effecting change, as some Native clients may expect immediate results and, therefore, be frustrated by a slow rate of change or the reluctance of the professional to supply answers (LaFromboise et al., 1994). In these cases, single session therapy that helps bolster the client's strengths, restore autonomy and confidence, and explore solutions for immediate implementation may be the treatment of choice (Talmon, 1991).

A number of conventional treatment techniques can be appropriate with Native clients. With female clients who have an adequate education level and English fluency, bibliotherapy may be used. As mentioned previously, a majority of Native women in therapy are sexual abuse victims and survivors. They can be encouraged to read books such as *Courage to Heal* (Bass & Davis, 1988), and both men and women should complete the exercises in the accompanying workbook (Davis, 1990). Another option would be to read stories and books about heroic survivors.

Stress reduction techniques (e.g., muscle relaxation and guided imagery) can be extremely useful with presenting problems such as a personal crisis or chronic stress. However, these methods need to reflect Native cultures and values. For example, when encouraging a Native client to imagine a peaceful place, "one might evoke images of a sanctuary adorned with works of art, poetry, or beadwork, birds and other wildlife, or the pleasing colors of the rainbow" (LaFromboise et al., 1994, p. 54).

Group Therapy and Counseling. Group work is becoming the treatment of choice for a number of agencies with programs serving Native peoples (Edwards & Edwards, 1984). One advantage of group therapy is that Native clients may share similar problems and frustrations. Group work also is congruent with the value most Native people place on cooperative activities. Disadvantages include Native clients' possible reluctance to share personal concerns and also their cultural tendency toward noninterference with others (Lum, 1992). Also, with Native clients, it is doubtful whether heterogeneous grouping will produce desired results (Lewis & Ho, 1989).

Dufrene and Coleman (1992) provided guidelines for group therapy with Native clients, which include the following: (a) Group therapy should respect the spiritual dimensions of Native cultures; (b) Group sessions should begin and end with a prayer that would be acceptable to Native tribes represented in the group; (c) Group counseling should be conducted by a Native professional; and (d) When a Native professional is unavailable, group counseling should be conducted by a non-Native professional with background knowledge of the particular tribe.

Structuring a group as an experiential class or workshop allows for the use of a theme, such as "Self-Esteem for Women," or "Native Adults in Transition." Many Native groups have also resulted from community attempts to cope with local crises. For example, when the Hopi faced the horror of the sexual abuse of more than 100 boys by a teacher ("Assault on the Peaceful," 1988), meetings of concerned parents turned into therapy sessions where adults, for the first time, revealed their own childhood experiences of abuse (LaFromboise et al., 1994).

Manson, Walker, and Kivlahan (1989) and Fleming (1989) suggested two Native American Indian group treatment strategies based on traditional healing practices: the "four circles" and the "talking circle." The four circles structures group exploration around issues related to individuals within each of the four increasingly larger concentric circles representing the Creator at the center, one's partner or spouse at the next level, one's immediate or "blended" family at the next level, and, in the outermost circle, one's extended family, co-workers or classmates, and community and tribal members.

The talking circle is a form of group therapy that includes elements of ritual and prayer, but does not depend on interaction between the participants. LaFromboise and colleagues (1994) cited talking or healing circles that were led by Alaska Native women for their three- and four-year-old grandchildren, teaching them to talk about their feelings through role playing and modeling. Ashby, Gilchrist, and Miramontez (1987) discovered that their group members selected the talking circle as the most helpful and useful activity in a program addressing sexual abuse.

Family Therapy

Family therapy with Native clients will have more positive results than will individual counseling sessions. It reflects not only the Native value of cooperation but also the value Native peoples place on talk.

In the world of psychology, the dominant assumption is that talk is good and can heal a person. Therapy has even been referred to as "the talking cure." In Sioux Indian culture, talking is actually proscribed in certain family relationships. A woman who has never exchanged a single word with her father-in-law may experience deep emotional intimacy with him, a relationship that is almost inconceivable in a pragmatic world. The reduced emphasis on verbal expression seems to free Native families for other kinds of experience of each other, of nature, and of the spiritual realm (McGoldrick & Giordano, 1996).

An indigenous "talking" technique, especially among the Navajo, is the "sing." A sing is a group of prayers and rituals engaged in to remove or neutralize the cause of disharmony and bring a return of harmony. A sing may include curing chants, dry paintings, massage and heat treatments, sweat baths, ceremonial baths in yucca suds, public dances, and other procedures, depending on the ailment and its cause (Kluckhohn & Leighton, 1962).

The "Indian Way" consists of families working together to solve problems. Family therapy, with its systemic approach and emphasis on relationships, is particularly effective in working with Native clients, whose life cycle orientation blends well with family therapy's approach (Sutton & Broken Nose, 1996). Studies show that Native clients come to treatment hoping that the therapist is an expert who can give them concrete, practical advice about their concerns and be sensitive to their cultural beliefs and differences (DuBray, 1993; LaFromboise et al., 1990). Culturally sensitive, nondirective approaches, which incorporate the use of storytelling, metaphor, and paradoxical interventions, are recommended. Networking and the use of ritual are favored over strategic interventions and brief therapy models.

The helping professional should also be aware of greeting patterns of Native people. Traditionally, when strangers meet, they often identify themselves through their relatives: "I am a Navajo. My name if Tiana Bighorn. My hometown is Tuba City, Arizona. I belong to the Deer Springs Clan, born for the Rocky Gap Clan" (Benet & Maloney, 1994, p. 9).

Just as one strives to be in harmony with one's human relatives, so should one try to be in harmony with one's spiritual and natural relatives: "My mother told me, every part of this earth is sacred to our people. Every pine needle. Every sand shore. Every mist in the dark woods. Every meadow and humming insect. The Earth is our mother" (Jeffers, 1991, p. 3).

In 1980, the American Medical Association revised its code of ethics, giving physicians permission to consult, and to take referrals from and make referrals to, nonphysician leaders, including Native medicine people (Polacca, 1995). Even practicing Christians may have an ongoing relationship with medicine people, which may positively or negatively affect a therapist's work with a family, as the following case reveals:

> The Jacobs, a biethnic (Catawba/English) family who relocated to a large urban area, and were practicing Christians, had two children—Judith (17) and Roger (16). The children were enrolled in a Christian parochial school system with a large Native American Indian population. They were referred by the school's guidance counselor because Roger clearly had a drug abuse problem. After initially feeling that things were going well, the therapist began to sense that the family had become resistant, particularly after Roger was placed in detention for a drug episode. The therapist had instructed the family to have Roger remain there so that he could really experience the consequences of his actions. Without notifying the therapist, the family had him released and brought back to the reservation to stay with an aunt and uncle. When the therapist contacted the family about this, they scheduled an appointment but did not show up. When Roger returned to school, the family resumed therapy, only to have the same pattern repeat itself.

The Jacobs family had brought their son home to be with an uncle, a person who traditionally plays an important role in a son's upbringing. They also used the services of a medicine man and were involved in the Native American Church. They were reluctant to discuss these involvements with the therapist, feeling that she would not understand their decision and would reject their traditional approach, so they tried to avoid her. Instead of presuming the family was rejecting treatment, the therapist began to explore why the family had chosen another path. Gradually, she began to integrate some of their Native health methods into therapy. After two years of experiencing this integrated therapy, Roger became drug-free and remains so today.

The Native American Church is "the most important pan-Indian movement in this country. It is political, cultural and spiritual, a source of pride, power,

Something to Consider 4.2

The Sweat Lodge Ritual

The sweat lodge, historically, was almost a universal ritual for all of the tribes north of Mexico. The lodge was usually a small round house made of sod, sticks, or hide. The individual entered and hot rocks and water were placed inside to cause steam. The individual would remain for a specified time and would then plunge into snow or cold water. The sweat lodge was used for religious purposes, to purify oneself, and also to cure disease. McCloud (1995) described one such experience in the following manner:

> When you are part of a sweat, you are connecting with the living laws of the Creator. . . . All the symbols—earth, air, fire and water—are sacred to use. When you go in there it must be dark—we think of it as going into a spiritual womb of the Great Mother. . . . We humans are linked together by the spirit of life. People say they're from different nations and put different labels on, but when I look, I see just another human being. There's an energy in the universe that links us to all other life forms. We are all children of the Earth. We have these earthquakes and other natural disasters because people are poisoning her bloodstreams and cutting off her hair. They're not following the living laws about caring for the earth. (p. 282)

and psychological health" (Hammerschlag, 1988, p. 60). It has many members, especially in the West. Among the Navajo people, the original religion, or spiritualism, is believed to have been brought by a woman and kept by a man (Quintero, 1995).

Religious and spiritual Native rituals are intended to help the participants become one with the Spirit, within and without the Native American Church. Okun, Fried, and Okun (1999) described it in this way:

> Native American Indian peoples have a holistic vision of the universe, in which two-legged creatures live with four-legged creatures, and with creatures that fly and creatures that swim, in the Mother Earth, beneath the Father Sky. All are part of a complete system, which is totally integrated and in which harm to any specific element harms all. Native beliefs . . . refer to an experience that monotheistic people would call 'God,' but there is simply no way to translate Wakantanka, or any of the other native terms for the Great Spirit, into a way of describing all the forces and powers in the universe . . . present everywhere, all the time; in all events, objects, persons, and relationships. Divinity is totally integrated into the belief systems of native peoples, and the self/community/spirit is One. (pp. 164-165)

Something to Consider 4.2 describes this integration process in the ritual of the sweat lodge.

Network Therapy

Network therapy, created by Carolyn Attneave, a Delaware Indian, involves recreating the clan network to mobilize a family's kin and social system to help a client (LaFromboise & Fleming, 1990). The sessions are conducted in the home and involve considerable numbers of people, including members of the intervention team, the extended family, and others unrelated but known to the family. Network therapy has been used not only for crisis intervention, but also in establishing support systems of elders in rural communities, in reviving traditional healing systems of clients, and in dealing with natural and human disasters (Speck & Speck, 1984). This approach has proved to be a viable approach for preventing and dealing with psychiatric problems in communities (Schoenfeld, Halevy-Martini, Hemley-Van der Velden, & Ruhf, 1985) and has been applied in various situations and settings with Native clients and non-Native clients alike (Rueveni, 1984).

Middleton-Moz (1986) offered several suggestions for counseling with traditional Native American Indian adult clients who have presented emotional and psychological scarring due to forced assimilation. The helping professional must be aware of the multigenerational disruption of positive development that is the result of 500 years of historical trauma for Native peoples. In addition, the persistent destructiveness of oppression and racism that Native peoples have experienced on a daily basis must be acknowledged, and Native clients must be educated about the multigenerational impact of the historical trauma and be supported through the process of grieving personal and tribal losses of language, tradition, and religion.

Helping professionals must assist Native clients to grow and move toward health and wellness by (a) providing positive, concrete, well-articulated, and well-defined role models as mental health professionals and human beings; (b) assisting clients to identify elements of personal mental well-being and to design their own model based on healthy traditional values and practices; and (c) assisting clients to discharge the anger, shame, and fear associated with oppression and historical trauma (Middleton-Moz, 1986). Moreover, Native clients need to recognize when denial is used as a strategy to avoid dealing with the consequences of the historical trauma.

Summary

This chapter has attempted to convey to present and future helping professionals ethnic-appropriate information relative to counseling with Native adults. In some instances, the information may have reflected negativism; however, much of reality is negative. Once again, the reader is cautioned to recall the risk of generalizations, particularly when applied to Native peoples. Implications for the future of these populations will be addressed in a subsequent chapter.

Another recollection is also pertinent as this discussion comes to an end. The warning nearly 30 years ago from Vine Deloria, Jr., in *We Talk, You Listen* (1970) remains relevant today:

> Further generalizations about how we are all alike—all people— are useless today. Definite points of view, new logic, and different goals define us. All we can do is try to communicate what we feel our group means to itself and how we relate to other groups. Understanding each other as distinct peoples is the most important thing. (pp. 15-16)

From another perspective, David Lester, executive director for the Council of Energy Resource Tribes, summed up the self-determination of Native people succinctly in an interview with J. J. Peregoy (1993) in June, 1992:

> We're not the vanishing Americans—the reservations are not halfway houses for assimilation or extermination. Indians/Natives are an integral part of 20th century America. As long as there are human beings in the Western Hemisphere, we're going to have Indian people governing themselves, making their own decisions for their own future. (p. 192)

5

Career Development and Counseling
With Native Populations

Culture and value systems directly influence the development of the constructs used to form identities, knowledge structures of the world of work, meanings derived from work, thought processes used to derive career options and evaluate prospects, and views of personal success (Peterson, Sampson, & Reardon, 1991). Such is the case with Native cultures. Whereas no specific theory links the growth and development in cultural and ethnical perspectives directly to career development, I propose the use of synergetic counseling to demonstrate how the emergence of these perspectives influences career problem solving and decision making with Native populations (e.g., Herring, 1997a, 1997b; Herring & Walker, 1993).

According to the Bureau of Indian Affairs (Bureau of Indian Affairs, 1993), there are 547 recognized tribes, not including 200 Alaska Native tribes. Each tribe may have its own language, religious beliefs, and social characteristics common to that tribe. However, almost two thirds of Native American Indians live in urban areas; they are there for training, college, or employment (Zunker, 1998). Many keep close contact with their family and friends who live on the reservations (Johnson, Swartz, & Martin, 1995).

On the reservations, many are involved in farming, ranching, fishing, and lumber production. Off the reservations, Native American Indians work in factories, on farms, and as skilled crafts workers. Some tribes are engaged in various enterprises, such as motel management; others offer bingo and lottery games to the general public (Axelson, 1999).

The career development literature on specific Native students is sparse and is not generally well grounded. This chapter synthesizes the available literature to present an appropriate portrait of Native groups. Although comparisons may be made across these groups, variations within groups will also be recognized.

Definitions, Demographics, and Theories

In addition to the terminology discussed in Chapter 1, aspects of career development and counseling require definition. Demographic data are also needed to establish the rationale for serving the career developmental needs of Native youth. Helping professionals also need to be cognizant of the degree of ethnic awareness displayed by potential counselees and clients.

Definitions

From a career development perspective, *culture* is defined as a system of beliefs, values, customs, and institutions shared and transmitted by members of a particular society, from which individuals derive meaning for their work, love, and leisure activities (Peterson et al., 1991).

Multicultural career development is defined by Stone (1984) as,

An intervention and continuous assessment process that prepares institutions and individuals to experience the realities of life, work, and leisure in a culturally diverse environment. In particular, multicultural career development considers the effect of and relationship among career options, ethnic-cultural demographics, and psychosocial factors that impact an individual's occupational choices in a pluralistic society. (p. 272)

Demographics

For the purposes of this chapter, several concerns will be emphasized. More than 170 Native groups currently reside in the Unites States (U.S. Department of Education, 1994). In addition, the population of bi- and multiethnic Native individuals is rapidly increasing. Interethnic marriage rates in the United States have doubled each decade since 1970, from 310,000 that year to 1.2 million in 1992. The number of multiracial youth has grown accordingly: from 31,200 born in 1968 to four times that number—128,000—in 1991 (Gross, 1996). Native youth make up a large segment of that population. As this population increases, career development programs may need to adapt to their unique needs.

Ethnic and cultural minority youth are the largest growing segment of the U.S. population. By the year 2000, ethnic minority youth will make up nearly 30% of the population, with the Native population having the largest percentage of children and adolescents—37.4% under 18 years of age (U.S. Bureau of the Census, 1992).

From a career developmental perspective, Native youth deserve a more appropriate and ethnic-specific perspective. Native groups have the lowest living standards of any ethnic group in this nation. Approximately 24% live below the poverty level (U.S. Bureau of the Census, 1991). Unemployment on some reservations is reported to be as high as 90% (Herring, 1997b). The pattern is one of bare subsistence, with some of the worst slums in the United States existing on federal reservations (Rice, 1993). This population also has numerous cultural traits or values that conflict with mainstream society (e.g., time orientation and collectivism).

Theories of Ethnic Awareness

To serve Native persons appropriately, helping professionals must know their own ethnic awareness, as well as that of the Native individual. Briefly, here are two theories of the development of ethnic awareness.

Sue's Model. Sue (1978, 1990) postulated that an individual's worldview includes two dimensions of personality: (a) internal and external locus of control (IC & EC; Rotter, 1966) and (b) internal and external locus of responsibility (IR & ER; Jones et al., 1971). These dimensions may be presented in combinations, which divide individuals into four distinct quadrants. Individuals in Quadrant 1 (IC-IR) are associated with middle-class values and believe that they have control over their decisions and the ability to implement them. Native families who live bicultural and assimilated lifestyles would be placed in this quadrant. Individuals in Quadrant II (EC-IR) are associated with the sense of being a scapegoat and believe that they are held responsible for events over which they have little control, such as the pantraditional Native family. Quadrant III (EC-ER) individuals are associated with a rigid and inflexible approach to life and often blame "the system" for their fate. Native individuals living on reservations in traditional families may have this view. Quadrant IV (IC-ER) is composed of individuals who believe that they are able to control their destiny if given the opportunity. The transitional Native family has members in this quadrant. An individual's quadrant, determined by culture and ethnicity, can affect the way one develops career alternatives in the career counseling process (Peterson et al., 1991).

Christensen's Model. Christensen (1989) advanced a five-stage model of ethnic awareness. In Stage 1 (unawareness), individuals have given no thought to cultural, ethnic, or racial differences, nor are they aware of how these differences affect their opportunities in society. In Stage 2 (beginning awareness), individuals begin to question why different groups, including their own, possess different statuses in society. In Stage 3 (conscious awareness), individuals experience disequilibrium, preoccupation, and pain as they become more aware of the injustice, inequality, and oppression experienced by culturally disadvantaged groups. In Stage 4 (consolidated awareness), individuals become fully aware of how cultural differences affect social status and opportunity and begin to establish a sense of acceptance of themselves and dissimilar ethnic groups. In Stage 5 (transcendent awareness), individuals of both majority and minority cultures attain a sense of peace with themselves and are able to perceive transcendent, unifying, human qualities that span cultures. They feel comfortable within other ethnic groups as well as their own, whether it be a dominant or a minority group (Peterson et al., 1991).

Effective cross-cultural and multicultural career counseling involves an understanding of the degree of cultural and ethnic awareness, not only of the counselee or client but also of oneself as a helping professional. For example, communication may be difficult when a school guidance counselor and counselee are at different levels of ethnic awareness, especially when the school counselor is unaware of his or her own level of development (Peterson et al., 1991). For example, a Stage 3 (conscious awareness) Native student and a Stage 5 (transcendent awareness) European American school counselor discussing the prospect of going to professional school may have different perceptions of the opportunities and risks of such a choice. The counselee may have fears and doubts that need to be acknowledged and appreciated by the school counselor, even though the school counselor may have progressed beyond this level of functioning.

Ethnic Awareness and Synergetic Theory

Information processing theory contends that two domains interact in the internalization of external data: self-knowledge and occupational knowledge. Culture and ethnic perspectives are the foundations of each domain (Peterson et al., 1991). This interaction reflects a basic premise of synergetic counseling (Herring, 1997b). In the self-knowledge domain, the essential constructs for forming a Native identity are received from one's cultural-ethnic environment, another synergetic tenet (Herring, 1997b). Whether Native individuals see themselves as the primary unit; whether independence and autonomy are valued; whether they believe that they can control their environment; whether the seeking of power and status is a life-orienting goal;

what value is placed on competency and on winning rather than losing—these are examples of values derived from individuals' cultural-ethnic backgrounds, which form the core of their value systems and identities (Herring, 1997a, 1997b; Katz, 1985).

In the occupational knowledge domain, individuals' cultural-ethnic backgrounds provide the essential constructs and attributes needed for determining relationships among occupations, particularly in terms of their relative worth and status. The culturally differentiating status of teachers and clergy illustrate this point. Consequently, in career decision making by Native youth or their families, cultural-ethnic environments influence the degree to which a career choice is determined.

At the executive processing level, culture influences the choice of reasoning process: rational, intuitive, or dependent (Maruyama, 1978). The synergetic paradigm provides a framework for understanding how an individual's culture and ethnic identity influences his or her development of knowledge structures and thought processes, through which information is transformed into career decisions.

Sociocultural Factors

Native individuals present unique career development issues because of their developmental status and membership in their cultures. Some of the issues are related to sociocultural conditions (e.g., poverty, prejudice, racism), whereas others are developmental issues faced by all people. Developmental tasks, however, are also influenced by cultural factors. Traditional Native youth are reared within the context of an extended family, whose members bear primary responsibility for the socialization process. Thus, understanding the culture's concept of family is vital to effective career interventions.

Sociocultural factors often interfere with the Native student's mastery of developmental tasks. Poverty, language barriers, and negative stereotypes restrict perceived as well as real access to available resources (Rivers & Morrow, 1995). The effective school or career counselor must appraise the Native youth's environment. Such practical issues may include developing options for transportation to school, arranging tutorial services for youth and adults and educational resources for parents, and openly discussing the impact of daily exposure to discrimination, conflicting values, ethnic stereotypes, and career mythologies (see discussion of Career Myths later in this chapter). School and career counselors who observe Native students in classrooms and home environments acquire more accurate data about peer relationship skills, attitudes toward authority, study habits, and the degree to which primary needs (e.g., safety, shelter, hygiene, and nutrition) are being met. The effective counselor must address sociocultural issues as well as intrapsychic concerns.

Poverty, Low Socioeconomic Status (SES), and Class

Socioeconomic concerns are frequently the least discussed, and therefore the least addressed, multicultural issue. Economic deprivation and workplace discrimination are only two of the issues faced by less advantaged Native youth. The effect of unemployed and underemployed parents on Native youth is tremendous. A central issue has been a tendency for male counselors to dominate female and minority students and direct them into stereotypical career choices (Cayleff, 1986; Jones, Krupnick, & Kerig, 1987).

The high rates of poverty in Native families has been well established in the census data and in the literature (U.S. Bureau of the Census, 1990). However, variations in poverty rates within Native groups need to be recognized (Liu, Yu, Chang, & Fernandez, 1990). Perhaps the most direct effect of poverty is restricted access to environmental resources with which to combat substandard housing, lack of comprehensive health care, and inadequate nutrition (Rivers & Morrow, 1995). Several studies lend strong support to the relationship of low SES, its concomitant stressors, and high rates of psychological maladjustment among Native youth (e.g., Myers, 1989).

Classism is another variable in the appropriate delivery of services to Native students. Classism is not often presented as a viable variable in discussions of the educational and career development of students. Nevertheless, classism does have an important influence on students, perhaps to a greater extent than race or ethnicity. For example, one study indicated that the lower the parents' income and education, the less likely a child is to acquire a bachelor's degree or even enter college (Reinolds, 1996).

Another interesting observation is found in students' membership in certain class structures, regarding perceived maternal warmth. Several speculations might explain this. Rohner, Hahn, and Koehn (1992) agreed that downwardly mobile parents may "extend closer attention and care to their children by making highly visible sacrifices (e.g., labor intensive jobs not commensurate with their education and experiences) than the middle class parent, because the former would like to make sure their children will succeed in what they have failed" (p. 375). Additional research is suggested to yield subsequent data on this question, particularly among Native populations.

However, other issues also complicate factors in studying ethnicity in relation to career development. One reflects the confounding of race and ethnicity. Considerable disagreement exists regarding what is meant by *race* and whether or not that concept is useful even if an acceptable definition can evolve (Yee et al., 1993). Another issue is the "overlap between being economically disadvantaged and being culturally disadvantaged, because poverty tends to cross racial and ethnic boundaries" (Herr & Cramer, 1996, p. 272). In addition, European Americans attitudes about Native peoples play a vital role in the educational process.

Language Issues

Children generally learn second languages more easily and more quickly than adults. As a result, the language skills of bilingual children may threaten the traditionally strict hierarchical role of monolingual parents and children (Ho, 1992; Huang, 1994). Language issues may also interfere with academic achievement. For example, traditional learning styles for Native children rely heavily on nonverbal communication, observation, and enactment, as well as linguistic structures that are entirely different from those of English (Herring, 1997a). As a result, the English skills of Native children are among the poorest of any group in the United States, which partially explains their historical academic underachievement (Ho, 1992).

Stereotypes

Stereotypes are perpetuated by overtly negative images and attitudes as well as by covert omissions of the positive aspects of ethnic minority cultures, such as the Native cultures. These pervasive messages can become internalized if not countered by evidence to the contrary (Rivers & Morrow, 1995). When they are internalized, identity exploration may be restricted and a dichotomous mode of thinking can result (e.g., White is "good," Native is "bad"). Native peoples must choose between identifying with mainstream values to achieve their goals, or retaining their Native value systems. Such dichotomies are represented in the derogatory slurs by which Native youth sometimes refer to one who has "sold out" to the dominant culture. For example, "apple" refers to a Native individual who is considered "Red on the outside but White on the inside."

The most common traditional occupational stereotype of Native American Indians is that "of the skilled structural steel worker, daringly risking his life as he adroitly maneuvers thousands of feet above the ground" (Herr & Cramer, 1996, pp. 281-282). Although Native American Indians do account for a disproportionately large percentage of structural steel workers, the total number so employed is a very small percentage of the Native American Indian work force.

Academic Underachievement and School Dropout

A primary concern of school personnel is lowering the dropout rates of students. The frequency of school dropout for the general population ranges from 5% to 30%, whereas Native students have a much higher rate of 60%, especially in inner cities (U.S. Bureau of the Census, 1991). Their value orientations and difficult socioeconomic and family conditions are not conducive to continuing education (Rice, 1993).

Career Myths

Most ethnic minority students display less satisfaction with program choices and give lower ratings on receiving help with job choice and career decisions than do European American students (Richmond, Johnson, Downs, & Ellinghaus, 1983). These weaknesses contribute to a lack of self-awareness when Native students contemplate career options. Research also indicates that ethnic minority students exhibit differences from European American students in background experience, values, and orientation, which occur even though ethnic minority students' aspirations may equal or surpass those of middle-class European American students (Hispanic Research Center, 1991). These differences also tend to restrict a Native student's awareness of available careers and of the skills required. As a result, disproportionate numbers of Native students enter traditional career areas or remain unemployed. For example, the Native peoples of the Southwest are noted for their blankets, pots, and jewelry. Although a few might realize substantial wealth, the majority receive small monetary reward.

Irrational beliefs held by Native, and other, students are referred to as *career myths*, most often generated from historical, familial patterns of career ignorance and negative career developmental experiences (Dorn, 1987; Herring, 1990a). An example of a career myth is the belief that a career choice must be made before senior high school. Irrational career beliefs generally result in dysfunctional cognitive schema when Native students contemplate career decisions (Herring, 1990a).

Another example of irrational beliefs is that some occupations are tainted and should be avoided. People like garbage collectors, dead animal removers, hospital attendants, bail bondspersons, strippers, and others who work in jobs most people find physically, socially, or morally tainted are not particularly bothered by the stigma (Ashford & Kreiner, 1998). Those persons who work in stigmatized jobs often form an "us" against "them" mentality and may socialize with fellow workers. Workers with "dirty" jobs also tend to marry people in the same line of work and pass the profession down to their children. For example, 60% of the 20,000 member National Funeral Directors Association are family operations, and many are second- and third-generation businesses (Ashford & Kreiner, 1998).

Research has also substantiated the relationship between irrational cognitions and indecisiveness in an ethnic minority student's career development experiences (Haase, Reed, Winer, & Bodden, 1979). Irrational thinking is also the basic component of the ethnic minority student's career mythology (Slaney, 1983). Finally, research has demonstrated that traditional career theorists neglect to emphasize ethnicity and culture in their concepts (June & Pringle, 1977).

Chronic poverty and inappropriate education contribute to the persistence of career myths and low career aspirations among Native youth (Herr & Cramer, 1996). The availability of positive career role models also limits career choices of Native youth. Such limitations continue the cycle of disproportionate employment and restrict the potential of Native youth, as well as other low SES youth. Like other ethnic minority groups, Native populations have not been exposed to a wide range of careers and have limited opportunities to attend college because of high unemployment rates. Herring (1990a) suggested that Native youth be introduced to more nontraditional occupations and be provided with career information using Native role models to expand their career considerations.

Major Psychosocial Factors

Native youth also face numerous psychosocial obstacles in their attempts to participate in the world of work. This section will review the major psychosocial factors affecting these youth: identity conflicts, substance use and abuse, teenage pregnancy, suicide, and delinquency. The impact of these factors has been, and continues to be, counterproductive to successful career development for Native youth.

Identity Conflicts

Ethnic identity is conceptually separate from personal identity and ethnicity. Ethnic identity is thought to be achieved through a process of crisis (exploration of alternatives) followed by commitment (decisions that reflect personal investment) (Phinney & Alipuria, 1990). One simple approach to operationalizing ethnicity is to ask students what they consider their ethnicity to be. The situation of Native students is somewhat more complex. As previously presented, Native individuals have to prove who they are. This proof may be either a certain blood quantum percentage or tribal enrollment card. The biethnic or multiethnic status of Native individuals reduces their chances of establishing their ethnic identity.

Dana (1998) documented the cultural competence a helping professional needs to provide adequate, credible, and potentially beneficial services for multicultural populations. He presented a model for effective culture-specific services, which emphasizes the description and understanding of cultural and racial identity and the use of this information to develop cultural formations to increase the accuracy of diagnoses.

Substance Abuse

The problem of alcohol and other drug abuse in the United States continues to be of great concern. Three factors need to be recognized in this problem: physiological, sociological, and psychological (Lawson & Lawson, 1989). Physiological studies have indicated a genetic factor for some forms of substance abuse, sociological research has demonstrated the influence of family and peers, and psychological factors have been found to play a role. Although substance experimentation is relatively common among all adolescents, additional characteristics are reflected among Native youth. Diversity within Native groups makes it difficult to generalize from a particular subgroup to the larger group. For example, differences exist between reservation and nonreservation Native American Indians, among tribes, and even within tribes.

Results from four years of survey data conducted on over 200,000 eighth- and twelfth-grade students indicated that Native American Indian, Mexican American, and European American youth had higher lifetime prevalence rates for a number of substances compared with African American and Asian American youth. One in every seven Native American Indian eighth graders was found to be using inhalants (Beauvais, 1992). Recent research has attributed this to use by peers, weak family bonding, poor school adjustment, weak family sanctions against drugs, positive attitudes toward alcohol use, cultural values, low educational achievement, low employment opportunity, and risk of school dropout (Swaim, Thurman, Beauvais, Oetting, & Wayman, 1993).

Teenage Pregnancy

Whereas teenage mothers account for 12% of all births among European Americans, comparable proportions among Native American Indians range from 18% to 25%, depending on the research effort (Malone, 1986). Teenage pregnancy and parenthood are associated with educational setbacks, unemployment, family problems, and welfare dependency (Herring, 1997a, 1997b). Given the lack of role models, skills, and self-confidence necessary to pursue alternative paths, many ethnic minority girls, especially those from low SES families, may actively seek the traditional role of mother as the only rite of passage by which to enter into adult womanhood (Rivers & Morrow, 1995).

Suicide

Native American Indians have the highest rate of completed suicide of any ethnic group (Herring, 1997a). Suicide is the second leading cause of death for Native American Indian youth, with 23.6 deaths per 100,000 in the 15 to 19 year cohort (U.S. Congress, 1986).

Delinquency

Youth under the age of 21 account for about 30% of police arrests in the United States (U.S. Department of Justice, 1991). Factors related to chronic delinquency include low verbal intelligence, poor school performance, peer rejection in childhood, and membership in antisocial groups. A consistent factor is a family environment low in warmth, high in conflict, and characterized by lax and inconsistent discipline. Nonpeer and nonfamilial factors also influence the adolescent's choice of gang membership and delinquency (e.g., schools that fail to meet appropriate developmental needs). Native delinquents are plentiful on reservations and in urban areas.

Impact of Psychosocial Factors

In summary, school counselors and career counselors must understand how sociocultural and ethnic group contexts influence the development of mental health problems in Native youth. Concurrently, the negative influences of these problems on Native students' career development must be understood. Some researchers (e.g., Phinney, Lochner, & Murphy, 1990) contend that the common element among ethnic youth at risk for future psychological maladjustment is the maintenance of a foreclosed or diffused identity status. In addition, cultural marginality and the stress associated with acculturation result in heightened anxiety, lowered self-esteem, and aggressive acting-out or withdrawal behavior, which can contribute to such problems among ethnic minority youth as substance abuse, academic underachievement or dropping out, teenage pregnancy, delinquency, suicide, and homicide (Rivers & Morrow, 1995).

Standardized Career Assessment

The use of standardized career assessment has received little research attention, and research results have been inconclusive. Some studies have reported that differences in the results of career interest assessment are so slight between Native American Indians and European American populations that routine use of existing instruments would be appropriate (Herr & Cramer, 1996). Other studies have found differences of sufficient magnitude to warrant the development of separate Native norms (Epperson & Hammond, 1981; Gade, Fuqua, & Hurlburt, 1984).

A more recent study of the Strong-Campbell Interest Inventory (Haviland & Hansen, 1987) found no differences between female European American and Native American Indian college students, but discovered substantial differences between male European American and Native American Indian students.

The use of narrative approaches represents an appropriate assessment technique for Native individuals. Such approaches challenge school and career counselors to examine the type and place of career assessment in their counseling. In essence, narrative assessment is intended to encourage Native individuals to tell their own career stories (Borgen, 1995) and to uncover their subjective careers in a qualitative way. The four most popular methods of qualitative assessment are autobiographies, early recollections, structured interviews, and card sorts. Gysbers, Heppner, and Johnston (1998) comprehensively described the use of genograms and occupational card sorts as qualitative assessment tools.

More empirical data are needed from research on Native populations. This research should include data relative to Native peoples on and off reservations, potential differences between rural and urban Native populations, and gender differences. In addition, differences between Native adult and Native youth need to be determined.

Career Counseling With Native Youth

Theoretical thinking about career development of racial and ethnic groups is at a particularly early stage of development (e.g., Arbona, 1996; Patton & McMahon, 1999). Although broader theories have attempted to acknowledge the influences of race and ethnicity (e.g., Gottfredson, 1981; Super, 1990), these perspectives generally have not been integrated into theoretical models (Patton & McMahon, 1999). Gottfredson's (1986) concept of "at-risk" factors in career choice, originally proposed as a framework for assessment and intervention in career choice, is especially useful in considering such barriers to career choice as gender, SES, and ethnicity.

The social cognitive career theory (SCCT), characterized as emergent and evolving, emphasizes the relevance of other person and contextual variables such as gender, race and ethnicity, genetic endowment, and SES (Lent & Brown, 1996). The SCCT views gender and race as socially constructed and emphasizes their relevance to how they are viewed in the sociocultural environment and their relationship to opportunity structure (Patton & McMahon, 1999).

> Framing gender and ethnicity as socially constructed aspects of experience leads naturally to a consideration of sociostructural conditions and processes that mould the learning opportunities to which particular individuals are exposed, the characteristic reactions they receive for performing different activities, and the future outcomes they anticipate. (Lent & Brown, 1996, p. 315)

Future empirical studies with this model will establish its efficacy in application with Native and other ethnic groups.

Both the theoretical and the practical career development literature of the 1990s have paid too little attention to groups other than European American, able-bodied, middle-class males (Patton & McMahon, 1999). In particular, the availability of empirical evidence relative to career education and development with Native populations is limited and, to some extent, dated. Some studies, however, have yielded vital information. Lee (1995) found that parental influence has a greater impact on the career choice attitudes of African American and Native American Indian students than on that of European American students. Using a sample of 520 tenth-grade students in five public high schools in rural North Carolina, Lee found that self-concept interacted with ethnicity to produce groups of predictors of career attitude maturity. His results indicated that, among these groups, cultural and ethnic differences in views about self had important implications for career behaviors. For example, the research suggested that, in the case of Native American Indian students, historic socioeconomic hardships and unique cultural traditions may "affect the development of self-perceptions and their influence on behavior and attitudes in ways that are different from the other two ethnic groups" (p. 192).

Beyard-Tyler and Haring (1984) found that nontraditional, gender-based occupations were clearly considered by Navajo students on reservations. However, these researchers attributed the findings of acceptance of nontraditional occupations to "limited contacts with the institutions and materials that transmit the biases of the majority culture" (p. 270). Thus the students were less aware of the sex types associated with certain jobs.

Steward (1993) demonstrated through case studies that a Native American Indian college student who is outgoing, active, and grateful is likely to have an advantage in both mentoring and hiring over an equally competent Native American Indian student who does not exhibit these characteristics. Helping professionals need to be sure that the latter type of student is not neglected (Herr & Cramer, 1996).

The self-efficacy of rural Native American Indian adolescents has been measured as lower than that of European American and Hispanic adolescents (Lauver & Jones, 1991). Such lack of confidence in one's ability to perform career-related tasks has clear implications for the type of intervention necessary to raise aspiration levels. Another implication for school and career helping professionals exists herein.

As mentioned previously, the use of narratives with Native clients or counselees represents a way of "identifying and analyzing life career themes" (Gysbers et al., 1998, p. 236), uncovering the meaning that individuals ascribe to interwoven parts of their lives, and focusing on individuals' subjective careers (Patton & McMahon, 1999). "The power of stories to capture attention and convey meaning is reemerging as an important component in career counseling" (Krumboltz, Blando, Kim, & Reikowski, 1994, p. 60). Helping professionals may look at the characteristics of the story being told—for example, if a story is meaningless, repetitive, life-denying, or carries a message of subservience (McLeod, 1996). The type of story provides clues to the themes and patterns of an individual's larger life story and the meaning he or she makes of his or her life. In using this approach, as in most other forms of counseling, counselors use microskills such as empathic reflection, interventions such as psychodramatic enactments, and metaphor (Patton & McMahon, 1999).

Several trends can be gleaned from the research on ethnic career counseling. One evolving and persistent theme involves values. Katz (1985) described a variety of culturally determined values that directly influence the career counseling process. Some of these values are: the status and power of the school counselor (i.e., authority figure versus facilitator); communication (e.g., reflecting feelings versus providing knowledge or advice); framing the problem in terms of cause and effect (i.e., degree of emphasis on family history, learned behavior, search for meaning); goals (insight oriented versus change oriented); emphasis of scientific method (degree of emphasis on testing, appraisal, linear problem solving, and labeling problems); and time orientation (structured versus unstructured). In each of these dimensions, the Native individual will possess a personal value orientation, which may differ from that of the school counselor or career counselor. Helping professionals should develop a sensitivity to the Native student values that influence the counseling process and should be able to adopt counseling goals and treatment strategies consistent with the Native student's cultural orientation or environment.

Something to Consider 5.1

Career Issues On and Off Reservations

Native American Indian counselees and clients who live on reservations will likely differ from those who are assimilated in terms of their knowledge of the world of work and external pressures (Martin, 1991). Some of those differences are listed here.

Career Issues On Reservations

- Vocational opportunities in and around reservations are limited, as most reservations are located in rural areas (Leung, 1995).
- A limited exposure to the world of work has resulted in a general lack of occupational information (Martin, 1991).
- Native individuals who choose not to adopt mainstream cultural and occupational values may not have adequate job search and job maintenance skills to survive in the occupational world (Leung, 1995).

Career Issues Off Reservations

- Many Native individuals leave reservations and go to urban areas for vocational reasons (Heinrich et al., 1990).
- Many Native individuals feel torn between European American cultural values and traditional Native values (Leung, 1995).
- Many Native individuals are burdened with a sense of guilt that they have abandoned their Native heritage for economic and vocational gains (Sue & Sue, 1990).

A second theme is that more than half the adults in this country who have enough information to express an opinion support increasing the emphasis placed on career development by public schools (Brown, Minor, & Jepsen, 1992). School counselors who do not incorporate career development activities in their programs run the risk of losing public support for their programs. Effective programs operate on the basis of carefully conceived plans predicated on the needs of students (Wiggins & Moody, 1987).

The degree of acculturation also affects Native individuals' career plans. Ethnic minority students displaying higher degrees of acculturation tend to have higher occupational aspirations and expectations than do less acculturated ethnic minority students (Mahoney, 1992; Manaster, Chan, & Safady, 1992). Something to Consider 5.1 presents career issues of reservation and nonreservation Native populations.

Biethnic Youth

Gibbs and Hines (1992) studied the psychosocial adjustment of a sample of nonclinical biethnic adolescents and their parents over a two-year period. For biethnic teens who identify with European American middle-class culture, academic achievement may be a way to gain acceptance and demonstrate values they share with European American peers. However, awareness of prejudice and fear of failure in the academic realm may lead some of these adolescents to impose limitations on their academic achievement and ambitions. For those identifying with the minority culture, academic aspirations and studious behavior may invite ostracism or provoke ridicule. Fear of rejection by their peers may cause these teens to become involved in truancy, deliberately fail their courses, or engage in other self-defeating behaviors.

In the realm of conflicts over educational and career aspirations, 75% of these biethnic teens were performing above average academically and were planning to go to college and graduate school. However, fewer than half had made specific plans about careers or future lifestyles. Their educational aspirations appeared to be influenced primarily by their parents, whose average educational and occupational level was high, rather than by specific occupational goals. Thus their biethnic identity did not appear to have had a negative effect on their future aspirations, which seemed realistic and congruent with their academic performance. However, as stated previously, such research efforts cannot automatically be applicable to all biethnic or multiethnic Native individuals.

Counseling Orientations to Consider

The initial decision for the helping professional is which theoretical model to select for interventions. Frequently, available models can be confusing, overlapping, or redundant. The school counselor or career counselor must make a wise choice. In review, models available for consideration include cross-cultural counseling, minority group counseling, multicultural counseling, and synergetic counseling. The choice of theoretical stance will determine the effectiveness of any attempted intervention. Something to Consider 5.2 offers some examples of appropriate initial strategies for this population.

Cross-Cultural Counseling. Any counseling relationship in which two or more of the participants are culturally different is called *cross-cultural counseling.* Atkinson, Morten, and Sue (1993) defined this relationship as "situations in which both the counselor and student(s) are ethnic minority individuals but represent different racial/ethnic groups . . . or the counselor is a racial/ethnic minority person and the student is European American . . . or the counselor is European American and the student is a minority" (p. 15).

Minority Group Counseling. Any counseling relationship in which the client or counselee is a member of an ethnic minority group, regardless of the status of the helping professional, is considered minority group counseling. The research literature has concentrated on ethnic minorities and has examined only the relationship of the European American school counselor to the ethnic minority student relationship. This limited view of minority group counseling has resulted in some criticism because it ignores the special conditions of a counseling relationship in which the school counselor is also an ethnic minority person. Furthermore, concern exists that the term "minority group counseling" suggests a minority pathology; this is perceived as analogous to "Black pathology," an attempt to explain African American behavior in terms of European American norms (Atkinson, Morten, et al., 1993, p. 6).

Multicultural Counseling. Multicultural counseling encompasses all the facets of the diverse ethnic and cultural environments in contemporary society. In some respects, all counseling is multicultural, taking into account the infinite number of possible combinations of counselor and student or client (Axelson, 1993). Helping professionals need to create a "cultural environment wherein two people can communicate with and relate to each other" (p. 12).

Synergetic Counseling. I suggest the use of synergetic counseling precepts. Stated simply, this model encourages the use of the most appropriate intervention for the individual(s) at the moment, with considerations for historical and environmental influences. Additional influences on the counseling session would include issues of gender, age, sexual orientation, and conditions of medical, mental, physical, or emotional challenge.

Native individuals' resistance to counseling in general is exemplified by their underuse of existing mental health services. Native peoples are the most neglected group in the mental health field (Manson, 1982). Miller (1982) suggested that more Native people would take advantage of counseling relationships if appropriate counseling strategies were used. Trimble and LaFromboise (1985) summarized Miller's strategies as follows:

1. Personal ethnic identity in itself is hardly sufficient for understanding the influence of culture on the client.

2. The client's history contains a number of strengths that can promote and facilitate the counseling process.

3. The counselor should be aware of his or her own biases about cultural pluralism—they might interfere with the counseling relationship.

4. The counselor should encourage the client to become more active in the process of identifying and learning the various elements associated with positive growth and development.

5. Most important are empathy, caring, and a sense of the importance of the human potential. (p. 131)

School and career counselors and other helping professionals who use a synergetic approach with Native students may consider the following examples of concepts, activities, and techniques (Axelson, 1993; Herring, 1997b; Herring & Walker, 1993):

1. Identifying and reinforcing self-perceived qualities and self movement
2. Blocking negative thoughts
3. Practicing positive visual imagery
4. Validating self through identification with others
5. Learning self-assertion skills
6. Understanding and using the system
7. Acquiring knowledge and information through career guidance and education

The initial counseling session must begin with conceptual and facilitating interventions to ensure a shared understanding of what the sessions are about. The helping professional must gain an understanding of the Native group membership (e.g., nation or tribe) of the student, and should exert time and effort to gather data (e.g., an assessment of class, acculturation, language, education, and subgroup membership) prior to its use in addressing the problem, rather than assuming a generic Native personality.

Native youth and adults, on the other hand, have to understand the limits of the counseling and be encouraged to be creative and persistent in their job search experiences by learning effective job-seeking techniques (Drummond & Ryan, 1995). Learning activities should include supervised practice, support services, and debriefings after students receive feedback from potential and actual employers. As in all areas of counseling, school and career counselors are required to engage in periodic and systematic follow-up activities on their Native students.

To assist school counselors in providing developmental strategies for Native students, the following strategies are designed to help Native students maintain their cultural heritage and at the same time introduce concepts of career development of the dominant society (Zunker, 1998).

1. *Using parents and relatives as counseling facilitators:* The rationale for this approach is embedded in the strong family ties of Native peoples.

2. *Using Native role models:* They should assist in helping to break down resistance to counseling objectives. Native students should react more favorably to other Native individuals.

3. *Emphasizing individual potential in the context of future goals:* Identity conflicts make it difficult for Native individuals to project themselves into other environments, including work environments. (p. 440)

Summary

Contemporary society (and future society even more so) reflects ethnic and cultural heterogeneity. Current Native groups will evolve into one of the ethnic majority groups of tomorrow. Helping professionals need to recognize the career development needs of Native students and adults and the types of interventions that are successful with them (Drummond & Ryan, 1995). Concurrently, helping professionals need to become more culturally sensitive and competent. Although Bowman (1995) argued that it is impossible for career counselors to be aware of all variables within a culture, the proper attitude is to be open to continued learning about cultural diversity (Zunker, 1998).

Native individuals are culturally conditioned to have different worldviews from those of European Americans. Traditional Native children are generally not motivated to achieve status through the accumulation of wealth. Their lifestyles are extremely democratic, and their cultures promote egalitarianism. Such examples of Native perspectives support the need for multicultural counseling efforts.

A multicultural perspective in career development and counseling is vital because of the diversity of Native peoples and their rapidly changing demographics. The need for an enhanced awareness of the importance that Native culture plays in the career development process is evident, as is the need for additional research in Native career development. Angry Native youth will remain as such until, within educative systems, peoples of all heritages and differences are valued and permitted to empower themselves through an egalitarian allocation of socioeconomic resources (Hernandez, 1995).

Experiential Activities

1. Try the following exercises to enhance Native students' understanding and awareness of ethnic stereotypes in the world of work (adapted from Aronson, 1994, p. 31):

   a. Ask students to close their eyes for a moment and imagine a lawyer, then a police officer, then a doctor, then a criminal. Ask them to raise their hands if they saw either a female lawyer, a Native American Indian police officer, an Alaska Native doctor, or a European American criminal. Explain that stereotypes operate so subtly that sometimes we don't even notice them.

   b. List the following "types of people" on the board and ask students to assign each to an ethnic group or nationality based on stereotypes. Have them fill in details about how these different people dress, how they talk, where they live, and what they value most in life.

chemistry professor	bank president
rap musician	hairstylist
gang member	political terrorist

   Now ask Native students to imagine the rap musician matching the description of the chemistry professor or the hairstylist fitting the description of the political terrorist. Discuss why it seems easy to think in terms of stereotypes. Consider the harm done by stereotypes when they are applied to entire groups of people.

2. Do a sociogram (survey) of the class to find out the degree of interaction among students of different ethnicities: "If your mother would only let you invite two kids to your birthday party, which two from one class would you choose?" Or ask a similar question about getting help with homework.

3. Survey career choices of students in the junior high, senior high, or community college. Compare the choices by ethnic or cultural group membership. Write a report of the results from your study.

4. Participate in a dyadic encounter with a Native adult individual about careers. Describe your experiences.

6

Using the Creative Arts in
Counseling Native Populations

Although all Native entities possess various creative art mediums, many forms are common across most Native groups. The use of music, dance, food, art, play, symbolism and metaphor, and literature as healing forces among Native peoples is well documented, especially with children (e.g., Appleton & Dykeman, 1996; Arnheim, 1990; Fleming, 1989). During the Middle Ages, Native creative arts (e.g., paintings, jewelry, masks, and architecture) flourished and helped give Native cultures and peoples in various geographical areas a distinctiveness and freedom unknown in Europe. It was during this time period in the Americas that creative arts became an integral part of Native healing (Dufrene & Coleman, 1992). The use of metaphor and healing stories became especially powerful.

The aim of this chapter is to suggest a few creative approaches that can be employed with Native clients and counselees. These approaches focus particularly on the use of culturally relevant ways of communicating. They should be considered ways to supplement the traditional role of counselor or therapist.

Creative Art Mediums and
Their Implications for Counseling

The use of art in general "does not rely on verbalization and therefore can be an ideal form of self-expression between a counselor and client or

104

counselee from different cultural backgrounds" (Alexander & Sussman, 1995, p. 380). The use of art also allows the helping professional to learn more about Native cultures and worldviews. An excellent example is to have Native clients and counselees create a collage linking current beliefs, life-style, and attitudes to their cultural heritage.

Space limitations prevent a comprehensive discussion of the numerous creative art forms within Native cultures. However, a cursory examination of the most pervasive of these art forms will be presented. Traditional arts range from those that are primarily auditory or written (e.g., music, drama, and literature) to those that are predominantly visual (e.g., painting, mime, dance, and movement). Many overlaps exist between these two categories, and in most cases two or more art forms are combined in counseling, such as literature and drama or dance and music. These combinations work because "music, art, dance/movement, drama therapy, psychodrama, and poetry therapy have a strong common bond" (Summer, 1997, p. 80). The impact of creative arts in counseling is largely dependent on the skills of the helping professional (Appleton & Dykeman, 1996). The following examples, therefore, are not intended to be inclusive but rather representative.

Symbolism and Metaphor

One of the main achievements of successful helping professionals is their ability to listen to and use the language of their clients or counselees, a procedure known as "minesis" (Gladding, 1998, p. 88). Such a process often involves hearing unique and universal metaphors employed by clients and counselees and then using these figures of speech in select ways to build rapport and foster change. "A metaphor is a figure of speech, containing an implied comparison—expressing an idea in terms of something else" (Meier & Davis, 1997, p. 30). It is common for Native peoples to express themselves in metaphorical stories, either verbal or written (Kincade & Evans, 1996). The significance of imagery in the life of an individual is also reflected in its importance in promoting everything from peace to love relationships (Gladding, 1998).

Traditional Native healers draw on a vast body of generational symbolism and metaphoric usages to construct a world in which the individual can feel safe and comfortable (e.g., myths, chants, dances, and sandpaintings; Dufrene & Coleman, 1994a). For example, among the Navajo, symbolism in healing is seen in the use of *mandalas*, such as the medicine wheel, a ceremonial circle of stones (Dufrene, 1990). Medicine wheels have horizontal and vertical lines through the center. The circle symbolizes the earth, lines represent the pathways, and the four colors (black, white, red, and yellow) symbolize the four races and the four directions. Color symbolism varies among tribes, but the concept is universal among Native groups.

In Cherokee teachings, the medicine wheel represents the individual and the clan as lessons in life for directions and guidance (Garrett & Garrett, 1994, 1996). The four directions are sacred, the number five refers to the Sun, and the number six is Mother Earth. The number seven is the sacred fire in the center of the circle and serves as the connection with the Great One in the Universal Circle of life. One elder described this relationship as, "The plants are your brothers and sisters, even the skunk is kin to you. We are all related and connected to each other" (Garrett & Garrett, 1996, p. 30).

An example of symbolism in healing is found in Lofgren's (1981) description of a Navajo client who divided a large sheet into quarters and began drawing scenes of her life history. Expecting the client to work in a left to right fashion, Lofgren was surprised at the client's different time line format. Unsure if the client understood, Lofgren repeated the directions. However, Lofgren learned that the Navajo way of depicting one's life in quadrants is symbolic of the four ages of humans: infancy, youth, maturity, and the transition of age. As the therapist began to overcome cultural barriers, a more culturally appropriate way was discovered to communicate with the client.

Another simple metaphoric intervention is to sit on a mountain, or an imaginary one, and take a couple of breaths and "see" what you feel. The body and mind can relax and come into balance with a focus on the center or spirit self. "It is wonderful to just be alone, because we then learn how not alone we really are," commented one Cherokee elder (Garrett & Garrett, 1996, p. 94).

The Zuni tribe uses *fetishes*, usually carvings of animals in stone or shell, which contain a spirit and provide supernatural assistance to the owner. In psychiatry, the term describes an object that a person has invested with magical or sexual powers. Such objects hold a key to the unconscious mind (Hammerschlag, 1988).

Pottery and Blankets

Native pottery and blankets reflect the refinement of techniques and materials over generations. For pottery, either the decoration is painted on or the surface is incised. Repeated distinctive designs reflect the perpetuation of Native history and culture. Pottery designs convey stories of hardship (e.g., relocation) and distinctive designs are associated with particular tribes (e.g., Eastern Woodmen pottery is distinctive from that of Northeastern pottery). The completion of the pottery equates with a spiritual giving and taking (Dufrene & Coleman, 1994a, 1994b).

Many Native tribes are proficient weavers and their blankets are prized for their designs and regional uniqueness. For example, among many Southwestern Native tribes, the number of blankets owned is a measure of wealth. Blankets are also the preferred gift for births and marriages and are often used as shrouds for Native burials. The intricate designs and colors often depict the spiritual forces that guided the process. The process itself often evolved into a spiritual venture to become rebalanced and aligned with nature (Ferrara, 1994).

Hammerschlag (1988) described Maria, a 16-year-old Pueblo apprentice weaver, who wanted to participate in her tribe's annual arts festival, which lasted several days. Her non-Native school principal viewed this as a "flimsy excuse" and advised Maria that her absence would be cause for suspension. Maria began to manifest signs of depression because she knew that the experience would have resulted in an increased spiritual connection with her art. Subsequently, her school guidance counselor mediated this conflict by arranging for cultural leave with the principal.

The school counselor's strategy allowed Maria to remain in school, yet respected her cultural values. This example also illustrates how Native values previously perceived as conflicting can be reframed to effect a positive result.

Dolls, Masks, and Clown Motifs

The length of this section reflects the inalienable use of dolls, masks, and clown motifs by Native peoples. In addition, most non-Native individuals are not aware of these aspects of Native culture.

The clown motif remains a viable component of the Native way (Herring, 1994). Common to most tribal groups, it is perhaps more strongly emphasized in the Plains and the Southwest. Clowns are an unusual expression of individuality within Native cultures, representing different treatment of those who do not fit the norm, and afford those who practice this art form a power, privilege, license, and expressiveness denied to other tribal members.

Humor via the clown motif in Native cultures is pervasive, and at times perverse. Clown humor is a special type of humor, whose linkage extends from pre-exploration times to the present day. Clown humor has, thus, been well conditioned over time to become an acceptable form of social intercourse and ceremonial rituals. Granted, clown humor can serve as an "ice-breaking" mechanism as individuals interact, within and between ethnic groups. However, the intent of this discussion is to emphasize the possibility of incorporating the clown motif into counseling and other helping relationships with Native adults and youth. Ultimately, this form of humor as a helping strategy is a question for empirical research to answer. Above all, practitioners must realize that clown humor is not just humorous. Some underlying message is almost always being carried in the humor response. And helping professionals should become aware of these underlying messages when assisting Native individuals.

The most widely researched clown (*Chuchnut*) figures of Native American Indian cultures are those of Southwestern tribal groups. For example, the *kachinas* of the Hopi Nation are supernatural spirits through which humankind and the Great Spirit communicate. They dwell in Kivas during their annual summer visits and are represented by dancers in Hopi ceremonies. Children are taught about these spirits through the use of kachina dolls carved and painted to resemble the dancers (e.g., a Sun kachina depicts the messenger of enlightenment). In that light, the major motifs will be described further. The following descriptions reflect the most common clown figures among Southwestern tribal groups (Colton, 1959, pp. 19-76; Mails, 1997, pp. 129-134, 250-252; Wright, 1977, pp. 78-90). Note the use of earth colors and the distinctive roles of each clown character and reflect on how these characteristics can be adapted to a helping relationship.

Kwikwilyak(q)a (Mocking Kachina). The Mocking Kachina has no personality of his own but merely reflects the actions of anyone who passes within his view. The humor of his action lies in the rapidity with which he imitates others and their efforts to get away from him. He is usually seen in the Bean Dance as a foil for the Ho-e (see below). The Ho-e finally rid themselves of this nuisance by pretending to set fire to their hair. The Kwikwilyaka imitates this action and touches off his cedar bark hair.

This kachina wears a brown case mask with juniper bark hair, has tubular eyes, a mouth painted with stripes, and may have a snout. Three white lines under the eyes are symbols. The clothing consists of a black and white cloth ruff, old shirt with trousers ("white man clothes"), and red moccasins. He carries a rattle and a cane.

Ho-e or Wo-e (No English translation). Ho-e is one of the principal characters in the Bean Dance. His antics are the delight of the crowd as he fights with the Mocking Kachina or runs afoul of the guards. A favorite pastime is imitating the songs and actions of others, usually with little regard for the important kachinas he accompanies. He is loud and boisterous and totally lacking in any sense of responsibility.

Ho-e wears a white face or sack mask, with a red chevron across the nose and a lambskin wig. Clothing consists of a kilt, sash, and fox skin, but he is barefooted. His shoulders are painted white and he carries a rattle.

Tasavu (Navajo Clown). The Navajo Clown is one of long standing among the Hopi. He performs much as the Piptuka (see next page) does, appearing during a pause in the dance to do something crazy.

Koshari, Paiyakyamu, Hano Chukuwai-upkia (Glutton). The multiple names of this clown give some indication of his origin. Koshari, or their variants, may be found in most of the pueblos. They are figures both sacred and profane. Their actions, although highly amusing, are not what the Hopi or anyone else would like to be caught doing in public. They are the ultimate example of overdoing everything.

The Glutton wears a face mask painted white with black eyes and mouth. Two soft black and white striped horns are on top of the head. He wears a rag ruff, a breech clout, and is barefooted. His body is painted in black and white horizontal stripes. No regular accessories are used.

Koyemsi (Mudhead). The Koyemsi is a multifaceted clown introduced from the Zuni culture. In Zuni legend, punishment for incest left individuals coated with mud, hence the name Mudhead (National Geographic Society, 1979). Koyemsi may appear as a chorus, and generally their songs are in the Zuni language. During rests in a dance, they may engage in games with children in the audience. At other times only a single Mudhead may appear as a drummer for a group. Should a dancer not have the proper mask or be late in arriving, he can easily become a Mudhead by donning that mask. These kachinas appear in almost every Hopi dance.

Koyemsi wear a reddish brown sack mask to which are fastened three gourds, one on top and one over each ear, all painted reddish brown. A rag ruff is worn along with a kilt made from a woman's old dress. His body is painted with red-brown clay and he carries a feather and a rattle.

Huhuwa (Cross-Legged Kachina). This kachina is supposed to represent a Mishongnovi man who was badly crippled but was so kind and gentle that he was made a kachina. He moves about during the Powamu ceremony, delivering presents to the children as he hobbles along and making wisecracks to all. He also appears during the mixed dances.

Huhuwa wears a white face mask with carved wooden nose and a tubular or painted mouth. His wig is made of lambskin with the wool left intact. No distinctive costume is used. He wears shells around his neck and carries a rattle.

Tsuku (Hopi Rio Grande Clown). The Tsuku, like the Koshari, have a ritual pattern of behavior, which they follow as they enter the village. They enter over the rooftops as though they were traversing great mountains and valleys.

Making their way to the plaza, they encounter incredible difficulties along the way, arriving more by accident than by careful planning. Once in the plaza they build a "house" of ashes and put their "sister," a stuffed coot, inside it. Their every action is untutored and irresponsible, as they don't know how to pray to the kachinas and must learn as the dance proceeds. Their actions are so unbridled that eventually kachina warriors come and threaten them for misbehaving. Exhibiting exaggerated cowardice, the Tsuku blame everyone but themselves, and when the warriors withdraw they forget it all. However, before the dance has ended the warriors return and thoroughly beat the clowns, drenching them with water as the clowns cower and promise to behave better. This play is re-enacted every time they appear, always interwoven with other humorous essays or interactions with kachinas, racers, and audience.

This clown wears a brown face mask with two horizontal red bands. A rag ruff and a breech cloth is worn with no body paint.

Piptuka (Caricature). The piptuka are not kachinas. They have been called grotesques, clowns, and comics, but could just as easily be called caricatures. They are off-the-cuff ad-lib dramatizations of Hopi humor. They can be produced in a moment using materials at hand and are then presented as humorous comments on Hopi subjects. They may appear in a skit about the rude behavior of European Americans or mimicking Hopi marital problems or whatever topic is current in the villages. There are both male and female Piptuka; the females are called Piptu Wuhti.

Piptuka wears a white face mask with hair of a white lamb's hide, a nose carved out of cottonwood, and red paint on the cheeks. A rag ruff is worn with the rest of the costume, made up any way to appear funny.

Tasap Yeibichai Kwa-um (Navajo Talking God Grandfather). This kachina is taken directly from the Navajo Yeibichai ceremony. The figure among the Navajo holds a position of great reverence. However, among the Hopi the kachina is given a sly twist. The personage is exaggerated both in actions and role. The entire performance is in pantomime, but the actions are overdone just enough to produce a humorous rather than a serious kachina.

A case mask painted white with a green corn painted in place of a nose is worn. The eyes and mouth are crescent-shaped or interlocking half-squares. Ears of corn are painted on the mask in place of ears. A fox skin or Douglas fir ruff is worn with a red kilt and no footwear. An alternate costume consists of a velvet shirt, trousers, leggings, red moccasins, and lots of silver jewelry.

Ushe (Hano Cactus Kachina). Ushe appears with a Koyemsi or other clowns at Hano and reputedly belongs to the Tewa. He is a tease more than a clown, or at best a practical joker. He holds a roll of "piki" in his hand but, when an unsuspecting person reaches for it, he quickly substitutes cactus and holds that out for the person to prick his fingers. The Navajo have a similar figure called Hush-yei or Chaschin-yei; this kachina may well have derived from them rather than the Tewa.

A sack mask painted white or green is worn with red ears and tube mouth. A rabbit skin blanket is about the waist and fringed red moccasins are on the feet.

Gans (Masked Dancers, Clown Dancers, Mountain Spirit Impersonators). The Clown Dancers of the White Mountain, Chiricahua, San Carlos, and Mescalero Apache impersonate the Mountain Spirits, principally for the purpose of curing certain illnesses. Four dancers, plus the clown (called "Gray One," "Long Nose," or "White Painted"), are in each set. The identity of the performers is kept secret and violators are severely rebuked. Masked dancers usually performed as clowns initially, to learn the appropriate dance routines. Clowns are not necessary with each set of dancers for social occasions, and sometimes a clown role is not used. But when they dance to cure sickness, clowns become the most important dancers, for they have more power than any other masked dancer (Opler, 1965). The clown(s) do not talk to the people while dancing, except when messages are carried for the Gans. Clowns only motion; they are there to make fun. The audience gives directions and the clowns follow them, making fools of themselves just for the fun of it. The clown has no special position in the dance line, and touching him is not dangerous. During performances, the clown is the servant and messenger of the masked dancers, carrying requests to the musicians for certain dance songs and attending to spectators with personal items.

Each dancer selects his own headdress and costume style, following directions from the medicine man as to materials and techniques. Mask and costume styles differ within tribal areas. Clown paint, however, symbolizes the deer, which is the clown's symbolic horse. Black, blue, yellow, and white are used for color and as symbols of the four directions.

Heyoka. The Heyoka, found in the Plains tribes (Assiniboin, Dakota, Lakota, Plains-Cree, Plains-Ojibwa, and Ponca) are "contraries" or "sacred clowns." They have had visions or dreams of the Thunder Beings, called *wakinyan* (Lyon, 1996b). Shamans who receive their power from the Thunder Beings are considered among the most powerful Lakota shamans. Those who have had such dreams are required to participate in ceremonies by acting and speaking backwards, or they will be struck by lightning (Lame Deer & Erdoes, 1972). They perform such antics as riding their horses backwards, washing themselves with dirt, saying the opposite of what they mean, and expressing joy by sighs and moans.

They are also known to perform a special dance, which involves dipping their arms into a kettle of boiling water to grab pieces of meat (Lyon, 1996b). As they perform this dance, they splash the hot water on one another. It has been reported that, to protect their skin from burns, the dancers apply the juice from either the whip root plant or the red false mallow to form a mucilaginous coating on the skin (Gilmore, 1977). They also wear special costumes during this dance, including a long-nosed mask made of buffalo hide or cloth.

Apart from the special dance they perform, the Heyoka appear at other ceremonies such as the Sun Dance. Their antics cause the participants to laugh and thus lighten the serious mood. Although no special healing powers are granted to the Heyoka, many prominent healers were, and are, known to be a Heyoka, such as the powerful Lakota shaman John Fire Lame Deer.

False Face Society. This society is based on the "false faces," or wooden masks, used by various nations for healing. The Seneca word for mask is "face" (*gagohsa'*), the Owondaga word is "hunchback" (*hadu'i*), and the Mohawk word is "face" (*gagu'wara*). Skinner (1961) observed that the easternmost group of Ojibwas, the Mississaugas, adopted the False Face Society from the Iroquois for use in healing. The masks are wooden portraits of several types of mythical beings that wander about in the forests. According to Fenton (1941):

> The Faces of the forest also claimed to possess the power to control sickness. They instructed the dreamers to carve likenesses in the form of masks, saying that whenever anyone makes ready the feast, invokes their help while burning Indian tobacco and sings the curing songs, supernatural power to cure disease will be conferred on human beings who wear the masks. (p. 406)

The masks are carved from a single block of basswood or other soft wood such as willow. In former times, each person carved his own mask on a living basswood, but today craftsmen most often carve the masks for society members. Because each mask reflects the visions or dreams of the person for whom it is carved, and because the craftsmen also give in to their artistic whims, there are as many False Face types as there are different people.

These masks are treated as sacred objects and are handled with great respect. If one is dropped, an offering of burning tobacco is given and a little bundle of sacred tobacco is tied near the ear or forehead of the mask. Also, when a mask is passed on or purchased, the new owner ties a bundle of sacred tobacco to it. Thus, older masks often have many bundles tied to them. When not in use, the mask is wrapped in a cloth or hung on a wall; the mask is hung facing the wall, or its face is covered.

The most variable feature of such masks is the mouth, and the Iroquois tend to name masks according to the expressions of the mouth, except when they are named for the spirit helpers they represent (e.g., "his mouth is twisted"). The eyebrows are arched and the forehead is usually deeply wrinkled. The face is usually painted red or black and framed by a wig of black hair from the tail of a horse.

The False Face Society has two main classes of false faces, each with a different healing ritual for patients (Lyon, 1996b). One is the False Face Company, whose masks represent the greatest doctor—known to the Seneca as "our defender the doctor" and to the Onondaga as "the great humpbacked one." Other masks from this group represent his underlings, "the common forest people whose faces are against the trees." The other class is the Common Faces, who live in the forests and are deformed—either hunch-backed or crippled below the waist. The members of the False Face Society are, for the most part, people who have been cured by the society's healing ceremonies. Other members are admitted as a result of their dreams.

In addition to curing individuals, members of the False Faces go through the settlement twice a year (spring and fall) to rid it of sickness. They shake their rattles and use brushes of pine boughs, accompanied by loud cries, to drive sickness away. They visit every room in a house, sweeping under the beds and peering into every nook and corner for disease spirits. If they happen upon a sick person, they blow ashes on him or her.

Harrington (1921) reported that "a vague tradition exists to the effect that the False Face Company of the Cayuga once put a stop to an epidemic of cholera among the Minsi (a branch of the Lenni Lenape or Delaware)" (p. 161). Among the Seneca, Parker (1909) termed the society *Jadigon-sashono* and reported that there are three divisions of the False Faces employing four classes of masks—doorkeeper or doctor masks, dancing masks, beggar masks, and secret masks. The secret masks are never used during public ceremonies. Their principal ceremonies include the Marching Song, the Doctor's Dance, and the Doorkeeper's Dance.

When a person becomes ill, he or she is first attended to by a shaman known to be clairvoyant, who diagnoses the case. Ailments of the head, shoulders, and joints are usually referred to the False Face Society. Thus, the masks are used to cure swellings of the face, toothaches, inflammations of the eyes, nosebleeds, sore chins, earaches, and so forth. There have been reported cases of hysterical possession among Iroquois women when the masked men approach: "On hearing the rumpus of whining and rattles, which marks their approach, one woman would fall into spasms, imitate their cry, and crawl toward the fire, and, unless she was restrained, plunge her hands into the glowing embers and scatter the fire as if she were a False-face (spirit) hunting tobacco" (Fenton, 1941, p. 422). The masked men would restore her to normal by blowing hot ashes on her.

Sandpainting

The art of sandpainting continues to be used by traditional Native healers in their rituals. For example, Navajo healers recite every word for the ceremony in the right order, each line with its appropriate melody. As they sing, they sprinkle sand on the ground with movements of their thumbs and forefingers, creating what many believe to be the greatest folk art on this continent (Hammerschlag, 1988). In one ritual to restore balance to a female who had been separated from her tribe since youth, the completed sandpainting depicted a Navajo legend about a child who was lost to the tribe, but returned in another form. The healer asked the subject to sit in the middle of the painting so she could actually mingle with the heroic figures and absorb their strengths (Highwater, 1976).

Storytelling, Poetry, and Folktales

Storytelling is an integral part of spiritual life and is also a way to transmit tribal legends or histories generationally. This art form is also used to teach children about morality and cultural values. The Cherokee story of "The Deer and the Bear" is a good example. This story explains the traditional view that the mind and body are united in Cherokee Indian medicine rather than separate entities (adapted from Garrett & Garrett, 1996, p. 93).

> The deer is a cunning animal, considered sacred, because it is the mind of the universe. It hears and sees all things, and you can talk to the deer. The bear, however, likes to sleep and eat when hungry. The bear is the body of the universe, just doing what comes naturally, without regard to anything or anybody, except for the messages received. Each cell of the body stores the messages and memory of all time. We can condition our bodies to listen and to receive those messages as the sacred deer does for mental healing. (p. 93)

Another example is found in the very special relationship based on mutual respect and caring that exists between Native elders and children as one moves through the Circle of Life from "being cared for" to "caring for" (Red Horse, 1980). Native elders transmit to children the tradition that they carry their ancestors' spirits. Children are held in reverence as carriers of traditions and as "little people" who are still very close to the spirit world and from whom adults have much to learn (Garrett & Garrett, 1994, 1996). A young Cree from Alberta, Canada, asked his aging grandfather, "Grandfather, what is the purpose of life?" After a long silence, he replied, "Grandson, children are the purpose of life. We were once children and someone cared for us, and now it's our time to care" (Garrett & Garrett, 1996, p. 192).

Storytelling in the form of folktales reflects the client's culture and can help provide a glimpse of the types of problems faced by the client, as well as available problem-solving skills. Native folktales communicate an appreciation for and relationship to the Earth and its animals. Native peoples believe that the earth is a member of one's family and should be respected and cherished and not controlled (Bruchac, 1991; Caduto & Bruchac, 1991). Caduto and Bruchac (1991) wrote that "to the native people of North America, what was done to a frog or a deer, to a tree, a rock or a river, was done to a brother or a sister" (p. xviii).

These beliefs are passed down from one generation to the next through experience and storytelling. Native folktales are meant to educate as well as to entertain. Bruchac (1991) wrote that if a child misbehaves, he or she will be told a story rather than being punished because "striking a child breaks that child's spirit, serves as a bad example and seldom teaches the right lesson, but a story goes into a person and remains there" (p. i).

Storytelling in the form of dramas can be an effective intervention as well. The power of drama highlights unequal and unjust actions of prejudice and can lead to greater sensitivity and fairness. For example, the movie *Dances With Wolves* had a positive effect on individuals in the audience and society as a whole.

Poetry also has therapeutic value. In addition, the background of a poet can make a difference in whether the poem is pertinent or relevant to a particular population. Poems that are most open to discussion have a greater universal appeal (Lessner, 1974). For example, in working with at-risk youth, Gardner (1993) used Native American Indian poet Joy Harjo's (1983) poem "I Give You Back" to express wisdom and strength in resolving their fear.

A final suggestion is to be sure to have Native music available for children to hear when you are reading or reenacting any stories. Excellent and authentic Native music can be found in most large music stores. Additional sources include Narada Media, 4650 North Port Washington Road, Milwaukee, WI 53212-1063; Talking Taco Records, P.O. Box 40576, San Antonio, TX 78229-1576; SEQUOIA, P.O. Box 280, Topanga, CA 90290-0280; Sound of America Records (SOAR), P.O. Box 8606, Albuquerque, NM 87198 (505-268-6110); and EarthBeat! Records, P.O. Box 1460, Redway, CA 95560-1460 (707-923-3991).

Play

Counselors need to engage children in counseling and therapy (Alexander & Sussman, 1995). They should also use games that are familiar to a child's culture. The traditional approach has been to use games such as puzzles, building blocks, or computer games. A different approach would be to use hopscotch to complete a number of "hops" successfully in a specified sequence. Others are hand clapping and rhymes.

Most people are aware of the games contributed by Native groups, which have evolved into contemporary "ball" games and wrestling formats. Historically, Native boys and girls engaged in very similar play until around four or five years of age, and for the most part they were also dressed identically. After that age, play included the carrying out of minor camp functions (e.g., gathering wood, getting water) by both genders, and parents were very indulgent as to whether assigned tasks were executed. The foundations for the sexual division of labor were laid early. Thus little girls were told (Opler, 1941):

> Your work will be to make baskets and build fires, my daughter. Keep busy like your mother. Watch your mother as she is going through her daily work. When you get older, you will do the same things. It doesn't hurt you to pick up little sticks of wood and carry them in. Stay there by the fire. Watch what your mother is doing. (p. 27)

Dreams and Visions

The significance of imagery in the life of a person and its importance in promoting everything from peace to love relationships can be traced to dreams (Gladding, 1998). Furthermore, the concept of "the dream" and envisioning a future is stressed in a variety of ways, such as the dream catcher idea in the Native American Indian tradition.

Historically, the *vision quest* was both a rite of passage for young boys and a rite of spiritual renewal for adult men (Herring, 1997b). "The vision quest, like psychotherapy, is a transforming ritual" (Hammerschlag, 1988, p. 53). The vision quest is now found in most tribes and nations, including the Sioux, Menominee, Winnebago, Crow, Cheyenne, and Alaskan Inuit.

Helping professionals can collaborate with indigenous healers in dreamwork by recreating dreams through various art mediums. They can also have Native clients record their dreams (e.g., chants). A 38-year-old Cree who was deaf (not hearing impaired) used a drawing to demonstrate how the night spirit protects the sleeping bush people and their prey. This drawing was motivated by a dream the Cree had while living in a bush camp (Ferrara, 1991).

Dance and Music

In Native cultures, dance and music are dramatic ways of invoking the favor of the spiritual world. Both can be used as a form of self- or group expression. Alexander and Sussman (1995) suggested four therapeutic purposes for the use of dance and music in the counseling relationship:

1. To enhance relaxation training by identifying different relaxing or anxiety-provoking stimuli
2. To help clients or counselees problem solve around issues of ethnic identification and ethnic conflict
3. To help students feel welcome on predominantly European American school and college campuses
4. To help clients or counselees feel welcome and comfortable in the waiting rooms of helping professionals

One example of Native dances is the Sun Dance, the most sacred ceremony of the Plains tribes. Performed annually in July (the Moon of Making Fat), the participants believe that if Native people come together in this sacred circle, civilization will endure. If they fulfill this commitment made by their ancestors to Wakan Tanka, the Great Spirit, then the earth will survive. Hammerschlag (1988) described it in this way:

> The dancers dance not for themselves alone, but for their families, their tribes, and for all of humankind. As a gesture of surrender to the Creator, warriors pierce their flesh with sticks. They believe their flesh is the only thing they can offer to the Creator that is truly their own.
> . . . This is the dancers' pledge: I give you this piece of my spirit, give me the peace of your presence. I touch your presence on this Mother Earth; treat me with kindness and give my people life. (pp. 149-150)

Food

The role of food is another excellent example of Native expression. As Brown and Mussell (1985) stated, "For old and new ethnic groups in America, foodways—the whole pattern of what is eaten, when, how, and what it means—are closely tied to individual and group ethnic identity" (p. 38). The use of food in holiday celebrations, potluck dinners, festivals, and numerous other special occasions can enhance ethnic awareness. The manner in which food is eaten and prepared can also help determine a Native individual's level of acculturation.

There are many Native contributions to the kinds of foods eaten around the world; one example is offered here. One of the most popular myths and historical misconceptions involves the use of alcohol. Many people believe that European explorers, colonists, and settlers introduced alcoholic "spirits" to Native American Indians. What they introduced was a more refined product. Historically, most Native American Indian tribes already knew the effects of alcohol. For example, the Apaches made, and some still do, a beverage with low alcohol content, *tulapai*, or *tiswin*, which they drank during parties and on ceremonial occasions (Boyer, 1979).

Humor

Humor can be a useful counseling strategy when working with Native peoples of all ages (Herring & Meggert, 1994). Contrary to the stereotypical belief that Native peoples are solemn, stoic figures poised against a backdrop of tepees, horses, tomahawks, and headdresses, or in the case of Alaska Natives, igloos and parkas, the reality is that they love to laugh. Humor is important in bringing Native peoples together and reaffirming bonds of kinship. Laughter relieves stress and creates an atmosphere of sharing and connectedness.

Native humor is unique in its pragmatism, especially in its observation of the obvious and the use of exaggeration. From the use of the clown motif in ceremonies and rituals (see discussion earlier in this chapter; Herring, 1994) to the use of practical jokes, humor is a prominent feature of Native culture. For example, this brief conversation illustrates the lightheartedness of Native humor:

> Person A: "Those are some good-looking bones you're working with."
> Person B: "These, here, are buffalo ribs."
> Person A: "Where did you get them from?"
> Person B: "A buffalo."
> Person A: "Did you get them yourself?"
> Person B: "No, the buffalo helped me."

Native people know the importance of not taking oneself too seriously. Native individuals who are not open to teasing or cannot handle laughing at themselves probably cannot handle being part of the group; they may be too wrapped up in themselves and their problems. Native humor serves to reaffirm and enhance the sense of connectedness that comes from being part of the group (Garrett & Garrett, 1993, 1994). Nevertheless, the helping professional is cautioned to use humor very discreetly and to ensure tribal specificity.

Advantages and Limitations of the
Use of Creative Arts in Counseling

As Gladding (1998) so aptly concluded:

> One key aspect of counseling that promotes the best within the helping arena is the use of the creative arts. By their very nature, the arts foster different ways of experiencing the world. They are enriching, stimulating, and therapeutic in their own right. When employed in clinical situations, they help counselors and clients gain unique and universal perspectives on problems and possibilities. (p. ix)

Advantages of the Use of Creative Arts in Counseling

There are numerous advantages to using the creative arts in counseling Native individuals. The most efficacious are the following:

1. The use of creative arts involves a playfulness that helps temper reactions to serious moments and gain a clearer perspective on life (Erikson, 1975).
2. The use of creative arts promotes a collegial relationship (Arnheim, 1990). Professional barriers are broken down, enhancing the ability of clients or counselees and counselors to understand and address present difficulties more clearly.
3. The use of creative arts promotes communication (Arnheim, 1990).
4. The use of creative arts "enables clients [and counselees] to recognize the multiple nature of themselves and the world" (Gladding, 1998, p. 9).
5. The use of creative arts allows clients and counselees to see their perceived objectivity as neutral or even fun, and therefore not resisted (Gladding, 1998).
6. These forms of expression allow, and even encourage, nonverbal clients to participate meaningfully in helping relationships (Herring, 1990c).
7. The creative arts give the helping professional one more tool to use in diagnosis, understanding, or dialogue in the professional relationship (Gladding, 1998).

Limitations of the Use of Creative Arts in Counseling

Whereas numerous advantages exist for using the creative arts in counseling, limitations are also inherent in that use.

1. Clients and counselees who are artists themselves may not benefit from such an approach and it may prove to be counterproductive (Fleshman & Fryrear, 1981).

2. Many artists and some clients may view counseling and activities associated with it as being nonartistic (Gladding, 1985).

3. Popular misperceptions are held about the creative arts, especially links between creative arts and mental health (e.g., creativity and mental illness) (Gladding, 1985).

4. In some instances, clients tend to avoid artistic enterprises because of an irrational fear that they will become too involved (Ellis, 1988).

5. The actual techniques used may become arts and crafts, which are much more mechanical and structured than the creative arts (Gladding, 1998).

6. Clients and counselees may become too introspective, passive, or overcritical of themselves or situations (Gladding, 1998).

7. The creative arts may be used in nontherapeutic ways. The release of emotions must be therapeutically channeled (Warren, 1984).

8. The creative arts may be used in nonscientific ways (e.g., the omission of the four common attributes of "honesty, parsimony, quality, and insight") (Burke, 1989, p. 27).

Summary

This chapter has presented suggestions to helping professionals for the use of the creative arts when working with Native individuals and groups. Use of the creative arts is another example of how synergetic counseling can enhance the lives of Native peoples. The myriad of creative arts affords the helping professional the luxury of being selective in technique and specific to the preferences of the client or counselee. The helping professional is once again cautioned not to generalize across Native groups to the point of being insensitive.

As Alexander and Sussman (1995) summarized,

Counselors can tap into the client's everyday life to aid in the therapeutic process . . . in no way is this intended to be an exhaustive list of all possible interventions, but is intended to stimulate counselors to explore different aspects of a client's life often ignored by counselors. (p. 583)

Experiential Activities

1. Play a tape or CD of Native music to a client or counselee and ask for general feedback.
2. Have small groups discuss the advantages of using folklore as a therapeutic intervention.
3. Read a Native story to a group and elicit feedback and interpretation (a projective technique).
4. Have students list some of the symbolism and metaphors that are found in their ethnic group.
5. Visit a public Native powwow and observe the various creative arts embedded in Native life.

7

Implications for Training, Practice, and Research

In general, the arena of intellectual and personality assessment appears destined to change. This change will have important implications for Native peoples. Influenced by technology and society, the future will bring more changes in the practices and procedures used in testing. Drummond (1996) predicted the following areas of change:

- The future will see continued reliance on tests as the primary means of establishing mastery of competencies.

- Schools, states, and institutions will share more in the future.

- The future will see more movement toward assessing cognitive aspects of intelligence.

- In personality measurement, behavioral assessment techniques will become more widely used, and traditional pencil-and-paper inventories will diminish in importance.

- Test authors and test publishers will need to withdraw some tests from public access since they do not meet the standards set by professional organizations.

- Criticism of testing will increase, especially when studies look at the long-term effects of accountability.

- The future will probably question whether established policies have led to better practice, quality education, or more competent professionals in the workforce. (pp. 456-457)

How these changes will affect Native populations is speculative. The hope is that the delivery of assessment processes to Native peoples will be enhanced. To reinforce that hope, four areas must be addressed: (a) the political and organizational involvement of Native nations, tribes, and individual members must be increased; (b) the training of helping professionals must be improved; (c) helping professionals must improve their delivery of services or practice; and (d) research agendas need to be redirected.

Expanding the Political Agenda

The future prospects for Native populations, especially those who choose to remain on reservations, hinges on the attitudes and political agendas of the U.S. Congress, which funds and administers the Bureau of Indian Affairs (BIA), the Indian Health Service (IHS), and the Office of Indian Education (OIE). Across Native country, community leaders, political activists, and tribal college administrators and staff are working hard, educating the public and getting people out to vote.

The recurrent theme in the Native struggle for greater political recognition is education. Native voter education plus education of public officials equals greater Native political power. Both parts of the equation stress education, which may explain why educational institutions such as tribal colleges take such an active role (Hill, 1996).

Federal budget and policy decisions have added impetus to the efforts of Native activists in voter education and registration. The impact of the Republican Party's "Contract with America" and efforts to reduce federal spending were felt keenly on reservations and in tribal colleges. Budgets that fund housing and a host of educational programs were cut or reduced. A major concern is the election and appointment of public officials who are insensitive to Native issues and concerns, or of public officials who are ignorant of tribal governments.

In the area of mental health and education, tribal governments must assume a more active stance in regulating the quality of psychological services (McShane, 1987). Those tribal members interested in improving the mental health status of Native peoples should become actively involved in all levels of professional and governmental organizations. In addition, tribal members need to put constant pressure on their tribal elders to become more involved in political and social organizations. In particular, increased federal funding and appropriate grant sources should be stressed.

Operating within the framework of political disinterest and insensitivity, Native peoples will continue to increase in population, to relocate to urban areas, and to marry outside their ethnic group. This will ensure a concurrent need for increased mental health services. To deliver these services effectively and appropriately, changes are needed in the areas of training, practice, and research.

Implications for Training

Two basic issues are included in the training of mental health counselors and therapists: (a) the need for increased numbers of Native mental health practitioners and (b) increased efforts to ensure that non-Native practitioners are adequately trained to work with Native populations.

Recruitment, Education, and Training of Native Students

Several research efforts have yielded appropriate suggestions for the recruitment, education, and training of Native students to become helping professionals and to return to their nations, tribes, and Native urban centers. These suggestions include the following:

1. Prospective Native students should be acquainted with the benefits of pursuing careers in psychology, and recruitment efforts to psychological training programs need to be increased and expedited (LaFromboise, 1998).
2. Psychological, social work, and counseling training programs need to revise their curricula to include the impact of culture on clients and counselees (Trimble, 1991).
3. Psychological, social work, and counseling training programs need to revise their curricula to include the impact of history and environment on Native clients and counselees (Herring, 1997a, 1997b).
4. Psychological, social work, and counseling training programs need to revise their curricula to include the impact of the degree of acculturation present in Native clients and counselees (Herring, 1997a, 1997b).
5. Training programs should include Native community-based practica and internships to develop a sensitivity to the effects of one's personal worldview (LaFromboise, 1998).
6. Training programs should emphasize building on the strength of Native clients and counselees, while helping Native clients maintain vital memberships in

social networks and remain in natural communities in the least restrictive environment (e.g., Swinomish Tribal Mental Health Project, 1991).

7. Training programs need to prepare additional personnel in culturally sensitive and geriatric care and medicine for elderly Native individuals, with or without disabling conditions (C. D. Cook, 1990; Saravanabhavan & Marshall, 1994).

Vocational Rehabilitation Services. Vocational rehabilitation (VR) services are another area of additional study and training. Fischer's (1991) study revealed the two most critical training needs identified by VR counselors who serve Native individuals on reservations or tribal lands. In short, these needs are (a) understanding Native attitudes toward health and disabling conditions and (b) interviewing and using counseling skills with Native individuals. However, these identified needs have not been addressed adequately nor in a timely manner. In a survey of VR counselor education programs offering master's degrees, a total of 71% of those responding did not address Native cultures (Dodd, Nelson, Ostwald, & Fischer, 1990).

To implement these recommendations, training and education programs must recognize their current weaknesses. They must then be willing to hire or train professional faculty members who possess expertise in Native peoples and Native cultures. Finally, training programs must be willing to commit to a continued effort to promote appropriate training of helping professionals.

Training of Non-Native Practitioners

The burden of responsibility for providing ethnic-appropriate training for preservice mental health practitioners and school guidance counselors rests on the shoulders of those involved in such education. The recent rise in the influence of the "fourth force" in counseling (i.e., multiculturalism) has generally been reflected in training programs. Courses addressing multiculturalism have been added to training programs. Although one course cannot adequately cover the entire scope of multiculturalism, that is all that most training programs offer.

Then, too, the much debated issue of inclusion versus exclusion has caused something of a ripple and, in my opinion, distracted efforts to increase multicultural awareness among students and in-service educators. One advantage of exclusion is that it limits the content thrust of a course which, in return, allows more in-depth coverage of fewer topics. A disadvantage, however, is that some topics are not covered at all.

Too often, discussions of Native populations are the omitted topics. Rationalization of this generally focuses on one of two views: either the Native population is too small statistically to be emphasized, or no Native peoples live in the area. In either case, no need exists for disseminating knowledge. Each of these perspectives can be debated elsewhere in appropriate forums.

Training programs must make some attempt to educate their non-Native students (and in some cases Native students) about Native populations. They need to be aware of the stereotypes, historical genocide, within-group variances, levels of acculturation, value and belief systems, and other pertinent information regarding this population. The increasing change of demographics in this nation implies an ever changing local population. As more and more Native individuals leave reservations and tribal trust lands to seek more diverse occupational options and improved living conditions, more and more Native youth and adults, with varying levels of acculturation, will seek the assistance of school guidance counselors and mental health professionals. These professionals need to be aware of the numerous, and frequently unique, Native issues if they are to be prepared to meet the needs of Native individuals and groups.

Implications for Practice

The increasing likelihood that helping professionals, private and educational, will interact with Native populations underscores the need for trained professionals who understand Native cultures and views of seeking mental health and who provide appropriate mental health and educational experiences. Although at-risk conditions continue to jeopardize the future of many Native children and adolescents, many programs and efforts provide evidence of progress. However, there is an urgent sense (fueled, for example, by low achievers, AIDS, STDs, teenage pregnancy, learning problems, health conditions, and a plethora of other conditions) that immediate action is needed to improve the lives and futures of Native youth.

Similar conditions affect the lives of Native adults and Native elders. Their plight is also pervasive and must be addressed. Action taken now has the potential for success; failure to respond or a mediocre response will result in more Native peoples being at risk, and in those already at risk receiving little substantive help.

General Issues and Concerns

On the basis of a belief in the importance of acculturation, social and professional experiences with Native peoples, and the literature with regard to counseling Native peoples, those helping professionals involved in providing mental health services are encouraged to consider the points below when working with Native clients and counselees (adapted from Choney, Berryhill-Paapke, & Robbins, 1995).

1. Some Native individuals, particularly those with strong traditional beliefs about mental health, may respond more appropriately to interventions if traditional healers are involved in the process.
2. The use of the extended family offers tremendous potential for improving counseling outcome. Counseling of the Native family, however, will involve a different process than counseling the non-Native family. Therapeutic sessions may occur in different settings and locations. The Native family may prefer to be active participants and may be less interested in "talk therapy."
3. Major consideration needs to be given to differences in communication styles, perceptions of trustworthiness, gender role differences, and social support networks.
4. Extreme caution should be taken in the use of standardized tests in the assessment of Native individuals, especially Native youth. The failure to include such variables as Native life experience, cognitive structure, use of nonstandard English, and economic conditions can detrimentally affect test results and assessment. Insensitive interpretations can result in increased numbers of school dropouts. (pp. 87-88)

Native Women's Issues

In addition, LaFromboise, Berman, and Sohi (1994) emphasized Native women's issues and concerns in their suggestions for improved mental health practice with Native populations.

1. Mental health practitioners must learn to appreciate the strengths (e.g., long-term coping mechanisms of victimized women) and adaptations of Native women.
2. Mental health practitioners must emphasize the importance of tradition and ritual in therapy and hint at the need for reexamination of the subtle dynamics of sex bias, gender role, and cultural stereotyping in therapy with Native women.
3. The number of existing community care givers (both Native on and off reservations and non-Native) who can better address Native women's issues needs to be increased.

The Older Native Individual With Disabilities

According to the census of 1990, nearly 8.5% of Native peoples were 60 years of age or older and about 20.5% were 45 years of age or older (U.S. Bureau of the Census, 1992). Quality of life is a tremendous concern for this population. Elderly Native people form the most underserved group of individuals in the United States (C. D. Cook, 1990). According to C. D. Cook (1990), 50% of the Native elderly receive social security benefits, fewer than 51% of Native elders receive Medicare, and fewer than 40% receive Medicaid.

Research has indicated that the aging Native individual is faced with poverty, poor health, and difficult living conditions. In a survey of Native individuals with disabilities in Denver, Colorado (Saravanabhavan & Marshall, 1994), the majority of those interviewed were found to be between the ages of 45 and 69. In general, they reported having multiple disabilities: they had functional limitations in basic areas (e.g., lifting, walking, and seeing), and reported needing basic health care devices (e.g., eyeglasses). Limited income was reflected in lack of home ownership, lack of transportation, and lack of comprehensive health care. Lack of transportation was frequently reported as a barrier to obtaining services, and was second only to disability in reported problems related to securing employment.

Health care and human service professionals concerned with the issue of aging, and interested in serving the older Native population better, must implement the following in their practice (C. D. Cook, 1990; Saravanabhavan & Marshall, 1994):

- Improve the quality of life a Native elder experiences (e.g., in the areas of housing, basic health care, economic security, and educational and employment opportunities).
- Serve Native individuals at a younger age than non-Natives.
- Provide outreach services to the older Native population, rather than expect, or demand, that people will come to the office.
- Use the informal networks of Native peoples (i.e., extended family and friends).
- Provide transportation to services when necessary.
- Assist with appropriate and necessary vocational services.

School Psychology

School psychology may have the greatest impact of all psychological specialties on the future of the mental health of Native peoples. School psychology also faces the most difficult challenges where it is most often practiced, in public schools where politics and policy often override science. *The Handbook of School Psychology* (3rd edition) by Reynolds and Gutkin (1999) will help the practitioner, the scholar, the teacher, and the student to overcome obstacles in delivering the best available health services and in improving practice skills, research, and thinking in and about psychology. No other single source exists with the breadth and depth of coverage of topics vital to school psychology, ranging from theory-based presentation to scholarly reviews of research to more directive, or how-to, chapters.

Understanding that there are tribal as well as individual differences within the same tribe in terms of acculturation (Attneave, 1982) is important for all mental health practitioners and school guidance counselors. Through such an understanding, helping professionals may be able to avoid stereotyping based on general assumptions (Herring, 1997a; Thomason, 1991).

Implications for Research

Culturally and ethnically sensitive research is based on the value and belief systems of the target group, in this case, Native populations. Appropriately sensitive research reflects Native attitudes, expectations, and norms, and has components that take into consideration Native behavioral preferences and expectations (Martin, 1992). Researchers cannot assume they possess cultural sensitivity just because they are Native. The within-group variations of Native populations are too diverse. Moreover, researchers from a dissimilar culture or ethnic group may find it especially difficult to establish cultural sensitivity (Schinke & Cole, 1995). Demands on academic researchers (e.g., dissertations, presentations, and publication needs) are evidence of a culture of science that routinely comes into contact with dissimilar ethnic and cultural groups, often resulting in awkwardness, if not outright discord (Beauvais, 1995).

Traditional Native peoples are frequently suspicious of scientific research and outside researchers due to past experiences of exploitation. Researchers have published findings that in no way reflected the realities in Native communities or influenced repressive governmental policies toward tribal communities, such as forced assimilation through boarding schools and land allotment (Stubben, 1995). Even well-intentioned researchers may not recognize cultural and ethnical dissimilarities. Applied or participatory research should be a component of any research project involving Native communities (Beauvais, 1995; Stubben, 1995).

Medicine's (1988) ten-year-old observations about research efforts involving Native populations still deserve consideration today. Those perspectives are:

1. The underdevelopment of research on Native peoples is mainly caused by placing all Native groups into a single classification when concentrating on Native problems.

2. The majority of research on Native populations is written from a male perspective that portrays Native women as "drudges" or "matriarchal matrons" or in the "princess/squaw" derogatory manner.

3. The research on Native groups has not been used to improve theoretical knowledge.

4. The research from non-Natives has many "truths" about Native peoples that should be challenged.

The most critical thrust of Medicine's observations is the existence of an urgent need for research agendas created and conducted by Native researchers (p. 87), rather than from the obvious etic perspective of non-Native scholars.

Research Relative to Acculturation Levels

The level or degree of acculturation has been a major thread weaving through the discussions in this book. It will continue to be an inalienable variable in helping Native youth and adults. To that end, Choney and colleagues (1995) offered the following suggestions for research involving acculturation levels of Native individuals:

1. Concerted efforts should be made to develop a means of measuring acculturation that accounts for the multifaceted nature of the process (i.e., across spiritual, cognitive, affective, and behavioral domains).

2. When thinking about the effects of acculturation, researchers should avoid making value judgments about the health status of any particular level of cultural response. All levels may be "healthy" or "unhealthy" depending on the situational context in which they are offered.

3. Group or individual "acculturation profiles" should be developed because defining a single acculturation level for any individual is an unrealistic goal given the possibility that a person may have cultural responses representative of differing levels for each domain.

4. The notion that acculturation is a naturally occurring unidirectional force should be discarded; in its place researchers must understand that although some degree of acculturation is indeed present in all Native peoples today, it represents the culmination of historic and current superimposition of values that are often alien to tribes and is not the natural result of cultural evolution. (p. 88)

Research Relative to Scientific Inquiry

In addition to the important variable of acculturation, the area of empirical data relative to Native populations needs to be addressed as well. Choney and colleagues (1995) offered the following suggestions for specific improvements in research efforts with Native populations:

1. Researchers should collaborate with Native community leaders in joint efforts to meet the needs of Native peoples. For example, Native youth could be aided by collaborative efforts in youth suicide, gang violence, and substance abuse.
2. Research is needed regarding consulting counseling process and outcome. Native values, attitudes, and beliefs about counseling should be known. In addition, the applicability of specific counseling techniques needs to be assessed. An extremely important area involves developing methods to increase use of mental health services.
3. Research emphasizing identification of variables related to adaptive functioning is minimal at best and is an area that needs increased efforts.
4. Native mental health research is developing the potential to be of great assistance to Native peoples. That potential needs to be met.

Research Relative to Gender Roles

In the area of gender roles and issues among Native populations, LaFromboise and colleagues (1994) suggested the following emphases:

1. Additional research is needed on the link between mental health and role conflict related to the family and the community.
2. Given the extent to which Native women are victims of physical and sexual violence, further research on anxiety disorders and post-traumatic stress disorder is also deemed appropriate.
3. Increased understanding of the factors that contribute to depression in Native women is warranted.
4. The relevance of diagnostic instruments with Native women needs to be increased.

Research Relative to Tribal Colleges

Tribally owned and administered colleges are constantly battling scholars and academicians who seek permission to conduct investigations with students and their families. Nason (1996) summarized their concerns in four key research policy problem areas:

1. Inappropriate use of culturally sensitive information, especially spiritual information.
2. Commercial or other exploitive use of information.
3. Unauthorized infringement of individual, family, or group ownership rights for songs, stories, or other information.
4. Potential conflicts or harm resulting from the research, including the harm that comes from inappropriate interpretation of information, inappropriate intrusions into community life, and breaches of confidentiality and friendships. (p. 19)

Tribal colleges also experience difficulties maintaining sufficient faculty. In addition, tribal colleges have frequent faculty turnover. Tribal colleges also have problems attracting Native faculty members. Tierney, Ahern, and Kidwell (1996) offered the following recommendations to address these concerns:

1. *Develop more regional tribal college interaction.* The tribal colleges in a region could pool some of their resources to have constant faculty interaction.

2. *Create an academic strategic plan.* Because funding is so precarious, long-range planning often seems fruitless. However, institutions need to have academic strategic plans with clearly delineated goals and plans for achieving those goals. Without such a plan, faculty development frequently becomes individualistic rather than cohesive.

3. *Demonstrate institutional commitment.* If faculty development is a priority, then institutional budgets should reflect such a concern.

4. *Develop institutional policies for all individuals to follow.* In particular, any individual who uses faculty development funds for further study should be asked to stay at the institution at least one year beyond the grant or reimburse the institution.

In an effort to address such concerns, the Association of Aboriginal Post-Secondary Institutions (Nason, 1996) has created a research proposal checklist with its ideas for guidelines in this area. This checklist contains the following ten points:

- Community members' rights as research participants
- Access to and copying of tribal data
- The involvement of tribal personnel in the research as collaborators
- Tribal control, access, and copyright to research data
- Tribal interests in the publication of research data
- Sensitive data collection and specialized research permits
- The identification of restricted data or subjects
- Mandatory community review and concurrence as a condition of research funding and research work
- Compliance procedures and/or contractual obligations
- The possibility of cooperative research agreements with individuals or the institutions (p. 19)

Research Relative to Career Development

As presented in Chapter 5, more research is needed in the area of career development, career education, and career counseling with Native youth and adults. Information is needed on how Native individuals living both on and off reservations perceive career topics such as career maturity. Empirical data regarding career assessment is also needed. In addition, the need is obvious for more appropriate delivery of career development and education to Native youth. For example, the differentiation between the world of work observed on and near reservations and the world of work in urban areas increases daily. All Native peoples, especially Native youth, deserve an improved and enhanced exposure to occupational options open to them.

Research Relative to Technology

Preliminary studies and research indicate that computer-adaptive and computer-assisted testing will be used more extensively in education and the helping professions. Psychological data and traditional test information can be stored in computer files; this can be both cost effective and laborsaving. This efficiency, in addition, allows for immediate feedback and remediation. More tests are being developed that use multiple input and output devices for displaying results. Whereas in the past, tests had to be transferred from pencil-and-paper format to computer format, various types of items unique to the use of the computer are now being devised. Video disk technology, CD-ROM, and virtual reality technology can simulate real situations. Test items are no longer dependent on words. For example, an item on a personality test can give a visual display of the choices. Distance learning has become more and more beneficial in education.

The effects of technological advancements on Native populations will hinge on other developments. Urban Native individuals will have an advantage in these developments because of where they reside. Urban schools and agencies are more apt to possess technology than are rural, reservation, or tribal land schools and agencies. Tribal governments will need to search for additional funds to provide these technological services to their peoples.

In particular, long distance learning opportunities are promising prospects for rural, reservation, and tribal land needs. Educational opportunities not available in these areas could be brought to the Native peoples by this method. The efficacy of this type of delivery service can be documented by the positive results of such endeavors in such widely dispersed areas as Wyoming and Alaska.

Research Relative to Vocational Rehabilitation

Providing VR services for Native populations, who are outside the dominant culture (i.e., the European American middle class), presents problems for VR counselors. The VR service delivery system emphasizes orderliness and accountability by using a plethora of forms, files, and appointments (Fischer, 1991). Such structure conflicts with the values of Native individuals, who place importance on cooperation and organization by space, not time (Herring, 1997d). A lack of English-language skills and communication problems may also inhibit successful rehabilitation.

Fischer's (1991) study indicated several other areas of research relative to the use of VR services by Native individuals.

- The need to measure the impact of the differences between Native individuals and non-Native individuals on the Native individual's successful vocational rehabilitation
- The need to determine the multicultural rehabilitation counseling approaches that would facilitate an increase in successful vocational rehabilitations of Native individuals
- The need to investigate the variables of closed Native VR cases categorized as not accepted for services due to lack of interest on the part of the client
- The need to compare particular reservation or tribal land Native individuals and non-Native individuals because Native females are underrepresented in proportion to non-Native females
- The need to investigate the possibility of establishing rehabilitation services (e.g., a reservation or tribal land VR agency) that would better address the needs of the Native individuals accessing the state VR agency

The necessity of these research agendas is even more evident when the success rate of Native clients is considered. Perhaps as a result of the conflict between VR service values and cultural values, Native individuals are not successfully rehabilitated at the rate of the general population (52.7% and 62.8%, respectively; Morgan & O'Connell, 1987).

Research Relative to Psychological and Intellectual Assessment

Assessment is at a crucial, if not critical, point of development. Vance (1998) concluded that,

assessment is in a state of flux and that in many educational and clinical settings psychological assessment has fallen into disrepute during the past 20 years. Some educational professionals, and others as well, find the results of tests irrelevant, untimely, and in general unresponsive to the clinical or educational needs of children. This problem has probably developed because psychologists have, in some cases, formed a misguided and self-destructive loyalty to the standard battery of tests (Draw-A-Person, WISC-II, Bender Gestalt, and WRAT-R) and administered them in situations where their use is inappropriate. (pp. 6-7)

One of the most vital concerns in current and future assessment is test bias. The issue of bias in mental testing is an important one with strong historical precedents in the social sciences and with strong social consequences. The psychometric community has been forced to refine its definition of bias further, to inspect practices in the construction of nonbiased measures, and to develop statistical procedures to detect when bias occurs (Reynolds et al., 1999). Although advancements in bias technology are undeniable, additional research is required.

Empirical data relative to bias research do suggest several guidelines to ensure equitable assessment: (a) investigation of possible referral source bias, (b) inspection of test developers' data for evidence that sound statistical analyses for bias across groups to be evaluated with the measure have been completed, (c) assessment with the most reliable measure available, and (d) assessment of multiple abilities with multiple techniques (Reynolds et al., 1999).

In addition, a philosophical perspective is emerging in the bias literature. This view requires test developers not only to demonstrate whether their measures have differential content, construct, and predictive validity across groups prior to publication, but also to incorporate in some form content analyses by interested groups to ensure that offensive materials are omitted (Reynolds et al., 1999). Interested groups would include ethnic and cultural minorities, gender advocates, persons with disabilities, alternative lifestyle advocates, and linguistic scholars.

Additional attention must also be directed toward training programs, especially school psychology training programs. Fagan and Wise (1994) have identified three potential challenges to training programs: (a) strains on program curricula caused by dual training standards, (b) weakened ties to schools of education because of the professional psychology model of training in clinical psychology, and (c) pressure on programs in schools of education to identify more with an educational than a psychological orientation.

Bias research in personality and intelligence testing must be expanded. Only recently have publishers begun to address this problem appropriately. Researchers in personality, intelligence, and psychodiagnostics must increase their efforts in this area of concern.

Summary

This chapter has attempted to offer some suggestions to the helping professional on how to improve the daily life of Native peoples. Suggestions were made for the enhancement of training practices and the improvement of practice, and recommendations were made for increased research efforts. An increase in efforts in these three areas is vital to the healthy development of Native peoples.

Helping professionals need to revisit their roles in the future. They need to develop the knowledge, skills, and competencies to be good consumers of tests. Many advocates have stressed the need for a decision-making model for using tests and have emphasized that tests are only one source of information, the results of which are not absolute. Therefore, many experts have also advocated using an approach with multiple components to obtain data needed for decision making. Such multiple sources of information and appropriate decision making need to be used with the extremely diverse Native populations.

Perhaps this statement from Wall (1993) is a fitting conclusion to this text on counseling Native American Indians and Alaska Natives: "It's hard being an Indian. You have to live up to such high standards as an Indian; plus you've got to live up to white man's standards" (p. 165).

Experiential Activities

1. What can you do, as an individual, to address the issues and concerns presented in this chapter?

2. Survey the educational institutions in your area and assess what is being done relative to Native populations.

3. In your personal educational history, how much exposure have you had regarding Native populations?

4. If you are currently in practice as a private, agency, community, or school helping professional, are there any Native clients or counselees among your clientele or school population? What specific attention have you given to those individuals? If you are not practicing, project your thoughts to your anticipated field of practice.

5. Visit a testing center or service and observe any actual or potential biases. Give a report on what you observed and generate alternatives.

6. What other suggestions would you give to improve the delivery of mental health services to Native individuals and groups?

Additional Resources

This Appendix provides the reader with resource material not specifically mentioned in previous discussions. The reader is cautioned always to be alert to the authenticity of materials purporting to be Native-authored or containing information relative to Native peoples. Contemporary materials should reflect contemporary Native peoples, not as they existed a century ago. The suggested resources are not inclusive, and some may have newer editions or volumes. Some addresses and telephone numbers may have changed. These resources are offered in hopes that the reader will follow up and expand his or her ethnic-appropriate resource collection.

For example, Hollywood movies historically have misportrayed Native peoples and their lifestyles, even though many did imply empathy on the part of European Americans. Such movies include *The Vanishing American* (1925), *Northwest Passage* (1940), *Broken Arrow* (1950), and *Little Big Man* (1972). More recent movies are more empathic, employ Native actors, and reveal what is unique and universal in Native life, such as *House Made of Dawn* (1972), *Three Warriors* (1977), *Spirit of the Wind* (1982), *Harold of Orange* (1984), *Dances With Wolves* (1990), *Incident at Oglala* (1991), *Thunderheart* (1992), *Geronimo* (1993), *Lakota Woman* (1994), and *Children of the Dust* (1995).

The reader is advised to consult the following sources to evaluate the treatment of Native peoples in curriculum materials:

Slapin, B., & Seale, D. (Eds.). (1992). *Through Indian eyes: The Native experience in books for children.* New Society Publishers; Oyate, 2702 Mathews St., Berkeley, CA 94702
The Council on Interracial Books for Children, *Chronicles of American Indian Protest*, New York
Instructional Development Program for the Institute of Indian Services and Research. (1972 or most recent). *Bibliography of nonprint instructional materials on the American Indian.* Provo, Utah: Brigham Young University Printing Service.

Reproducible Resources

Aten, J. *Americans, too: Understanding American minorities through research-related activities.* Carthage, IL: Good Apple.
Big multicultural tales for grades K-3. Scholastic, P. O. Box 11457, Des Moines, IA 50380-1457; (800) 325-6149.

Finney, S., & Kindle, P. *North American Indians: Integrated activities for whole language and thematic teaching* (CTP 2422 - Grades 2-3). Creative Teaching Press.

Finney, S., & Kindle, P. *North American Indians: Integrated activities for whole language and thematic teaching* (CTP 2423 - Grades 4-6). Creative Teaching Press.

The multicultural activities set. Scholastic, P.O. Box 11457, Des Moines, IA 50380-1457; (800) 325-6149.

Films and Videos

The following may be purchased or rented from Insight Media, 2162 Broadway, New York, NY 10024; (212) 721-6316, FAX (212) 799-5309, (800) 233-9910:

More than bows and arrows (1992, 60 min.)

The American Indian collection (1990) (Sioux, Apache, Navajo) (5 volumes, 60 min. each)

Indians of North America (1993, 5 volumes, 30 min. each)

Live and remember (1986) (Dakota Sioux, 29 min.)

Native American cultures (1992, 2 volumes, 60 min. each)

The Faith Keeper (1991) (Turtle Clan of Onondaga Nation, 58 min.)

Inughuit (1985) (Inuit, 85 min.)

The eternal drum (1994, 25 min.)

Emergence (1981) (Navajo, 14 min.)

Native American history (1993) (Columbian & North America, 2 volumes, 50 min. each)

Cede, yield, and surrender (1991, 25 min.)

How the West was lost (1993) (Navajo, Nez Perce, Apache, Cheyenne, Lakota, 6 segments, 50 min. each)

Columbus didn't discover us (1992, 24 min.)

Surviving Columbus (1990) (Pueblo, 60 min.)

Other media resources include:

Racial and sexual stereotyping (28 min., Films for the Humanities & Sciences, P.O. Box 2053, Princeton, NJ 08543-2053; (800) 257-5126, FAX (609) 275-3767)

An eagle must fly (Brigham Young University, 1226 Spring Street, NW, Provo, UT 84560)

Differences (Windwalker Cinema Associates, Inc.)

Sacred Ground (Swank Motion Pictures, P.O. Box 9232, Seattle, WA 98109)

Good to be Indian: Proud and free (Robeson County Title IV Indian Education Project, Box 1328, Lumberton, NC 28358)

Land of the eagle (1991, 8 vols., Time-Life Video, 777 Duke St., Alexandria, VA 22314)

Shenandoah Film Productions, 538 G St., Arcata, CA 95521 (Native American owned)

Canyon Records, 4143 N. 16th St., Phoenix, AZ 85016

Indian House, Box 472, Taos, NM 87571

Reservations

A unique resource for information about reservations is Tiller, V. E. V. (Ed.). (1996). *Tiller's guide to Indian country: Economic profiles of American Indian reservations.* Albuquerque, NM: Bow Arrow Publishing. This source provides basic and current information about every reservation, rancheria, and Alaska Native village in the United States. It describes climate, community facilities, education (each tribal college is identified), the local economy, and the location. It cites statistics on population, enrollment, land holdings, and employment. Each entry contains a brief summary of local historical and cultural information. Source materials were drawn from tribal records, BIA labor force reports, telephone interviews with tribal staffs, and visits to many tribal communities. Nowhere else is so much basic information gathered in one place nor made so accessible.

Literature

Native Contributions

Editors of Time-Life Books. (1997). *The way of the spirit.* Del Mar, CA: Author.

Jones, B., & Jones, G. (1995). *Listen to the drum.* Salt Lake City, UT: Commune-A-Key.

Jones, B., & Jones, G. (1995). *The healing drum.* Salt Lake City, UT: Commune-A-Key.

Lyon, W. S. (1996). *Encyclopedia of Native American healing.* New York: Norton.

Mails, T. E. (1997). *The Hopi survival kit.* New York: Stewart, Tabori & Chang.

Meadows, K. (1991). *Earth medicine: Revealing hidden teachings of the Native American medicine wheel.* Rockport, MA: Element.

Meadows, K. (1991). *The medicine way: A shamanic path to self-mastery.* Rockport, MA: Element.

Weatherford, J. (1989). *Indian givers: How the Indians of the Americas transformed the world.* New York: Fawcett.

Weatherford, J. (1991). *Native roots: How the Indians enriched America.* New York: Fawcett.

Native Place Names

Huden, J. C. (1962). *Indian place names of New England.* New York: Museum of the American Indian, Heye Foundation.

Native Life in 1492

Dorris, M. (1992). *Morning girl.* New York: Hyperion.

Fradin, D. (1993). *Hiawatha: Messenger of peace.* New York: McElderry.

Fritz, J., Highwater, J., Mahy, M., McKissack, F., McKissack, P., & Paterson, K. (1992). *The world in 1492.* New York: Henry Holt.

Native Life After 1492

Costabel, E. (1993). *The early peoples of Florida.* New York: Atheneum. (Florida)

Friedman, R. (1992). *An Indian winter.* New York: Holiday House. (North Dakota)

Goble, P. (1993). *Death of the iron horse.* New York: Aladdin. (Plains)

Leacock, E. L., & Rothschild, N. (Ed.). (1994). *Labrador winter: The ethnographic journals of William Duncan Strong, 1927-1928.* Washington, DC: Smithsonian Institution Press. (Inuit)

Marrin, A. (1993). *Cowboys, Indians, and gunfighters: The story of the cattle kingdom.* New York: Atheneum.

Ortiz, S. (1988). *The people shall continue.* Children's Book Press. (Overview from Native perspective)

Nies, J. (1996). *Native American history: A chronology of the vast achievements of a culture and their links to world events.* New York: Ballantine.

Savilla, E. M. (1995). *Along the trail.* Yuma, AZ: Author. (Quechan)

Contemporary Native Life

A good source for softcover books on contemporary Native peoples is Pemmican Publishing Inc., Unit # 2-1635 Burrows Avenue, Winnipeg, Manitoba, Canada R2XOTI.

Armitage, P. (1991). *The Innu.* New York: Chelsea House.

Ata, T., & Moroney, L. (1989). *Baby rattlesnake.* San Francisco: Children's Book Press. (Chickasaw)

Bruchac, J. (1993). *Dawn land.* Fulcrum. (Abenaki)

Begaye, L. S. (1992). *Ma'ii and Cousin Horned Toad.* (1992). New York: Scholastic. (Navajo)

Begaye, L. S., & Tracy, L. (1993). *Building a bridge.* Flagstaff, AZ: Northland. (Navajo-European American)

Buchanan, K. (1994). *It rained on the desert today.* Flagstaff, AZ: Northland. (Chapter 11, Native American Indian)

Casler, L. (1994). *The boy who dreamed of an acorn.* New York: Philomel Books. (Chinook)

Cowcher, K. (1988). *Rain forest.* New York: Farrar Straus & Giroux. (South America)

DePaola, T. (1983). *The legend of the bluebonnet.* New York: Putnam. (Plains Indian)

DePaola, T. (1988). *The legend of the Indian paintbrush.* New York: Putnam. (Plains Indian)

Edmiston, J. (1993). *Little Eagle Lots of Owls.* Boston: Houghton Mifflin. (Native American Indian)

Ekoomiak, N. (1990). *Arctic memories.* New York: Henry Holt. (Quebec, Inuit; text in Inuktitut and English)

Eyvindson, P. (1990). *Jem and the great one.* Winnipeg, Canada: Pemmican. (Native American Indian)

Eyvindson, P. (1992). *The yesterday stone.* Winnipeg, Canada: Pemmican. (Native American Indian)

Franklin, K. L. (1994). *The shepherd boy.* New York: Maxwell/Macmillan. (Navajo)

George, J. C. (1987). *Water sky.* New York: HarperCollins. (Alaska Eskimo [Inuit])

Goble, P. (1988). *Iktomi and the boulder.* New York: Orchard Books. (Lakota Sioux)

Goble, P. (1989). *Iktomi and the berries.* New York: Orchard Books. (Lakota Sioux)

Goble, P. (1990). *Iktomi and the ducks.* New York: Orchard Books. (Lakota Sioux)

Goble, P. (1993). *The lost children.* New York: Bradbury Press. (Blackfoot)

Goble, P. (1994). *Iktomi and the buzzard.* New York: Orchard Books. (Lakota Sioux)

Green, R. (1991). *The mystery of the Navajo moon.* Flagstaff, AZ: Northland. (Navajo)

Hirschi, R. (1992). *Seya's song.* Seattle, WA: Sasquatch Books. (S'Klallam, Washington and British Columbia)

James, B. (1994). *The mud family.* New York: Putnam. (Anasazi Pueblo)

James, B. (1995). *Blow away soon.* New York: Putnam. (Chapter 11, Native American Indian)

Joose, B. M. (1991). *Mama, do you love me?* San Francisco: Chronicle Books. (Inuit)

Kendall, R. (1992). *Eskimo boy: Life in an Inupiaq village.* New York: Scholastic. (Inuit)

Kusugak, M. A. (1993). *Northern lights, soccer trails.* Toronto, Canada: Annick Press. (Inuit)

Loewen, I. (1986). *My mom is so unusual.* Winnipeg, Canada: Pemmican. (Inuit)

Loewen, I. (1993). *My Kokum called today.* Winnipeg, Canada: Pemmican. (Cree)

Markle, S. (1992). *The fledglings.* New York: Bantam. (North Carolina Cherokee)

Martin, B., & Archambault, J. (1987). *Knots on a counting rope.* New York: Henry Holt. (Navajo)

Medearis, A. S. (1991). *Dancing with the Indians.* New York: Holiday House. (Seminole)

McDermott, G. (1994). *Coyote: A trickster tale from the American Southwest.* San Diego, CA: Harcourt Brace. (Native American Indian)

McLellan, J. (1994). *Nanabosho: How the turtle got its shell.* Winnipeg, Canada: Pemmican. (Ojibwa)

Miles, M. (1971). *Annie and the old one.* Boston: Little, Brown. (Navajo)

Momaday, N. S. (1994). *House made of dawn.* New York: Fire Keepers. (Walatowa Pueblo)

Owen, R. (1994). *My night forest.* New York: Four Winds Press. (Native American Indian)

Paulsen, G. (1978). *The night the white deer died.* New York: Delacorte. (Pueblo)

Pennington, D. (1994). *Itse Selu, Cherokee harvest.* Watertown, MA: Charlesbridge. (Frontier Cherokee)

Rodanas, K. (1991). *Dragonfly's tale.* New York: Clarion. (Zuni)

Sanderson, E. (1990). *Two pairs of shoes.* Winnipeg, Canada: Pemmican. (Cree)

Seattle, Chief, & Jeffers, S. (1991). *Brother Eagle, Sister Sky.* New York: Dial. (Illustrated text of Chief Seattle's speech)

Seymour, T. V. N. (1993). *The gift of Changing Woman.* New York: Henry Holt. (Apache)

Scott, A. H. (1992). *On mother's lap.* New York: Clarion. (Inuit)

Thompson, P. (1991). *Song of the wild violets.* Chicago: Laurel Leaf. (Chippewa)

Titus, A. W. (1994). *Young goat's discovery.* Santa Fe, NM: Red Crane Books. (Hopi)

Wadden, M. (1991). *Nitassinan, the Inuit struggle to reclaim their homelands.* Toronto, Canada: Douglas & McIntyre.

Waterton, B. (1980). *A salmon for Simon.* Toronto, Canada: Douglas & McIntyre. (Canadian Native peoples)

Wood, T. (1992). *A boy becomes a man at Wounded Knee.* Cheyenne, WY: Walker & Company Library. (Lakota Sioux)

Native Folklore (Excellent sources for storytelling)

Begay, S. (1992). *Ma'ii and Cousin Horned Toad.* New York: Scholastic. (Navajo text included)

Belting, N. (1992). *Moon was tired of walking on air.* Boston: Houghton Mifflin. (South American)

Caduto, M., & Bruchac, J. (1992). *Keepers of the animals: Native American stories and wildlife activities for children.* Golden, CO: Fulcrum.

Goble, P. (1992). *Crow chief.* New York: Orchard.

Goble, P. (1993). *The girl who loved wild horses.* New York: Aladdin.

Retold by Tony Hillerman. (1986). *The boy who made dragonfly.* Albuquerque: University of New Mexico Press.

Hinton, L. (trans.). (1992). *Ishi's tale of lizard.* New York: Farrar Straus & Giroux. (Yahi)

Retold by J. London with L. Pinola. (1993). *Fire race.* San Francisco: Chronicle Books.

McDermott, G. (1993). *Raven: A trickster tale from the Pacific Northwest.* New York: Harcourt Brace.

Sports

Whitney, A. (1977). *Sports and games the Indians gave us.* New York: David McKay. (How to make gaming equipment for use in the games described)

Native Masks

Begin a study of masks by showing *The Loon's Necklace* (Britannica Films, 11 minutes).
Peters, J., & Sutcliffe, A. (1975). *Creative masks for stage and school.* New York: Plays, Inc. (Making masks)

Native Poetry

Bierhorst, J. (1971). *In the trail of the wind: American Indian poems and ritual orations.* New York: Holt, Rinehart & Winston.
Bierhorst, J. (1983). *The sacred path: Spells, prayers and power songs of the American Indians.* New York: William Morrow.
Brandon, W. (1971). *The magic world: American Indian songs and poems.* New York: William Morrow.
Bruchac, J. (Ed.). (1989). *Voices from the longhouse: An anthology of contemporary Iroquois writing.* New York: Greenfield Review Press.
Bruchac, J. (1991). *Native American stories.* Golden, CO: Fulcrum.
Bruchac, J., & London, J. (1992). *Thirteen moons on Turtle's back: A Native American year of the moon.* New York: Philomel.
Bruchac, J., & Locker, T. (1995). *The earth under Sky Bear's feet: Native American poems of the land.* New York: Philomel.
Caduto, M. J., & Bruchac, J. (1991). *Keepers of the animals: Native American stories and wildlife activities for children.* Golden, CO: Fulcrum.
Erdoes, R. (1972). *The Sun Dance People, the Plains Indians, their past and present.* New York: Knopf.
Erdoes, R., & Ortiz, A. (1984). *American Indian myths and legends.* New York: Pantheon.
Fletcher, A. C. (1970). *Indian story and song from North America.* New York: AMS Press. (Reprinted from 1900 edition, New York: Duffield & Company)
Harjo, J. (1983). *She had some horses.* New York: Thunder's Mouth.
Hirschfelder, A., & Singer, B. (Eds.). *Rising voices: Writings of young Native Americans.* New York: Scribner.
Jones, H. (1993). *The trees stand shining: Poetry of the North American Indians.* New York: Dial.
Levitas, G., Vivelo, F. R., & Vivelo, J. J. (1974). *American Indian prose and poetry: We wait in the darkness.* New York: Putnam.
Rothenberg, J. (1972). *Shaking the pumpkin, traditional poetry of the Indian North Americas.* New York: Doubleday.

Native Authors

Selected Native authors, writing from emic-idioemic views, include the following (tribal affiliation in parentheses):

Luther Standing Bear (Lakota Sioux); Ignatia Broker (Ojibwa); Joseph Bruchac (Abenaki); Ella Cara Deloria (Dakota Sioux); Vine Deloria (Dakota Sioux); Michael Dorris (Modoc); Black Elk (Oglala Lakota Sioux); Louise Erdrich (Chippewa); Eric

L. Gansworth (Onondaga); Michael Garrett (Eastern Cherokee); Roger Herring (Cherew/Catawba); Geary Hobson (Cherokee/Chickasaw/Quapaw); Linda Hogan (Chickasaw); Sara Winnemucca Hoplins (Paiute); Basil Johnston (Ojibwa); Francis La Flesche (Omaha); Lame Deer (Lakota Sioux); Lee Maracle (Metis); John J. Mathews (Osage); N. Scott Momaday (Kiowa); Simon Ortiz (Acoma); Louis Owens (Choctaw-Cherokee); Vickie Sears (Cherokee); Leslie M. Silko (Laguna); Anna L. Walters (Pawnee-Otoe-Missouria); James Welch (Blackfeet/Gros Ventre).

General Knowledge

The American Indians (1994, 16 vols.). Time-Life Education, P.O. Box 85026, Richmond, VA 23285.

Ballantine, B., & Ballantine, I. (Eds.). (1993). *America's fascinating Indian heritage.* Pleasantville, NY: Reader's Digest Association.

Cahape, P., & Howley, C. B. (1992). *Indian nations at risk: Listening to the people.* Charleston, WV: Appalachia Educational Laboratory (ERIC Clearinghouse on Rural Education & Small Schools).

Callahan, C. M., & McIntire, J. A. (1994). *Identifying outstanding talent in American Indian and Alaska Native students.* Washington, DC: Office of Educational Research and Improvement.

Stoutenburgh, J., Jr. (1990). *Dictionary of the American Indian: An A-to-Z guide to Indian history, legend and lore.* New York: Wings Books.

Unlearning "Indian" stereotypes. Stereotypes in U.S. History Books, CIBS Resource Center, 1841 Broadway, Room 300, New York, NY 10023.

U.S. Congress, Office of Technology Assessment. (1990, January). *Indian adolescent mental health* (OTA-H-446). Washington, DC: Government Printing Office.

Healing

Boyer, L. B. (1979). *Childhood and folklore: A psychoanalytic study of Apache personality.* New York: The Library of Psychological Anthropology.

Bradley, R. K. (1967). *Weavers of Tales.* Cherokee, NC: Betty Dupree.

Brown, V., & Johnson, P. (1981). *Return of the Indian spirit.* Berkeley, CA: Celestial Arts.

Chief Seattle. (1988). *How can one sell the air? A manifesto for the earth.* Summertown, TN: Book Publishing Company.

Four Worlds Development Project. (1984). *The sacred tree: Reflections on Native American spirituality.* Wilmot, WI: Loyus Light.

Garrett, J. T., & Garrett, M. T. (1996). *Medicine of the Cherokee: The way of right relationship.* Santa Fe, NM: Bear & Company.

Hammerschlag, C. A. (1988). *The dancing healers: A doctor's journey of healing with Native Americans.* San Francisco: HarperSan Francisco.

Lake, M. G. (1991). *Native healer: Initiation into an ancient art.* Wheaton, IL: Quest Books.

Locust, C. (1985). *American Indian beliefs concerning health and unwellness.* Native American Research and Training Center Monograph, Flagstaff: University of Arizona.

McFadden, S. (Ed.). (1991). *Profiles in wisdom: Native elders speak about the earth.* Santa Fe, NM: Bear & Company.

Mooney, J. (1972). *Myths of the Cherokee and sacred formulas of the Cherokees.* Nashville, TN: Charles Elder.

Sams, J., & Carson, D. (1988). *Medicine cards: The discovery of power through the ways of animals.* Santa Fe, NM: Bear & Company.

Ywahoo, D. (1987). *Voices of our ancestors: Cherokee teachings from the Wisdom Fire.* Boston: Shambhala.

Picture Books

Ata, T., & Moroney, L. (1989). *Baby rattlesnake.* San Francisco: Children's Book Press. (Frontier days)

Beaty, J. J. (1997). *Building bridges with multicultural picture books for children 3-5.* Upper Saddle River, NJ: Prentice Hall. (Combination of various ethnic groups)

Buchanan, K., & Buchanan, D. (1994). *It rained on the desert.* Flagstaff, AZ: Northland. (Modern Arizona)

Eyvindson, P. (1988). *Chester Bear, where are you?* Winnipeg, Canada: Pemmican. (Modern Canada)

Franklin, K. L. (1994). *The shepherd boy.* New York: Maxwell/Macmillan. (Navajo)

Sanderson, E. (1992). *Two pairs of shoes.* Winnipeg. Canada: Pemmican. (Contemporary)

Music

"Authentic Indian Dances and Folklore" and "Songs about Native Americans" can be obtained from Kimbo Educational, P.O. Box 477, Long Branch, NJ 07740-0477.

"American Indian Songs and Chants," "Earth Spirit," "Moving within the Circle," "Walk in Beauty," and "Thundercord" can be obtained from Claudia's Caravan, Multicultural/ Multilingual Materials, P.O. Box 1582, Alameda, CA 94501.

Carlstrom, N. W. (1992). *Northern lullaby.* New York: Philomel.

Medearis, A. S. (1991). *Dancing with the Indians.* New York: Holiday House.

Education

Annual College Guide for American Indians, 1994-1995. 96 pp. AISES Publishing, Inc., 1630 30th St., Suite 301, Boulder, CO 80301 (1-9 copies: $5 each postpaid; 10-19 copies: $4.50 each; 20-29 copies: $4 each; 30 or more copies: $3 each).

Billman, J. (1992). The Native American curriculum: Attempting alternatives to tepees and headbands. *Young Children, 47*(6), 22-25.

The *Journal of American Indian Education* is a refereed journal (three issues annually) that publishes papers directly related to the education of North American Indians and Alaska Natives, with an emphasis on basic and applied research. College of Education, Arizona State University, P.O. Box 871311, Tempe, AZ 85287-1311.

Native Peoples Magazine is dedicated to the sensitive portrayal of the arts and lifeways of Native peoples of the Americas. Issued quarterly by Media Concepts Group, Inc., 5333 N. Seventh Street, Suite C-224, Phoenix, AZ 85014; (888) 2NATIVE (262-8483) or (602) 252-2236.

Patterson-Rudolph, C. (1993). *Petroglyphs and Pueblo myths of the Rio Grande.* Albuquerque, NM: Avanyu.

Reyhner, J. (1988). *Teaching the Indian child: A bilingual/multicultural approach* (2nd ed.). Billings, MT: Bilingual Education Program, Eastern Montana College.

Reyhner, J. (Ed.). (1992). *Teaching American Indian students.* Norman: University of Oklahoma Press.

Rhodes, R. W. (1994). *Nurturing learning in Native American students.* Hotevilla, AZ: Sonwai Books.

Schaafsma, P. (1980). *Indian rock art of the Southwest.* Albuquerque: University of New Mexico Press.

Shaffer, D. D. (1993, Summer). Making Native American lessons meaningful. *Child Education,* 201-203.

Tribal College: Journal of American Indian Higher Education addresses broad subjects relevant to education and the future of Native communities, using both journalistic and scholarly articles. It serves the tribal colleges, Native higher education in the Western Hemisphere, Indian education, and members of other communities. Issued quarterly by the American Indian Higher Education Consortium, an organization of 30 Indian-controlled colleges in the United States and Canada. Tribal College, P.O. Box 720, Mancos, CO 81328. (970) 533-9170.

Selected Native Organizations

American Indian Law Center
Box 4456, Station C
Albuquerque, NM 87109
(505) 277-5462

Association on American Indian Affairs
432 Park Avenue South
New York, NY 10016
(212) 689-8720

The Indian Family Circle Project
N. M. Department of Social Services
P.O. Drawer 5160
Santa Fe, NM 87502
(505) 827-8400

National Indian Social Worker's Association
1740 West 41st Street
Tulsa, OK 74107
(918) 446-8432

Native American Adoption Resource Exchange
200 Charles Street
Dorseyville, PA 15238
(412) 782-4457

Native American Rights Fund
National Indian Law Library
1506 Broadway
Boulder, CO 80302
(303) 447-8760

Northwest Indian Child Welfare Association
c/o RR I, Box 751
Portland, OR 97207
(503) 725-3038

Southwest Indian Court Judges Association
College of Law, Arizona State University
Tempe, AZ 85287-7906
(602) 965-6181

Three Feathers Associates
Box 5508
Norman, OK 73070
(405) 360-2919

Urban Indian Child Resource Center
390 Euclid Avenue
Oakland, CA 94610
(510) 356-2121

References

Achterberg, J. (1987). The shaman: Master healer in the imaginary realm. In S. Nicholson (Ed.), *Shamanism: An expanded view of reality* (pp. 103-124). Wheaton, IL: Theosophical Publishing House.

Aiken, L. R. (1989). *Assessment of personality.* Needham Heights, MA: Allyn & Bacon.

Alexander, C. M., & Sussman, L. (1995). Creative approaches to multicultural counseling. In J. G. Ponterotto, J. M. Casas, L. A. Suzuki, & C. M. Alexander (Eds.), *Handbook of multicultural counseling* (pp. 375-384). Thousand Oaks, CA: Sage.

Allen, B. P., & Adams, J. Q. (1992). The concept "race": Lets go back to the beginning. *Journal of Social Behavior and Personality, 7,* 163-168.

American Indian Education Handbook Committee. (1982). *American Indian education handbook.* Sacramento: California State Department of Education.

American Psychological Association. (1992). *Ethical principles of psychologists and code of conduct.* Washington, DC: Author.

American Psychological Association. (1993). Guidelines for providers of psychological services to ethnic, linguistic, and culturally diverse populations. *American Psychologist, 48,* 45-48.

Anastasi, A. (1988). *Psychological testing* (6th ed.). New York: Macmillan.

Anastasi, A., & Cordova, F. A. (1953). Some effects of bilingualism upon the intelligence test performance of Puerto Rican children in New York City. *Journal of Educational Psychology, 44,* 1-19.

Appleton, V. E., & Dykeman, C. (1996). Using art in group counseling with Native American youth. *Journal for Specialists in Group Work, 21,* 224-231.

Arbona, C. (1996). Career theory and practice in a multicultural context. In M. L. Savickas & W. B. Walsh (Eds.), *Handbook of career counseling theory and practice* (pp. 45-54). Palo Alto, CA: Davies-Black.

147

Arnheim, R. (1990). The artist as healer. *Arts in Psychotherapy, 17,* 1-4.

Aronson, D. (1994). Changing channels. *Teaching Tolerance, 3*(2), 28-31.

Arredondo, P. M. (1986). Immigration as a historical moment leading to an identity crisis. *Journal of Counseling and Human Service Professionals, 1,* 79-87.

Ashby, M. R., Gilchrist, L. D., & Miramontez, A. (1987). Group treatment for sexually abused American Indian adolescents. *Social Work With Groups, 10,* 21-32.

Ashford, B., & Kreiner, G. (1998, August). *How can you do it? Dirty work and the dilemma of identity.* Paper presented at the annual Academy of Management Conference, San Diego, CA.

Assault on the peaceful: Indian child abuse. (1988, December 26). *Newsweek,* p. 31.

Atkinson, D. R., Morten, G., & Sue, D. W. (1993). *Counseling American minorities: A cross-cultural perspective* (4th ed.). Dubuque, IA: William C. Browne.

Atkinson, D. R., Morten, G., & Sue, D. W. (1998). *Counseling American minorities* (5th ed.). Boston: McGraw-Hill.

Atkinson, D. R., & Thompson, C. E. (1992). Racial, ethnic, and cultural variables in counseling. In S. D. Brown & R. W. Lent (Eds.), *Handbook of counseling psychology* (2nd ed., pp. 349-382). Dubuque, IA: William C. Brown.

Atkinson, D. R., Thompson, C. E., & Grant, S. K. (1993). A three-dimensional model for counseling racial/ethnic minorities. *Counseling Psychologist, 21,* 257-277.

Attneave, C. (1969). Therapy in tribal settings and urban network interventions. *Family Process, 8,* 192-210.

Attneave, C. L. (1982). American Indian and Alaska native families: Emigrants in their own homeland. In M. McGoldrick, J. K. Pearce, & J. Giordana (Eds.), *Ethnicity and family therapy* (pp. 55-83). New York: Guilford.

Axelson, J. A. (1993). *Counseling and development in a multicultural society* (2nd ed.). Pacific Grove, CA: Brooks/Cole.

Axelson, J. A. (1999). *Counseling and development in a multicultural society* (3rd ed.). Pacific Grove, CA: Brooks/Cole.

Baruth, L. C., & Manning, M. L. (1999). *Multicultural counseling and psychotherapy: A lifespan perspective* (2nd ed.). Columbus, OH: Merrill.

Bass, M., & Davis, L. (1988). *Courage to heal: A guide for women survivors of child sexual abuse.* New York: Harper & Row.

Bateson, M. C. (1994). *Peripheral visions.* New York: HarperCollins.

Beard-Williams, D. (1994, December 1). We speak English in L.A.: Don't apologize. *Los Angeles Times,* p. 12A.

Beauvais, F. (1992). Trends in Indian adolescent drug and alcohol use. *American Indian and Alaska Native Mental Health Research Journal, 5,* 1-12.

Beauvais, F. (1995). Ethnic communities and research: Building a new alliance. In *The challenge of participatory research CSAP cultural competence series* (pp. 129-147). Special collaboration NIAAA/CSAP Monograph. Department of Health and Human Services: Washington, DC.

Bellak, L. & Bellak, S. S. (1949). *Children's Apperception Test.* New York: Children's Psychological Services, Inc.

Benet, N., & Maloney, S. (1994). *Keeper of the culture* (Collector's Edition). Boulder, CO: Intertribal America.

Berkhoffer, R. (1978). *The White man's Indian: Images of the American Indian from Columbus to the present.* New York: Vintage.

Bernal, M. E. (1990). Ethnic minority mental health training: Trends and issues. In F. C. Serafica, A. I. Schwebel, R. K. Russell, P. D. Isaac, & L. B. Myers (Eds.), *Mental health of ethnic minorities* (pp. 249-274). New York: Praeger.

Bernstein, B. (1967). Social structure, language, and learning. In A. H. Passow, M. Goldberg, & A. J. Tannenbaum (Eds.), *Education of the disadvantaged* (pp. 225-244). New York: Holt, Rinehart & Winston. (Reprinted from Educational Research, 3, 1961, pp. 163-176)

Berry, J., Trimble, J., & Olmedo, E. (1986). Assessment of acculturation. In W. Lonner & J. Berry (Eds.), *Field methods in cross-cultural research* (pp. 291-324). Beverly Hills, CA: Sage.

Berry, J. W., & Bennett, J. (1989). Syllabic literacy and cognitive performance among the Cree. *International Journal of Psychology, 24,* 429-450.

Berry, J. W., Kim, U., & Boski, P. (1988). Psychological acculturation of immigrants. In Y. Y. Kim & B. Gudykunst (Eds.), *Cross-cultural adaptations: Current approaches* (pp. 62-89). Newbury Park, CA: Sage.

Betz, N. E., & Fitzgerald, L. F. (1995). Career assessment and intervention with racial and ethnic minorities. In F. T. L. Leong (Ed.), *Career development and vocational behavior of racial and ethnic minorities* (pp. 263-277). Mahwah, NJ: Erlbaum.

Beyard-Tyler, K., & Haring, M. J. (1984). Navajo students respond to traditional occupations: Less info, less bias? *Journal of Counseling Psychology, 31,* 270-273.

Borgen, F. H. (1995). Leading edges of vocational psychology: Diversity and vitality. In W. B. Walsh & S. H. Osipow (Eds.), *Handbook of vocational psychology* (2nd ed., pp. 427-441). Mahwah, NJ: Erlbaum.

Boucsein, W. (1992). *Electrodermal activity.* New York: Plenum.

Bowman, S. L. (1995). Career intervention strategies and assessment issues for African Americans. In F. T. L. Leong (Ed.), *Career development and vocational behavior of racial and ethnic minorities* (pp. 137-161). Mahwah, NJ: Erlbaum.

Boyer, L. B. (1979). *Childhood and folklore: A psychoanalytic study of Apache personality.* New York: The Library of Psychological Anthropology.

Broken Nose, M. A. (1992). Working with the Oglala Lakota: An outsider's perspective. *Families in Society, 73*(6), 380-384.

Brown, D., Minor, C. W., & Jepsen, D. A. (1992). Public support for career development activities in America's schools. Report of the 1989 NCDA survey. *School Counselor, 39,* 257-262.

Brown, J. E. (1964). *The spiritual legacy of the American Indian* [Pamphlet No. 135]. Wallingford, PA: Pendle Hill.

Brown, L. K., & Mussell, K. (Eds.). (1985). *Ethnic and regional foodways in the United States: The performance of group identity.* Knoxville: University of Tennessee Press.

Bruchac, J. (1991). *Native American stories.* Golden, CO: Fulcrum.

Bureau of Indian Affairs. (1993, October 21). *Indian entities recognized and eligible to receive services from the United States Bureau of Indian Affairs.* Federal Register (58 FR 54364). Washington, DC: Government Printing Office.

Burke, J. F. (1989). *Contemporary approaches to psychotherapy and counseling.* Pacific Grove, CA: Brooks/Cole.

Burnam, M. A., Telles, C. A., Hough, R. L., & Escobar, J. I. (1987). Measurement of acculturation in a community population of Mexican Americans. *Hispanic Journal of Behavioral Sciences, 9,* 105-130.

Butcher, J. N., & Pancheri, P. (1976). *A handbook of cross-national MMPI research.* Minneapolis: University of Minnesota Press.

Butcher, J. N., & Williams, C. L. (1992). *Essentials of MMPI-2 and MMPI-A interpretation.* Minneapolis: University of Minnesota Press.

Caduto, M. J., & Bruchac, J. (1991). *Keepers of the animals: Native American stories and wildlife activities for children.* Golden, CO: Fulcrum.

Casas, E. (1992, August). *Multicultural counseling research: Proposing an agenda for the 90's.* Paper presented at the annual meeting of the American Psychological Association, Washington, DC.

Cayleff, S. E. (1986). Ethical issues in counseling gender, race, and culturally distinct groups. *Journal of Counseling & Development, 64,* 345-347.

Choney, S. K., Berryhill-Paapke, E., & Robbins, R. R. (1995). The acculturation of American Indians. In J. G. Ponterotto, J. M. Casas, L. A. Suzuki, & C. M. Alexander (Eds.), *Handbook of multicultural counseling* (pp. 73-92). Thousand Oaks, CA: Sage.

Christensen, C. P. (1989). Cross-cultural awareness development: A conceptual model. *Counselor Education and Supervision, 28,* 270-287.

Chung, D. K. (1992). Asian cultural commonalities: A comparison with mainstream American culture. In D. K. Chung, K. Murase, & F. Ross-Sheriff (Eds.), *Social work practice with Asian Americans* (pp. 27-44). Newbury Park, CA: Sage.

Colton, H. S. (1959). *Hopi Kachina dolls.* Albuquerque: University of New Mexico Press.

Constantino, G., Malgady, R. G., & Rogler, L. H. (1988). *Technical manual: The TEMAS thematic apperception test.* Los Angeles: Western Psychological Services.

Cook, C. D. (1990). American Indian elderly and public policy issues. In M. S. Harper (Ed.), *Minority aging: Essential curricula content for selected health and allied health professions* (pp. 137-143). (DHHS Publication No. HRS P-DV-90-4). Washington, DC: Government Printing Office.

Cook, S. W. (1990). *Information Test: Form C-4.* Boulder, CO: Institute of Behavioral Science, University of Colorado.

Cox, O. C. (1948). *Caste, class, and race.* Garden City, NY: Doubleday.

Cuellar, I., Harris, L. C., & Jasso, R. (1980). An acculturation scale for Mexican-American normal and clinical populations. *Hispanic Journal of Behavioral Sciences, 2*(3), 199-217.

Dana, R. H. (1988). Culturally diverse groups and MMPI interpretation. *Professional Psychology: Research and Practice, 19*(5), 490-495.

Dana, R. H. (1993a, November 5). *Can "corrections" for culture using moderator variables contribute to cultural competence in assessment?* Paper presented at the annual convention of the Texas Psychological Association, Austin, TX.

Dana, R. H. (1993b). *Multicultural assessment perspectives for professional psychology.* Boston: Allyn & Bacon.

Dana, R. H. (1998). *Understanding cultural identity in intervention and assessment.* Thousand Oaks, CA: Sage.

Darou, W. G. (1992). Native Canadians and intelligence testing. *Canadian Journal of Counseling, 26,* 96-99.

Dauphinais, P., Dauphinais, L., & Rowe, W. (1981). Effects of race and communication styles on Indian perceptions of counselor effectiveness. *Counselor Education and Supervision, 21,* 72-80.

Davis, G. L., Hoffman, R. G., & Nelson, K. S. (1990). Differences between Native Americans and whites on the California Psychological Inventory. *Psychological Assessment, 2*(3), 238-242.

Davis, L. (1990). *Courage to heal workbook: For men and women survivors of child sexual abuse.* New York: Harper & Row.

Deloria, V., Jr. (1970). *We talk, you listen.* New York: Dell.

Deloria, V., Jr. (1988). *Custer died for your sins: An Indian manifesto.* Norman: University of Oklahoma Press.

DeVos, G. A., & Boyer, L. B. (1989). *Symbolic analysis cross culturally: The Rorschach Test.* Los Angeles: University of California Press.

Dixon, J. K. (1989). *Group treatment for Native American women survivors of child sexual abuse.* New York: Harper & Row.

Dodd, J. M., Nelson, J. R., Ostwald, S. W., & Fischer, J. M. (1990). *Rehabilitation counselor education programs response to cultural pluralism.* Unpublished manuscript.

Dole, A. A. (1995). Why not drop race as a term? *American Psychologist, 50,* 40-54.

Domino, G., & Acosta, A. (1987). The relation of acculturation and values in Mexican Americans. *Hispanic Journal of Behavioral Sciences, 9,* 191-250.

Dorn, F. J. (1987). Dispelling career myths: A social influence approach. *School Counselor, 34,* 263-267.

Draguns, J. G. (1996). Humanly universal and culturally distinctive: Charting the course of cultural counseling. In P. B. Pedersen, J. G. Draguns, W. J. Lonner, & J. E. Trimble (Eds.), *Counseling across cultures* (4th ed., pp. 1-20). Thousand Oaks, CA: Sage.

Drummond, R. J. (1996). *Appraisal procedures for counselors and helping professionals* (3rd ed.). Columbus, OH: Merrill.

Drummond, R. J., & Ryan, C. W. (1995). *Career counseling: A developmental approach.* Columbus, OH: Merrill.

DuBray, W. (1993). *American Indian values: Mental health interventions with people of color.* St. Paul, MN: West.

Dufrene, P. M. (1990). Utilizing the arts for healing from a Native American perspective: Implications for creative arts therapies. *Canadian Journal of Native Studies, 10,* 121-131.

Dufrene, P. M., & Coleman, V. D. (1992). Counseling Native Americans: Guidelines for group process. *Journal for Specialists in Group Work, 17,* 229-235.

Dufrene, P. M., & Coleman, V. D. (1994a). Art and healing for Native American Indians. *Journal of Multicultural Counseling and Development, 22,* 145-152.

Dufrene, P. M., & Coleman, V. D. (1994b). Art therapy with Native American clients: Ethical and professional issues. *Art Therapy: Journal of the American Art Therapy Association, 11*(3), 191-193.

Eberhard, D. R. (1989). American Indian education: A study of dropouts, 1980-1987. *Journal of American Indian Education, 29,* 32-40.

Educational Testing Service. (1995). *Performance assessment: Difficult needs, difficult answers* (Trustees' colloquy)[Pamphlet]. Princeton, NJ: Author.

Edwards, E. D., & Edwards, M. E. (1984). Group work practice with American Indians. *Social Work With Groups, 7,* 7-21.

Eldredge, N. M. (1993). Culturally affirmative counseling with American Indians who are deaf. *Journal of Rehabilitative Counseling, 26*(4), 1-18.

Ellis, A. (1988). *How to stubbornly refuse to make yourself miserable about anything—yes, anything!* Secaucus, NJ: Lyle Stuart.

Epperson, D., & Hammond, K. (1981). Use of interest inventories with Native Americans: A case for local norms. *Journal of Counseling Psychology, 28,* 213-220.

Erikson, E. H. (1975). *Life history and the historical moment.* New York: Norton.

Escobar, J. E. (1993). Psychiatric epidemiology. In A. C. Gaw (Ed.), *Culture, ethnicity, and mental illness* (pp. 43-73). Washington, DC: American Psychiatric Press.

Exner, J. E. (1990). *A Rorschach workbook for the comprehensive system* (3rd ed.). Asheville, NC: Rorschach Workshops.

Eysenck, H. J., & Eysenck, S. B. S. (1975). *Manual for the Eysenck Personality Questionnaire.* San Diego, CA: Educational and Industrial Testing Service.

Fagan, T. K., & Wise, P. S. (1994). *School psychology.* White Plains, NY: Longman.

Feagin, J. R. (1989). *Racial and ethnic relations.* Englewood Cliffs, NJ: Prentice Hall.

Fenton, W. N. (1941). Masked medicine societies of the Iroquois. In *Smithsonian Institution Annual Report for 1940* (pp. 397-429). Washington, DC: Smithsonian Institution.

Ferrara, N. (1991). Lukes map of the journey: Art therapy with a Cree Indian boy. *Journal of Child and Youth Care, 6,* 73-78.

Ferrara, N. (1994). Native American experience of healing through art. *Art Therapy: Journal of the American Art Therapy Association, 11*(3), 216-217.

Fischer, J. M. (1991). A comparison between American Indian and non-Indian consumers of vocational rehabilitation services. *Journal of Applied Rehabilitation Counseling, 22*(1), 43-45.

Fischer, L., & Sorenson, G. P. (1996). *School law for counselors, psychologists, and social workers.* White Plains, NY: Longman.

Flaherty, J. H., Gaviria, G. M., Pathak, D., Michell, T., Wintrob, R., Richman, J. A., & Birz, S. (1988). Developing instruments for cross-cultural psychiatric research. *Journal of Nervous and Mental Disease, 176,* 256-263.

Fleming, C. (1989, August). *Mental health treatment of American Indian women.* Paper presented at the annual meeting of the American Psychological Association, New Orleans, LA.

Fleshman, B., & Fryrear, J. L. (1981). *The arts in therapy.* Chicago: Nelson-Hall.

Ford, R. (1983). *Counseling strategies for ethnic minority students.* Tacoma: University of Puget Sound. (ERIC Document Reproduction Service No. ED 247 504)

French, L. A. (1993). Adapting projective tests for minority children. *Psychological Reports, 72,* 15-18.

Fuller, G. B., & Vance, B. (1995). A comparison of the MPDT-R and Bender-Gestalt in predicting achievement. *Psychology in the Schools, 32,* 12-17.

Gade, F., Fuqua, D., & Hurlburt, G. (1984). Use of the Self-Directed Search with Native American high school students. *Journal of Counseling Psychology, 31,* 584-587.

Gardner, J. (1993). Runaway with words: Teaching poetry to at-risk teens. *Journal of Poetry Therapy, 6,* 213-227.

Garrett, J. T. (1991). Where the medicine wheel meets medical science. In S. McFadden (Ed.), *Profiles in wisdom: Native elders speak about the earth* (pp. 167-179). Santa Fe, NM: Bear & Company.

Garrett, J. T., & Garrett, M. (1996). *Medicine of the Cherokee: The way of right relationship.* Santa Fe, NM: Bear & Company.

Garrett, M. T. (1996). "Two people": An American Indian narrative of bicultural identity. *Journal of American Indian Education, 36*(1), 1-21.

Garrett, M. W., & Garrett, J. T. (1993). *Full circle: A path to healing and wellness.* Unpublished manuscript, University of North Carolina-Greensboro.

Garrett, M. W., & Garrett, J. T. (1994). The path of good medicine: Understanding and counseling Native Americans. *Journal of Multicultural Counseling and Development (Special Issue), 22,* 134-144.

Gibbs, J. T., & Hines, A. M. (1992). Negotiating ethnic identity: Issues for Black-White biracial adolescents. In M. P. P. Root (Ed.), *Racially mixed people in America* (pp. 223-238). Newbury Park, CA: Sage.

Gilmore, M. R. (1977). *Uses of plants by Indians of the Missouri River region.* Lincoln: University of Nebraska Press.

Giordano, J., & Giordano, M. A. (1995). Ethnic dimensions in family therapy. In R. Mikesell, D. Lusterman, & S. McDaniel (Eds.), *Integrating family therapy* (pp. 34-61). Washington, DC: American Psychological Association.

Gladding, S. T. (1985). Counseling and the creative arts. *Counseling and Human Development, 18,* 1-12.

Gladding, S. T. (1998). *Counseling as an art: The creative arts in counseling* (2nd ed.). Alexandria, VA: American Counseling Association.

Good, B. J., & Good, M. J. D. V. (1986). The cultural context of diagnosis and treatment: A view from medical anthropology. In M. R. Miranda & H. H. L. Kitano (Eds.), *Mental health research and practice in minority communities: Development of culturally sensitive training programs* (pp. 1-27). Rockville, MD: National Institute of Mental Health. (ERIC Document Reproduction Service No. ED 278 754)

Good Tracks, J. G. (1973). Native American non-interference. *Social Work, 18,* 30-34.

Goodluck, C. T. (1993). Social services with Native Americans: Current status of the Indian Child Welfare Act. In H. P. McAdoo (Ed.), *Family ethnicity: Strength and diversity* (pp. 217-226). Newbury Park, CA: Sage.

Gordon, M. M. (1964). *Assimilation in American life.* New York: Oxford University Press.

Gottfredson, L. S. (1981). Circumscription and compromise: A developmental theory of occupational aspirations. *Journal of Counseling Psychology, 28,* 545-579.

Gottfredson, L. S. (1986). Special groups and the beneficial use of vocational interest inventories. In W. B. Walsh & S. H. Ospipow (Eds.), *Advances in vocational psychology: Assessment of interests* (pp. 127-198). Hillsdale, NJ: Erlbaum.

Gough, H. G. (1987). *Manual for the California Psychological Inventory.* Palo Alto, CA: Consulting Psychologists Press.

Grady, E. (1992). *The portfolio approach to assessment.* Bloomington, IN: Phi Delta Kappa Educational Foundation.

Graham, J. R. (1987). *The MMPI: A practical guide* (2nd ed.). New York: Oxford University Press.

Graves, T. (1967). Psychological acculturation in a tri-ethnic community. *Southwestern Journal of Anthropology, 23,* 337-350.

Gronlund, N. E. (1998). *Assessment of student achievement* (6th ed.). Boston: Allyn & Bacon.

Gross, J. (1996, January 14). Groups encourage redefining America's view of race. *Arkansas Democrat Gazette,* p. 12A.

Gysbers, N. C., Heppner, M. J., & Johnston, J. A. (1998). *Career counseling: Process, issues and techniques.* Needham Heights, MA: Allyn & Bacon.

Haase, R. F., Reed, C. F., Winer, J. L., & Bodden, J. L. (1979). Effect of positive, negative, and mixed occupational information on cognitive and affective complexity. *Journal of Vocational Behavior, 15,* 294-301.

Hall, R. L. (1986). Alcohol treatment in American Indian populations: An indigenous treatment modality compared with traditional approaches. In T. F. Babor (Ed.), *Alcohol and culture: Comparative perspectives from Europe and America.* New York: New York Academy of Sciences.

Hambleton, R. K. (1993). Guidelines for adapting educational and psychological tests: A progress report. *European Journal of Psychological Assessment, 10,* 229-244.

Hammerschlag, C. A. (1988). *The dancing healers: A doctor's journey of healing with Native Americans.* New York: HarperCollins.

Hannon, J. W., Ritchie, M. R., & Rye, D. A. (1992, September). *Class: The missing dimension in multicultural counseling and counselor education.* Paper presented at the Association for Counselor Education and Supervision National Conference, San Antonio, TX.

Harjo, J. (1983). *She had some horses.* New York: Thunder's Mouth.

Harjo, S. S. (1993). The American Indian experience. In H. P. McAdoo (Ed.), *Family ethnicity: Strength in diversity* (pp. 199-216). Newbury Park, CA: Sage.

Harper, K. (1986). *Give me my father's body: The life of Minik, the New York Eskimo.* Iqaluit (Frobisher Bay), North West Territory: Blacklead Books.

Harras, A. (1987). *Issues in adolescent Indian health: Suicide* (Division of Medical Systems Research and Development Monograph Series). Washington, DC: U.S. Department of Health and Human Services.

Harrington, M. R. (1921). *Religion and ceremonies of the Lenape.* Indian Notes and Monographs, Heye Foundation. New York: Museum of the American Indian.

Haviland, M. G., & Hansen, J. I. C. (1987). Criterion validity of the Strong-Campbell Interest Inventory for American Indian college students. *Measurement and Evaluation in Case and Development, 20,* 196-201.

Hayne, B. (1993). An eagles view: Sharing successful American Indian/Alaska Native alcohol and other drug prevention programs. Vol. I and The drug-free schools and communities (Vol. II). (Clearinghouse No. CG547678) Portland, OR: Regional Center for Drug-Free Schools and Communities.

Heinrich, R. K., Corbine, J. L., & Thomas, K. R. (1990). Counseling Native Americans. *Journal of Counseling and Development, 69*(2), 128-133.

Helms, J. E. (1992). Why is there no study of cultural equivalence in standardized cognitive ability testing? *American Psychologist, 47*(9), 1083-1101.

Hernandez, T. J. (1995). The career trinity: Puerto Rican college students and their struggle for identity and power. *Journal of Multicultural Counseling and Development, 23,* 103-115.

Herr, E. L., & Cramer, S. H. (1996). *Career guidance and counseling through the life span: Systematic approaches* (5th ed.). New York: HarperCollins.

Herring, R. D. (1989). The American Native family: Dissolution by coercion. *Journal of Multicultural Counseling and Development, 17,* 4-13.

Herring, R. D. (1990a). Attacking career myths among Native Americans: Implications for counseling. *School Counselor, 38,* 13-18.

Herring, R. D. (1990b). Counseling Native American children: Implications for elementary guidance. *Elementary School Guidance & Counseling: Special Issue on Cross-Cultural Counseling, 23,* 272-281.

Herring, R. D. (1990c). Nonverbal communication: A necessary ingredient of cross-cultural counseling. *Journal of Multicultural Counseling and Development, 18,* 172-179.

Herring, R. D. (1990d). Understanding Native American values: Process and content concerns for counselors. *Counseling and Values, 34,* 134-137.

Herring, R. D. (1991). Counseling Native American youth. In C. C. Lee & B. L. Richardson (Eds.), *Multicultural issues in counseling: New approaches to diversity* (pp. 37-47). Alexandria, VA: American Association for Counseling and Development.

Herring, R. D. (1992). Seeking a new paradigm: Counseling Native Americans. *Journal of Multicultural Counseling and Development, 20,* 35-43.

Herring, R. D. (1994). The clown or contrary figure as a counseling intervention strategy with Native American Indian clients. *Journal of Multicultural Counseling and Development, 22,* 153-164.

Herring, R. D. (1995). Developing biracial ethnic identity: A review of the increasing dilemma. *Journal of Multicultural Counseling and Development, 23*(1), 29-38.

Herring, R. D. (1997a). *Counseling diverse ethnic youth: Synergetic strategies and interventions for school counselors.* Fort Worth, TX: Harcourt Brace.

Herring, R. D. (1997b). Counseling indigenous American youth. In C. C. Lee (Ed.), *Multicultural issues in counseling: New approaches to diversity* (2nd ed., pp. 53-70). Alexandria, VA: American Counseling Association.

Herring, R. D. (1997c). *Multicultural counseling in schools: A synergetic approach.* Alexandria, VA: American Counseling Association.

Herring, R. D. (1997d). Synergetic counseling and Native American Indian students. *Journal of Counseling and Development, 74,* 542-547.

Herring, R. D., & Meggert, S. (1994). The use of humor as a counseling intervention with Native American Indian children. *Elementary School Guidance and Counseling, 29,* 67-76.

Herring, R. D., & Walker, S. S. (1993). Synergetic counseling: Toward a more holistic model with a cross-cultural specific approach. *Texas Counseling Association Journal, 22,* 38-53.

Highwater, J. (1976). *Song from the earth: American Indian painting.* Boston: Little, Brown.

Hill, A. (1989). Treatment and prevention of alcoholism in the Native American family. In G. Lawson & A. W. Lawson (Eds.), *Alcoholism and substance abuse in special populations* (pp. 247-265). Rockville, MD: Aspen.

Hill, M. J. (1996). Indian voices rising: Native activists aim at '96 elections. Tribal College: *Journal of American Indian Higher Education, 7*(11), 12-17.

Hispanic Research Center. (1991). *Background and demand for engineering training and need for professional engineers in South Texas.* San Antonio: University of Texas Press.

Ho, M. K. (1992). *Minority children and adolescents in therapy.* Newbury Park, CA: Sage.

Hodgkinson, H. L. (1990). *The demographics of American Indians: One percent of the people; fifty percent of the diversity.* Washington, DC: Institute for Educational Leadership.

Hoffmann, T., Dana, R., & Bolton, B. (1985). Measured acculturation and MMPI-168 performance of Native American adults. *Journal of Cross-Cultural Psychology, 16,* 243-256.

Holtzman, W. H. (1988). Beyond the Rorschach. *Journal of Personality Assessment, 52,* 578-609.

Hornblower, M. (1995, October 9). Putting tongues in cheek. *Time,* 40-42.

Huang, L. N. (1994). An integrative view of identity formation: A model for Asian Americans. In E. P. Salett & D. R. Koslow (Eds.), *Race, ethnicity, and self-identity in multicultural perspective* (pp. 42-61). Washington, DC: National MultiCultural Institute.

Hultkrantz, A. (1992). *Shamanic healing and ritual drama: Health and medicine in Native American religious traditions.* New York: Crossroads.

Hunt, J. M. (1967). The psychological basis for using pre-school enrichment as an anecdote for cultural deprivation. In A. H. Passow, M. Goldberg, & A. J. Tannenbaum (Eds.), *Education of the disadvantaged* (pp. 174-213). New York: Holt, Rinehart & Winston.

Ibrahim, F. A. (1991). Contribution of cultural worldview to generic counseling and development. *Journal of Counseling and Development, 70,* 13-19.

Indian Fellowship Program. (1989). *Final Regulations, 34 CFR Part 263.* Washington, DC: Office of Indian Education.

Indian Health Service (IHS). (1988). *A progress report on Indian alcoholism activities.* Rockville, MD: U.S. Department of Health and Human Services, Public Health Service.

Indian Health Service (IHS). (1991). *Indian women's health care: Consensus statement.* Rockville, MD: U.S. Department of Health and Human Services, Public Health Service.

Indian Health Service (IHS). (1994). *Trends in Indian health.* Rockville, MD: U.S. Department of Health and Human Services.

Ivey, A. E., Ivey, M. B., & Simek-Morgan, L. (1993). *Counseling and psychotherapy: A multicultural perspective* (3rd ed.). Boston: Allyn & Bacon.

Jeffers, S. (1991). *Brother Eagle, Sister Sky: A message from Chief Seattle.* New York: Dial Books.

Jenkins, J. O., & Ramsey, G. A. (1991). Minorities. In M. Hersen, A. E. Kazdin, & A. S. Bellack (Eds.), *The clinical psychology handbook* (pp. 724-740). New York: Pergamon.

John, V. P., & Goldstein, L. S. (1967). The social context of language acquisition. In M. Deutsch, R. Bloom, B. Brown, C. Deutsch, L. Goldstein, V. John, P. Katz, A. Levinson, E. Peisach, & M. Whiteman (Eds.), *The disadvantaged child* (pp. 163-175). New York: Basic Books.

Johnson, M. E., & Lashley, K. H. (1989). Influence of Native-Americans cultural commitment on preference for counselor ethnicity and expectations about counseling. *Journal of Multicultural Counseling and Development, 17,* 115-122.

Johnson, M. J., Swartz, J. L., & Martin, W. E., Jr. (1995). Applications of psychological theories for career development with Native Americans. In F. T. L. Leong (Ed.), *Career development and vocational behavior of racial and ethnic minorities* (pp. 103-129). Mahwah, NJ: Erlbaum.

Johnson, S. D. (1990). Toward clarifying culture, race, and ethnicity in the context of multicultural counseling. *Journal of Multicultural Counseling and Development, 18,* 41-50.

Johnson-Powell, G., & Yamamoto, J. (Eds.). (1997). *Transcultural child development: Psychological assessment and treatment.* New York: John Wiley.

Jones, E. E., Kanouse, D., Kelley, H. H., Nisbett, R. E., Valins, S., & Weiner, B. (Eds.). (1971). *Attribution: Perceiving the causes of behavior.* Morristown, NJ: General Learning Press.

Jones, E. E., Krupnick, J. L., & Kerig, P. K. (1987). Some gender effects in a brief psychotherapy. *Psychotherapy, 24,* 337-352.

Josephy, A. M. (1968). *The Indian heritage of America.* New York: Knopf.

June, L. N., & Pringle, G. D. (1977). The concept of race in the career development theories of Roe, Super, and Holland. *Journal of Non-White Concerns, 6,* 17-24.

Kallen, H. M. (1956). *Cultural pluralism and the American idea.* Philadelphia: University of Pennsylvania Press.

Kaplan, B., & Johnson, D. (1964). The social meaning of Navaho psychopathology and psychotherapy. In A. Kiev (Ed.), *Magic, faith, and healing* (pp. 203-229). New York: Macmillan.

Katz, P. (1981). Psychotherapy and Native adolescents. *Canadian Journal of Psychiatry, 26,* 455-459.

Katz, J. H. (1985). The sociopolitical nature of counseling. *Counseling Psychologist, 13,* 615-624.

Kaufman, A. S. (1990). *Assessing adolescent and adult intelligence.* Boston: Allyn & Bacon.

Kaufman, A. S., & Kaufman, N. L. (1983). *Kaufman Assessment Battery for Children Manual.* Circle Pines, MN: American Guidance Service.

Kaufman, J. S., & Joseph-Fox, Y. K. (1996). American Indian and Alaska Native women. In M. Bayne-Smith (Ed.), *Race, gender, and health* (pp. 68-93). Thousand Oaks, CA: Sage.

Kaufman, S., Kamphaus, R. W., & Kaufman, N. L. (1985). New directions in intelligence testing: The Kaufman Assessment Battery for Children (K-ABC). In B. B. Wolman (Ed.), *Handbook of intelligence: Theories, measurements, and applications* (pp. 663-698). New York: John Wiley.

Kincade, E. A., & Evans, K. M. (1996). Counseling theories, process and interventions in a multicultural context. In J. L. DeLucia-Waack (Ed.), *Multicultural counseling competencies: Implications for training and practice* (pp. 89-112). Alexandria, VA: American Counseling Association.

Klineberg, O. (1935). *Race differences.* New York: Harper.

Kluckhohn, C., & Leighton, D. C. (1962). *The Navajo* (Rev. ed.). Garden City, NY: Anchor.

Krashen, S. (1996, Winter). Is English in trouble? *Multicultural Education,* 16-19.

Krumboltz, J. D., Blando, J. A., Kim, H., & Reikowski, D. J. (1994). Embedding work values in stories. *Journal of Counseling and Development, 73,* 57-62.

LaFromboise, T. D. (1988). American Indian mental health policy. *American Psychologist, 43,* 388-397.

LaFromboise, T. D. (1990). *Circles of women: Professionalization training for American Indian women.* Newton, MA: Women's Educational Equity Act Press.

LaFromboise, T. D. (1998). American Indian mental health policy. In D. R. Atkinson, G. Morten, & D. W. Sue (Eds.), *Counseling American minorities* (5th ed., pp. 137-158). Boston: McGraw-Hill.

LaFromboise, T. D., Berman, J. S., & Sohi, B. K. (1994). American Indian women. In L. Comas-Diaz & B. Greene (Eds.), *Women of color: Integrating ethnic and gender identities in psychotherapy* (pp. 30-71). New York: Guilford.

LaFromboise, T. D., & Bigfoot, D. (1988). Cultural and cognitive considerations in the prevention of American Indian adolescent suicide. *Journal of Adolescence, 11,* 139-153.

LaFromboise, T. D., & Dixon, D. N. (1981). American Indian perceptions of trustworthiness in a counseling interview. *Journal of Counseling Psychology, 28,* 135-139.

LaFromboise, T. D., & Fleming, C. (1990). Keeper of the fire: A profile of Carolyn Attneave. *Journal of Counseling and Development, 68,* 537-547.

LaFromboise, T. D., & Graff Low, K. (1998). American Indian children and adolescents. In J. T. Gibbs & L. N. Huang (Eds.), *Children of color: Psychological interventions with culturally diverse youth* (pp. 112-142). San Francisco: Jossey-Bass.

LaFromboise, T. D., & Rowe, W. (1983). Skills training for bicultural competence: Rationale and application. *Journal of Counseling Psychology, 30,* 589-595.

LaFromboise, T. D., Trimble, J. E., & Mohatt, G. V. (1990). Counseling intervention and American Indian tradition: An integrative approach. *Counseling Psychologist, 18,* 628-654.

Lame Deer, J., & Erdoes, R. (1972). *Lame Deer: Seeker of visions.* New York: Simon & Schuster.

Lauver, P. J., & Jones, R. M. (1991). Factors associated with perceived career options in American Indian, White, and Hispanic rural high school students. *Journal of Counseling Psychology, 38,* 159-166.

Lawson, G. W., & Lawson, A. W. (1989). *Alcoholism and substance abuse in special populations.* Rockville, MD: Aspen.

Lazarus, A. A., & Beutler, L. E. (1993). On technical eclecticism. *Journal of Counseling and Development, 71,* 381-385.

Lazarus, P. (1982). Counseling the Native American child: A question of values. *Elementary School Guidance and Counseling, 17,* 83-88.

Lee, C. C. (1984). Predicting the career choice attitudes of rural Black, white and Native American high school students. *Vocational Guidance Quarterly, 32*(3), 177-184.

Lee, C. C. (1995). Multicultural literacy: Imperatives for culturally responsive school counseling. In C. C. Lee (Ed.), *Counseling for diversity: A guide for school counselors and related professionals* (pp. 191-198). Boston: Allyn & Bacon.

Lent, R. W., & Brown, S. D. (1996). Social cognitive approach to career development: An overview. *Career Development Quarterly, 44,* 310-321.

Lessner, J. (1974). The poem as a catalyst in group counseling. *Personnel and Guidance Journal, 53,* 33-38.

Leung, S. A. (1995). Career development and counseling: A multicultural perspective. In J. G. Ponterotto, J. M. Casas, L. A. Suzuki, & C. M. Alexander (Eds.), *Handbook of multicultural counseling* (pp. 549-566). Thousand Oaks, CA: Sage.

Lewis, R. G., & Ho, M. K. (1989). Social work with Native Americans. In D. R. Atkinson, G. Morten, & D. W. Sue (Eds.), *Counseling American minorities* (3rd ed., pp. 65-72). Dubuque, IA: William C. Brown.

Lieblich, A., & Josselson, R. (Eds.). (1997). *The narrative study of lives.* Thousand Oaks, CA: Sage.

Lieblich, A., Tuval-Mashiach, R., & Zilber, T. (1998). *Narrative research: Reading, analysis, and interpretation.* Thousand Oaks, CA: Sage.

Linn, R. L., & Burton, E. (1994). Performance-based assessments: Implications of task specificity. *Educational Measurement Issues and Practice, 13,* 5-8,15.

Linton, R. W. (1968). *The cultural background of personality.* New York: Appleton-Century.

Littlefield, A., Lieberman, L., & Reynolds, L. T. (1982). Redefining race: The potential demise of a concept in anthropology. *Current Anthropology, 23,* 641-647.

Littrell, M. A., & Littrell, J. M. (1983). Counselor dress cues: Evaluations by American Indians and Caucasians. *Journal of Cross-Cultural Psychology, 14,* 109-121.

Liu, W. T., Yu, E. S. H., Chang, C. F., & Fernandez, M. (1990). The mental health of Asian American teenagers: A research challenge. In A. R. Stiffman & L. E. Davis (Eds.), *Ethnic issues in adolescent mental health* (pp. 92-112). Newbury Park, CA: Sage.

Locust, C. L. (1985). *American Indian beliefs concerning health and unwellness* (Native American Research and Training Center Monograph). Tucson, AZ: University of Arizona Press.

Locust, C. L. (1988). Wounding the spirit: Discrimination and traditional American Indian belief systems. *Harvard Educational Review, 58*(3), 315-330.

Lofgren, D. (1981). Art therapy and differences. *American Journal of Art Therapy, 21,* 25-30.

Lonner, W. J., & Ibrahim, F. A. (1996). Appraisal and assessment in cross-cultural counseling. In P. B. Pedersen, J. G. Draguns, W. S. Lower, & J. E. Trimble (Eds.), *Counseling across cultures* (4th ed., pp. 293-322). Thousand Oaks, CA: Sage.

Lum, D. (1992). *Social work practice and people of color: A process-stage approach.* (2nd ed.). Monterey, CA: Brooks/Cole.

Lyon, W. S. (1996a). Back from the edge of chaos: A psychotherapeutic use of the Lakota Yuwip. *Shaman's Drum, 40,* 50-65.

Lyon, W. S. (1996b). *Encyclopedia of Native American healing.* New York: Norton.

Mahoney, F. E. (1992). Adjusting the interview to avoid cultural bias. *Journal of Career Planning and Employment, 52*(23), 41-43.

Mails, T. E. (1997). *The Hopi survival kit.* New York: Stewart, Taberi & Chang.

Malgady, R. G., Constantino, G., & Rogler, L. H. (1984). Development of a thematic appercep-tion test (TEMAS) for urban Hispanics. *American Psychologist, 42,* 228-234.

Malone, T. E. (1986). *Report of the Secretary's Task Force on Black and Minority Health: Volume V: Homicide, suicide, and unintentional injuries* (GPO Publication No. 491-313/44710). Washington, DC: Government Printing Office.

Manaster, G. J., Chan, J. C., & Safady, R. (1992). Mexican-American migrant students' academic success: Sociological and psychological acculturation. *Adolescence, 27*(105), 124-135.

Manson, N. M. (Ed.). (1982). *Topics in American Indian mental health prevention.* Portland: Oregon Health Services University Press.

Manson, S. M. (1986). Recent advances in American Indian mental health research: Implications for clinical research and training. In M. R. Miranda & H. H. L. Kitano (Eds.), *Mental health research and practice in minority communities: Development of culturally sensitive training programs* (pp. 51-89). Rockville, MD: National Institute of Mental Health. (ERIC Document Reproduction No. ED 278 754)

Manson, S. M. (1994). Culture and depression: Discovering variation in the experience of illness. In W. J. Lonner & R. S. Malpass (Eds.), *Psychology and culture* (pp. 285-290). Boston: Allyn & Bacon.

Manson, S. M., Shore, J., Baron, A., Ackerson, L., & Neligh, G. (1992). Alcohol abuse and dependence among American Indians. In J. E. Helzer & G. J. Canino (Eds.), *Alcoholism in North America, Europe, and Asia* (pp. 113-130). Oxford, UK: Oxford University Press.

Manson, S. M., Shore, J., Bloom, J., Keepers, G., & Neligh, G. (1987). Alcohol abuse and major affective disorders: Advances in epidemiologic research among American Indians. In D. Spiegler, D. Tate, S. Aitken, & C. Christian (Eds.), *Alcohol use and abuse among ethnic minorities* (Research Monograph No. 18, pp. 292-300, DHHS Publication No. ADM 89-1435). Rockville, MD: National Institute on Alcohol Abuse and Alcoholism.

Manson, S. M., Walker, R. D., & Kivlahan, D. R. (1989). Psychiatric assessment and treatment of American Indians and Alaska Natives. *Hospital and Community Psychiatry, 38,* 165-173.

Marsh, F. E., & Horns-Marsh, V. (1998). For the record. *Kappa Delta Pi Record, 34*(1), 124.

Marsh, H. W., Richards, G. E., & Barnes, J. (1986). Multidimensional self-concepts: The effect of participation in an Outward Bound program. *Journal of Personality and Social Psychology, 50,* 195-204.

Martin, J. (1992). Your new global work force. *Fortune, 126*(13), 52-68.

Martin, W. E., Jr. (1995). Career development assessment and intervention strategies with American Indians. In F. T. L. Leong, (Ed.), *Career development and vocational behavior of racial and ethnic minorities* (pp. 227-246). Mahwah, NJ: Lawrence Erlbaum.

Martin, W. E., Sr. (1991). Career development and American Indian living on reservations: Cross-cultural factors to consider. *Career Development Quarterly, 39,* 273-283.

Maruyama, M. (1978). Psychotherapy and its applications to cross-disciplinary, cross-professional, and cross-cultural communication. In R. E. Holloman & S. A. Arutiunov (Eds.), *Perspectives on ethnicity* (pp. 131-156). The Hague: Mouton.

Maxwell, J. A. (Ed.). (1990). *America's fascinating Indian heritage.* Pleasantville, NY: Reader's Digest Association.

McCloud, J. (1995). You defend what's sacred to you. In J. Katz (Ed.), *Messengers of the wind* (pp. 272-283). New York: Ballantine.

McFee, M. (1968). The 150% man: A product of Blackfeet acculturation. *American Anthropologist, 70,* 1096-1103.

McGoldrick, M., & Giordano, J. (1996). Overview: Ethnicity and family therapy. In M. McGoldrick, J. Giordano, & J. K. Pearce (Eds.), *Ethnicity and family therapy* (2nd ed., pp. 1-27). New York: Guilford.

McLemore, S. D. (1983). *Racial and ethnic minorities in America* (2nd ed.). Boston: Allyn & Bacon.

McLeod, J. (1996). The emerging narrative approach to counseling and psychotherapy. *British Journal of Guidance and Counseling, 24,* 173-184.

McShane, D. (1987). Mental health and North American Indian/Native communities: Cultural transactions, education, and regulation. *American Journal of Community Psychology, 15,* 95-116.

McShane, D. A., & Plas, J. M. (1984). The cognitive functioning of American Indian children: Moving from the WISC to the WISC-R. *School Psychology Review, 13,* 61-73.

Medicine, B. (1988). Native American (Indian) women: A call for research. *Anthropology and Education Quarterly, 19*(1), 86-92.

Meier, S. T., & Davis, S. R. (1997). *The elements of counseling* (3rd ed.). Pacific Grove, CA: Brooks/Cole.

Mercer, C. D. (1987). *Students with learning disabilities* (3rd ed.). Columbus, OH: Merrill.

Mercer, J., & Lewis, J. (1978). *System of multicultural pluralistic assessment.* New York: Psychological Corporation.

Metcalf, A. (1979). Family reunion: Networks and treatment in a Native American community. *Group Psychotherapy, Psychodrama & Sociometry, 32,* 179-189.

Middleton-Moz, J. (1986). Wisdom of the elders. In R. J. Ackerman (Ed.), *Growing up in the shadow: Children of alcoholics* (pp. 57-70). Deerfield Beach, FL: Health Communications.

Miller, N. B. (1982). Social work services to urban Indians. In J. W. Green (Ed.), *Cultural awareness in the human services* (pp. 233-276). Englewood Cliffs, NJ: Prentice Hall.

Moran, J. R., Fleming, C. M., Somervell, P., & Manson, S. M. (1995). Measuring ethnic identity among American Indian adolescents. *Journal of Research on Adolescence, 92*(7), 390-413.

Morgan, J., & O'Connell, J. C. (1987). The rehabilitation of disabled Native Americans. *International Journal of Visual Impairment & Blindness, 81*(4), 1512-1555.

Morris, W. (Ed.). (1980). *The American Heritage dictionary of the English language.* Boston: Houghton Mifflin.

Mulhern, B. (1988, September 26-October 1). Wisconsin's Indians: Their progress, their plight. *Capital Times,* p. 1.

Murray, H. A. (1943). Thematic Apperception Test. Cambridge, MA: Harvard University Press.

Myers, H. F. (1989). Urban stress and mental health of Afro-American youth: An epidemiologic and conceptual update. In R. L. Jones (Ed.), *Black adolescents* (pp. 123-152). Berkeley, CA: Cobbs & Henry.

Nagel, J. (1995). Resource competition theories. *American Behavioral Scientist, 38,* 442-458.

Nason, J. D. (1996). Tribal models for controlling research. *Tribal College: Journal of American Indian Higher Education, 8*(2), 17-20.

National Geographic Society. (1979). *The world of the American Indian* (2nd ed.). Washington, DC: Author.

Neisser, U., Boodoo, G., Bouchard, T. J., Boykin, A. W., Brody, A. W., Brody, N., Cesi, S. J., Halpern, D. F., Loehlin, J. C., Perloff, R., Sternberg, R. J., & Ubina, S. (1996). Intelligence: Knowns and unknowns. *American Psychologist, 51,* 77-98.

Neukrug, E. (1994). *Theory, practice, and trends in human services.* Pacific Grove, CA: Brooks/Cole.

O'Brien, S. (1989). *American Indian tribal governments.* Norman: University of Oklahoma Press.

Okun, B. F., Fried, J., & Okun, M. L. (1999). *Understanding diversity: A learning-as-practice primer.* Pacific Grove, CA: Brooks/Cole.

Opler, M. E. (1941). *An Apache life-way.* Chicago: University of Chicago Press.

Opler, M. E. (1965). *An Apache life way.* New York: Cooper Square.

Ozer, E. (1986). *Health status of minority women* (A summary and response to the DHHS report of the Secretary's Task Force on Black and Minority Health). Washington, DC: American Psychological Association.

Paniagua, F. A. (1994). *Assessing and treating culturally diverse clients: A practical guide.* Thousand Oaks, CA: Sage.

Parham, T. A., & Helms, J. E. (1982). The influence of Black students' racial identity attitudes on preferences for counselor's race. *Journal of Counseling Psychology, 28,* 250-257.

Parker, A. C. (1909). Secret medicine societies of the Seneca. *American Anthropologist, 11*(2), 161-185.

Patton, W., & McMahon, M. (1999). *Career development and systems theory: A new relationship.* Pacific Grove, CA: Brooks/Cole.

Pedersen, P. B. (1977). The triad model of cross-cultural counselor training. *Personnel and Guidance Journal, 56,* 94-100.

Pedersen, P. B., Fukuyama, M., & Heath, A. (1989). Client, counselor, and contextual variables in multicultural counseling. In P. B. Pedersen, J. G. Draguns, W. J. Lonner, & J. E. Trimble (Eds.), *Counseling across cultures* (3rd ed., pp. 23-52). Honolulu: University of Hawaii Press.

Peregoy, J. J. (1991). *Stress and the sheepskin: An exploration of the Indian/Native experience in college.* Unpublished doctoral dissertation, Syracuse University.

Peregoy, J. J. (1993). Transcultural counseling with American Indian and Alaskan Natives: Contemporary issues for consideration. In J. McFadden (Ed.), *Transcultural counseling: Bilateral and international perspectives* (pp. 163-192). Alexandria, VA: American Counseling Association.

Peregoy, J. J. (1999). Revisiting transcultural counseling with American Indians and Alaskan Natives: Issues for consideration. In J. McFadden (Ed.), *Transcultural counseling* (2nd ed., pp. 137-170). Alexandria, VA: American Counseling Association.

Peterson, G. W., Sampson, J. P., Jr., & Reardon, R. C. (1991). *Career development and services: A cognitive approach.* Pacific Grove, CA: Brooks/Cole.

Pewewardy, C. (1997, January 13-20). Melting pot, salad bowl, multicultural mosaic, crazy quilt, orchestra or Indian stew: For Native peoples, it's your choice! Or is it? *Indian Country Today,* p. A7.

Phinney, J. S., & Alipuria, L. L. (1990). Ethnic identity in college students from four ethnic groups. *Journal of Adolescence, 13,* 171-183.

Phinney, J. S., Lochner, B. T., & Murphy, R. (1990). Ethnic identity development and psychological adjustment in adolescence. In A. R. Stiffman & L. E. Davis (Eds.), *Ethnic issues in adolescent mental health* (pp. 53-72). Newbury Park, CA: Sage.

Polacca, M. (1995). *Cross cultural variation in mental health treatment of aging Native Americans.* Unpublished manuscript, School of Social Work, Arizona State University.

Porter, J. (1998, August 22). Principals go to head of class in study. *Arkansas Democrat Gazette,* pp. 1A, 15A.

Quintero, G. A. (1995). Gender, discord, and illness: Navajo philosophy and healing in the Native American church. *Journal of Anthropological Research, 51*(1), 69-89.

Radloff, L. S. (1977). The CES-D scale: A self-report depressions scale for research in the general public. *Applied Psychological Measurement, I,* 385-401.

Red Horse, J. (1980). Family structure and value orientation in American Indians. *Social Casework, 61,* 462-467.

Rehab Brief. (1986). *Cross-cultural rehabilitation: Working with the Native American population, IX(5).* Washington, DC: National Institute of Handicapped Research.

Reinolds, C. (1996, June 20). Study: Income, not race, fuels education gap. *Arkansas Democrat Gazette,* pp. 1A, 11A.

Reschly, D. (1978). WISC-R factor structures among Anglos, Blacks, Chicanos, and Native American Papagos. *Journal of Consulting and Clinical Psychology, 46,* 417-422.

Reschly, D., & Sabers, D. (1979). Analysis of test bias in four groups with the regression definition. *Journal of Educational Measurement, 16,* 1-9.

Reyhner, J., & Eder, J. (1992). A history of Indian education. In J. Reyhner (Ed.), *Teaching American Indian students* (pp. 33-58). Norman: University of Oklahoma Press.

Reynolds, C. R., & Gutkin, T. B. (Eds.). (1999). *The handbook of school psychology* (3rd ed.). New York: John Wiley.

Reynolds, C. R., Lowe, P. A., & Saenz, A. L. (1999). The problem of bias in psychological assessment. In C. R. Reynolds & T. B. Gutkin (Eds.), *The handbook of school psychology* (3rd ed., pp. 549-595). New York: John Wiley.

Rice, F. P. (1993). *The adolescent: Development, relationships, and culture.* Boston: Allyn & Bacon.

Richardson, E. H. (1981). Cultural and historical perspectives in counseling American Indians. In D. S. Sue (Ed.), *Counseling the culturally different: Theory & practice* (pp. 216-255). New York: John Wiley.

Richmond, L. J., Johnson, J., Downs, M., & Ellinghaus, A. (1983). Needs of non-Caucasian students in vocational education: A special minority group. *Journal of Non-White Concerns, 12,* 13-18.

Rivers, R. Y., & Morrow, C. A. (1995). Understanding and treating ethnic minority youth. In J. F. Aponte, R. Y. Rivers, & J. Wohl (Eds.), *Psychological interventions and cultural diversity* (pp. 164-180). Boston: Allyn & Bacon.

Roberts, S. (1995). *Who we are: A portrait of America based on the latest U.S. Census.* New York: Times Books.

Rogers, M. R. (1993a). Best practices in assessing minority or ethnically different children. In H. B. Vance (Ed.), *Best practices in assessment for school and clinical settings* (pp. 399-440). Brandon, VT: Clinical Psychology Publishing.

Rogers, M. R. (1993b). Psychoeducational assessment of racial/ethnic minority children and youth. In H. B. Vance (Ed.), *Best practices in assessment for school and clinical settings* (pp. 39-94). Brandon, VT: Clinical Psychology Publishing.

Rohner, R. P., Hahn, B. C., & Koehn, U. (1992). Occupational mobility, length of residence, and perceived maternal warmth among Korean immigrant families. *Journal of Cross-Cultural Psychology, 23*(3), 366-376.

Rorschach, H. (1921). *Psychodiagnostik.* Bern: Bircher.

Rotter, J. (1966). Generalized expectancies for internal versus external control of reinforcement. *Psychological Monographs, 80,* 1-28.

Rueveni, U. (1984). Network intervention for crisis resolution: An introduction. *Family Therapy, 6*(2), 65-67.

Rushton, J. P. (1995). Construct validity, censorship, and the genetics of race. *American Psychologist, 50,* 40-41.

Russo, N. F., Olmedo, E. L., Stapp, J., & Fulcher, R. (1981). Women and minorities in psychology. *American Psychologist, 36,* 1315-1363.

Sage, G. P. (1991). Counseling American Indian adults. In C. C. Lee & B. L. Richardson (Eds.), *Multicultural issues in counseling: New approaches to diversity* (pp. 23-35). Alexandria, VA: American Association for Counseling and Development.

Sage, G. P. (1997). Counseling American Indian adults. In C. C. Lee (Ed.), *Multicultural issues in counseling* (2nd ed., pp. 33-52). Alexandria, VA: American Counseling Association.

Samuda, R. J. (1998). *Psychological testing of American minorities: Issues and consequences* (2nd ed.). Thousand Oaks, CA: Sage.

Samuda, R. J., & Associates. (1998). *Advances in cross-cultural assessment.* Thousand Oaks, CA: Sage.

Sanders, D. (1987). Cultural conflicts: An important factor in the academic failures of American Indian students. *Journal of Multicultural Counseling and Development, 15,* 81-90.

Saravanabhavan, R. C., & Marshall, C. A. (1994). The older Native American Indian with disabilities: Implications for providers of health care and human services. *Journal of Multicultural Counseling and Development, 22,* 182-194.

Sattler, J. M. (1988). *Assessment of children* (3rd ed.). San Diego: Author.

Schaefer, R. T. (1988). *Racial and ethnic groups* (3rd ed.). Glenview, IL: Scott, Foresman.

Schafer, C. (1990). Natividad cautions counselors to guard against stereotypes. *Guidepost, 32,* 4, 22.

Schinke, S., & Cole, K. (1995). Methodological issues in conducting alcohol abuse prevention research in ethnic communities. In *The challenge of participatory research CSAP cultural competence series* (pp. 148-170). Special collaboration NIAAA/CSAP Monograph. Washington, DC: Department of Health and Human Services.

Schoenfeld, P., Halevy-Martini, J., Hemley-Van der Velden, E., & Ruhf, L. (1985). Network therapy: An outcome study of twelve social networks. *Journal of Community Psychology, 13,* 281-287.

Seymour-Smith, C. (1986). *Macmillan dictionary of anthropology.* New York: Macmillan.

Simmons, B. J. (1998). The importance of being tested. *Kappa Delta Pi Record, 34*(4), 129-131.

Simons, R. C., & Hughes, C. C. (1993). Cultural-bound syndromes. In A. C. Gaw (Ed.), *Culture, ethnicity, and mental illness* (pp. 75-93). Washington, DC: American Psychiatric Press.

Skinner, B. F. (1961). *Cumulative record.* New York: Appleton-Century-Crofts.

Slaney, R. B. (1983). Influence of career indecision on treatments exploring the vocational interests of college women. *Journal of Counseling Psychology, 30,* 55-63.

Smolkin, L. B., & Suina, J. H. (1996). Lost in language and language lost: Considering Native language in classrooms. *Language Arts, 73,* 166-172.

Snipp, C. M. (1996). The size and distribution of the American Indian population: Fertility, mortality, residence, and migration. In G. Sandefur, R. Rondfuss, & B. Cohen (Eds.), *Changing numbers, changing needs: American Indian demography and public health* (pp. 17-52). Washington, DC: National Academy Press.

Speck, R. V., & Speck, J. L. (1984). Family networking in the 1980s: A postscript. *Family Therapy, 6*(2), 136-137.

Steward, R. J. (1993). Two faces of academic success: Case studies of American Indians on a predominantly Anglo university campus. *Journal of College Student Development, 34,* 191-196.

Stiggins, R. (1997). *Student-centered classroom assessment.* Columbus, OH: Merrill.

Stone, W. O. (1984). Servicing ethnic minorities. In H. D. Burck & R. C. Reardon (Eds.), *Career development interventions* (pp. 267-291). Springfield, IL: Charles C. Thomas.

Stubben, J. (1995). American Indian alcohol prevention research: A community advocate's perspective. In *The challenge of participatory research CSAP cultural competence series* (pp. 259-279). Special collaboration NIAAA/CSAP Monograph. Department of Health and Human Services: Washington, DC.

Sue, D. W. (1978). World views and counseling. *Personnel and Guidance Journal, 56,* 458-463.

Sue, D. W. (1990). Culture-specific strategies in counseling: A conceptual framework. *Professional Psychology, 21,* 423-433.

Sue, D. W., & Sue, D. (1990). *Counseling the culturally different: Theory and practice* (2nd ed.). New York: John Wiley.

Suinn, R. M., Ahuna, C., & Koo, G. (1992). The Suinn-Lew self-identity acculturation scale: Concurrent and factorial validation. *Educational and Psychological Measurement, 52,* 1041-1046.

Summer, L. (1997). Considering the future of music therapy. *Arts in Psychotherapy, 24,* 75-80.

Super, D. E. (1990). A life-span, life-space approach to career development. In D. Brown & L. Brooks (Eds.), *Career choice and development: Applying contemporary theories to practice* (2nd ed., pp. 197-261). San Francisco: Jossey-Bass.

Sutton, C. T., & Broken Nose, M. A. (1996). American Indian families: An overview. In J. G. Ponterotto, J. M. Casas, L. A. Suzuki, & C. M. Alexander (Eds.), *Handbook of multicultural counseling* (pp. 31-44). Thousand Oaks, CA: Sage.

Suzuki, L. A., & Kugler, J. F. (1995). Intelligence and personality assessment: Multicultural perspectives. In J. G. Ponterotto, J. M. Casas, L. A. Suzuki, & C. M. Alexander (Eds.), *Handbook of multicultural counseling* (pp. 493-515). Thousand Oaks, CA: Sage.

Swaim, R. C., Thurman, P. J., Beauvais, F., Oetting, E. R., & Wayman, J. (1993). *Indian adolescent substance use as a function of number of risk factors.* Unpublished manuscript.

Swinomish Tribal Mental Health Project. (1991). *A gathering of wisdom: Tribal mental health. A cultural perspective.* Mount Vernon, WA: Veda Vangarde.

Tafoya, T. (1989). Circles and cedar: Native Americans and family therapy. *Journal of Psychotherapy and the Family, 6*(1-2), 71-98.

Talmon, M. (1991). *Single session therapy.* San Francisco: Jossey-Bass.

Thomason, T. C. (1991). Counseling Native Americans: An introduction for non-Native American counselors. *Journal of Counseling and Development, 69,* 321-327.

Thompson, C. L., & Rudolph, L. B. (1988). *Counseling children* (2nd ed.). Monterey, CA: Brooks/Cole.

Thompson, J. W., Walker, R. D., & Silk-Walker, P. (1993). Psychiatric care of American Indians and Alaska Natives. In A. C. Gaw (Ed.), *Culture, ethnicity, and mental illness* (pp. 189-243). Washington, DC: American Psychiatric Press.

Thorndike, R. L., Hagen, E. P., & Sattler, J. M. (1986). *The Stanford-Binet Intelligence Scale: Fourth Edition.* Chicago: Roverside.

Tierney, W. G., Ahern, B., & Kidwell, C. S. (1996). Enhancing faculty development at tribal colleges. *Tribal College: Journal of American Indian Higher Education, 7*(3), 36-41.

Trimble, J. E. (1981). Value differentials and their importance in counseling American Indians. In P. Pedersen, J. Draguns, W. Lonner, & J. Trimble (Eds.), *Counseling across cultures* (2nd ed., pp. 203-226). Honolulu: University of Hawaii Press.

Trimble, J. E. (1991). The mental health service and training needs of American Indians. In H. Myers, P. Wohlford, L. P. Guzman, & R. J. Echemendia (Eds.), *Ethnic minority perspectives on clinical training and services in psychology* (pp. 43-48). Washington, DC: American Psychological Association.

Trimble, J. E., & Fleming, C. M. (1989). Providing counseling services for Native American Indians: Client, counselor, and community characteristics. In P. B. Pedersen, J. G. Draguns, W. J. Lonner, & J. E. Trimble (Eds.), *Counseling across cultures* (3rd ed., pp. 177-204). Honolulu: University of Hawaii Press.

Trimble, J. E., Fleming, C. M., Beauvais, F., & Jumper-Thurman, P. (1996). Essential cultural and social strategies for counseling Native American Indians. In P. B. Pedersen, J. G. Draguns, W. J. Lonner, & J. E. Trimble (Eds.), *Counseling across cultures* (4th ed., pp. 177-242). Thousand Oaks, CA: Sage.

Trimble, J. E., & LaFromboise, T. D. (1985). American Indians and the counseling process: Culture, adaptation, and style. In P. Pedersen (Ed.), *Handbook of cross-cultural counseling and therapy* (pp. 125-134). Westport, CT: Greenwood.

Trimble, J. E., LaFromboise, T. D., Mackey, D., & France, G. (1982). American Indians, psychology and curriculum development: A proposal reform with reservations. In J. Chunn & F. Ross-Sheriff (Eds.), *Mental health and people of color* (pp. 43-64). Washington, DC: Howard University Press.

Trimble, J. E., Manson, S. M., Dinges, N., & Medicine, B. (1984). American Indian concepts of mental health. In P. Pedersen, N. Sartorius, & A. Marsella (Eds.), *Mental health services: The cross-cultural context* (pp. 199-220). Beverly Hills, CA: Sage.

Tucker, M. B., & Mitchell-Kernan, C. (1990). New trends in Black American interracial marriage: The social structural context. *Journal of Marriage and the Family, 52,* 209-218.

Turbak, G. (1994). Let's hear it in English. *Reader's Digest, 145*(869), 177-180.

U.S. Bureau of the Census. (1981). *Census of the population: 1980.* Washington, DC: Government Printing Office.

U.S. Bureau of the Census. (1990). *Statistical abstracts of the United States: 1990* (110th ed.). Washington, DC: Government Printing Office.

U.S. Bureau of the Census. (1991). *Statistical abstracts of the United States: 1991* (111th ed.). Washington, DC: Government Printing Office.

U.S. Bureau of the Census. (1992). *Current population reports: Population projections of the United States by age, sex, race, and Hispanic origin 1992-2050.* Washington, DC: Government Printing Office.

U.S. Bureau of the Census. (1993a). *1990 Social and economic characteristics, United States.* Washington, DC: Government Printing Office.

U.S. Bureau of the Census. (1993b). *We the first Americans.* Washington, DC: Author.

U.S. Bureau of the Census. (1996). *Statistical Abstract of the United States: 1996* (116th edition). Washington, DC: Government Printing Office.

U.S. Congress. (1986). *Indian health care* (OTA-H-290). Washington, DC: Government Printing Office.

U.S. Department of Commerce. (1992). *Census Bureau resources for the Congress: 1990 summary.* Washington, DC: Government Printing Office.

U.S. Department of Education. (1994). *Sixteenth annual report to Congress on the implementation of the Individuals with Disabilities Act.* Washington, DC: Government Printing Office.

U.S. Department of Health and Human Services. (1996). *Trends in the well-being of America's children and youth: 1996.* Washington, DC: General Accounting Office.

U.S. Department of Justice. (1991). *Crime in the United States.* Washington, DC: Government Printing Office.

Valle, R. (1986). Cross-cultural competence in minority communities: A curriculum implementation strategy. In M. R. Miranda & H. H. L. Kitano (Eds.), *Mental health research and practice in minority communities: Development of culturally sensitive training programs* (pp. 29-49). Rockville, MD: National Institute of Mental Health. (ERIC Document Reproduction Service No. ED 278 754)

Vance, H. B. (Ed.). (1998). *Psychological assessment of children: Best practices for school and clinical settings* (2nd ed.). New York: John Wiley.

Walker, R. D., & LaDue, R. (1986). An integrative approach to American Indian mental health. In C. B. Wilkerson (Ed.), *Ethnic psychiatry* (pp. 143-199). New York: Plenum.

Wall, S. (1993). *Wisdoms daughters: Conversations with women elders of Native America.* New York: HarperCollins.

Walsh, W. B., & Betz, N. E. (1990). *Tests and assessment* (3rd ed.). Englewood Cliffs, NJ: Prentice Hall.

Ward, C. J. (1995, May). *Recent trends in educational attainment and employment among American Indians and Alaska Natives.* Paper presented at the workshop on Demography of American Indians, National Research Council, Washington, DC.

Warren, B. (1984). Introduction. In B. Warren (Ed.), *Using the creative arts in therapy* (pp. 3-8). Cambridge, MA: Brookline.

Wax, M., Wax, R., & Dumont, R. V., Jr. (1989). *Formal education in an American Indian community* (Rev. ed.). (Cooperative Research Project No. 1361. A Study of Social Problems Monograph). Prospect Heights, IL: Waveland Press.

Wechsler, D. (1981). *Manual for the Wechsler Adult Intelligence Scale-Revised.* San Antonio, TX: Psychological Corporation.

Wechsler, D. (1989). *Manual for the Wechsler Preschool and Primary Scale of Intelligence-Revised.* San Antonio, TX: Psychological Corporation.

Wechsler, D. (1991). *Manual for the Wechsler Intelligence Scale for Children-Third Edition.* San Antonio, TX: Psychological Corporation.

Wehrly, B. (1995). *Pathways to multicultural counseling competence: A developmental journey.* Pacific Grove, CA: Brooks/Cole.

Weinbach, R. W., & Kuehner, K. M. (1985). Selecting the provider of continuing education for child welfare agencies. *Child Welfare, 64,* 477-488.

Westermeyer, J. J. (1993). Cross-cultural psychiatric assessment. In A. C. Gaw (Ed.), *Culture, ethnicity, and mental illness* (pp. 125-144). Washington, DC: American Psychiatric Press.

Whitfield, W., McGrath, P., & Coleman, V. (1992, October). *Increasing multicultural sensitivity and awareness.* Paper presented at the annual conference of the National Organization for Human Services Education, Alexandria, VA.

Wiggins, J. D., & Moody, A. H. (1987). Student evaluations of counseling programs: An added dimension. *School Counselor, 34,* 353-361.

Wilson, T. P. (1992). Blood quantum: Native American mixed bloods. In M. P. Root (Ed.), *Racially mixed people in American* (pp. 108-125). Newbury Park, CA: Sage.

Winthrop, R. H. (1991). *Dictionary of concepts in cultural anthropology.* New York: Greenwood.

Wise, F., & Miller, N. B. (1983). The mental health of American Indian children. In G. J. Powell, J. Yamamoto, A. Romero, & A. Morales (Eds.), *The psychosocial development of minority group children* (pp. 344-361). New York: Brunner/Mazel.

Witt, S. H. (1980, Spring). Pressure points in growing up Indian. *Perspectives,* pp. 24-31.

Wolf, F. A. (1991). *The eagle's quest: A physicist's search for truth in the heart of the Shamanic world.* New York: Summit Books.

Wolpe, J., & Lang, P. J. (1964). A fear survey schedule for use in behavior therapy. *Behavior Research and Therapy, 2,* 27-30.

Woodside, M., & McClam, T. (1998). *Generalist case management: A method of human services delivery.* Pacific Grove, CA: Brooks/Cole.

Wright, B. (1977). *Hopi Kachinas: The complete guide to collecting Kachina dolls.* Flagstaff, AZ: Northland Press.

Yee, A. H., Fairchild, H. H., Weizmann, F., & Wyatt, G. E. (1993). Addressing psychologys problems with race. *American Psychologist, 48,* 1132-1140.

Youngman, G., & Sadongei, M. (1983). Counseling the American Indian child. In D. R. Atkinson, G. Morten, & D. W. Sue (Eds.), *Counseling American minorities: A cross-cultural perspective* (pp. 73-76). Dubuque, IA: William C. Brown.

Zitzow, D., & Estes, G. (1981). The heritage consistency continuum in counseling with Native American students. *Proceedings from the Forum on Contemporary American Issues, 3,* 133-142. Los Angeles: University of California-Los Angeles Publication Services.

Zuckerman, M. (1990). Some dubious premises in research and theory on racial differences. *American Psychologist, 45,* 1297-1303.

Zunker, V. G. (1998). *Career counseling: Applied concepts of life planning* (5th ed.). Pacific Grove, CA: Brooks/Cole.

Author Index

Achterberg, J., 26
Ackerson, L., 71
Acosta, A., 14, 69
Adams, J. Q., 13
Ahern, B., 132
Ahuna, C., 30
Aiken, L .R., 42
Alexander, C. M., 105, 116-117, 120
Alipuria, L. L., 92
Allen, B. P., 113
American Indian Education Handbook
    Committee, 3
American Psychological Association, 26
Anastasi, A., 33, 47
Appleton, V. E., 104-105
Arbona, 95
Arnheim, R., 104, 119
Arredondo, P. M., 63
Aronson, D., 103
Ashby, M. R., 79
Ashford, B., 91-92
Assault on the Peaceful, 78
Atkinson, D. R., 2, 8-13, 15-17, 100

Attneave, C. L., 43, 73, 129
Axelson, J. A., 85, 100, 101

Barnes, J., 64
Baron, A., 71
Baruth, L. C., 54, 62, 68, 73, 77
Bass, M., 78
Beard-Williams, D., 16
Beauvis, F., 2, 93, 129
Bellak, L., 42
Bellak, S. S., 42
Bennett, J., 43, 80
Berkhoffer, R., ix, x
Berman, J. S., 70, 127
Bernal, M. E., 14
Bernstein, B., 33
Berry, J. W., 15, 17, 43
Berryhill-Paapke, E., 127
Betz, N. E., 41
Beutler, L. E., 44
Beyard-Tyler, K., 96
Bigfoot, D., 62-63

Blando, J. A., 97
Bloom, J., 70
Bodden, J. L., 92
Bolton, B., 30
Borgen, F. H., 95
Boski, P., 15
Bouchard, T. J., 35
Boucsein, W., 45
Bowman, S. L., 102
Boyer, L. B., 22-23, 42, 118
Broken Nose, M. A., 58, 65, 76-77, 79
Brown, D., 98
Brown, J. E., 64
Brown, S. D., 95, 96
Bruchac, J., 22, 115
Bureau of Indian Affairs, 9, 84
Burke, J. F., 120
Burnam, M. A., 14, 69
Burton, E., 29
Butcher, J. N., 32, 41

Caduto, M. J., 22, 115
Cayleff, S. E., 89
Chan, J. C., 98
Chang, C. F., 89
Choney, S. K., 127, 130
Christensen, C. P., 87
Chung, D. K., xi
Cole, K., 129
Coleman, V. D., 11, 78, 104-106
Colton, H. S., 108
Constantino, G., 46-47
Cook, C. D., 125, 128
Cook, S. W., 47
Corbine, J. L., 64
Cordova, F. A., 33
Cox, O. C., 13
Cramer, S. H., 90, 92, 95, 97
Cronbach, 38
Cuellar, I., 30

Dana, R. H., 21, 23, 30, 37, 41-42, 45-46, 93
Darou, W. G., 56
Davis, G. L., 41
Davis, L., 78

Davis, S. R., 105
Dauphinais, L., 61
Dauphinais, P., 61
Deloria, V., Jr., 68, 69, 83
DeVos, G. A., 42
Dinges, N., 73
Dixon, D. N., 56, 60
Dixon, J. K., 71
Dodd, J. M., 125
Dole, A. A., 13
Domino, G., 14, 69
Dorn, F. J., 91
Downs, M., 91
Draguns, J. G., 12
Drummond, R. J., 101-102, 122
DuBray, W. H., 79
Dufrene, P. M., 78, 104-106
Dumont, R. V., Jr., 4
Dykeman, C., 104-105

Eberhard, D. R., 50
Eder, J., 69
Educational Testing Service, 27-29
Edwards, E. D., 78
Edwards, M. E., 78
Eldredge, N. M., 5
Ellinghaus, A., 91
Ellis, A., 120
Endicott, J., 47
Epperson, D., 95
Erdoes, R., 111
Erikson, E. H., 119
Escobar, J. E., 23
Escobar, J. I., 14, 69
Estes, G., 55
Evans, K. M., 105
Exner, J. E., 42
Eysenck, H. J., 47
Eysenck, S. B. S., 47

Fagan, T. K., 135
Fairchild, H. H., 13
Feagin, J. R., 14
Fenton, W. N., 112, 114
Fernandez, M., 89

Ferrara, N., 107, 116
Fischer, J. M., 34, 125, 134
Flaherty, J. H., 23
Fleming, C. M., 2, 22, 31, 52, 54, 56, 72, 75-76, 78, 82, 104
Fleshman, B., 120
Ford, R., 51
France, G., 50
French, L. A., 42, 47
Fryrear, J. L., 120
Fukuyama, M., 58
Fulcher, R., 21
Fuller, G. B., 40
Fuqua, D., 95

Gade, F., 95
Gardner, J., 115
Garrett, J. T., 9, 51, 60, 61, 62, 66, 70, 72, 73, 106, 114, 115, 118
Garrett, M. T., 30, 69
Garrett, M. W., 9, 51, 60, 61, 62, 66, 70, 72, 73, 106, 114, 115, 118
Gibbs, J. T., 99
Gilchrist, L. D., 79
Gilmore, M. R., 112
Giordano, J., 74, 79
Giordano, M. A., 74
Gladding, S. T., 105, 116, 119-120
Goldstein, L. S., 34
Good, B. J., 65
Good, M. J. D. V., 65
Good Tracks, J. G., 61
Goodluck, C. T., 23-24
Gordon, M. M., 15
Gough, H. G., 41
Graff Low, K., 2-3, 63
Graham, J. R., 41
Grant, S. K., 17
Graves, T., 15
Gronlund, N. E., 29
Gross, J., 85
Gutkin, T. B., 128
Gysbers, N. C., 95, 97

Haase, R. F., 92
Hagen, E. P., 38
Hahn, B. C., 89
Halevy-Martin, 82
Hall, R. L., 65
Hambleton, R. K., 46
Hammerschlag, C. A., 66, 81, 106-107, 114, 116-117
Hammond, K., 95
Hannon, J. W., 17
Hansen, J. I. C., 95
Haring, M. J., 96
Harjo, J., 115
Harjo, S. S., 22
Harper, F. D., 5
Harras, A., 52
Harrington, M. R., 113
Harris, L. C., 30
Haviland, M. G., 95
Hayne, B., 65
Heath, A., 58
Heinrich, R. K., 64, 68, 76, 98
Helms, J. E., 13, 29
Hemley-Van der Velden, E., 82
Heppner, M. J., 95
Hernandez, T. J., 102
Herr, E. L., 90, 92, 95, 97
Herring, R. D., xi, 2, 4, 8-9, 12, 43-44, 49-51, 55, 60, 63, 68-72, 75, 84, 86-88, 90-94, 101, 107, 116, 118-119, 124, 129, 134
Highwater, J., 114
Hill, A., 71
Hill, M. J., 123
Hines, A. M., 99
Hispanic Research Center, 91
Ho, M. K., 14, 37, 90
Hodgkinson, H. L., 8
Hoffman, R. G., 41
Hoffmann, T., 30
Holtzman, W. H., 47
Hornblower, M., 16
Horns-Marsh, V., 20
Hough, R. L., 69
Huang, L. N., 90
Hughes, C. C., 24

Hultkrantz, A., 25
Hurlburt, G., 95

Ibrahim, F. A., 26, 43, 58
Indian Fellowship Program, 3
Indian Health Services, 70-71
Ivey, A. E., 43
Ivey, M. B., 43

Jasso, R., 30
Jeffers, S., 80
Jenkins, J. O., 46
Jepsen, D. A., 98
Johnson, D., 57
Johnson, J., 91
Johnson, M. J., 84
Johnson, M. E., 17, 69
Johnson, S. D., 11, 12, 14
Johnson-Powell, G., 49
Johnston, J. A., 95
Jones, E. E., 86, 89, 97
Joseph-Fox, Y. K., 10
Josephy, A. M., 7
Josselson, R., 46
Jumper-Thurman, P., 2
June, L. N., 92

Kallen, H. M., 16
Kamphaus, R.W., 47
Kaplan, B., 57
Katz, J. H., 88, 97
Katz, P., 56
Kaufman, A. S., 39
Kaufman, J. S., 10
Kaufman, N. L., 47
Kaufman, S., 47
Keepers, G., 70
Kerig, P. K., 89
Khoo, G., 30
Kidwell, C. S., 132
Kim, U., 15, 97
Kincade, E. A., 105
Kivlahan, D. R., 78

Klineberg, O., 33
Kluckhohn, C., 79
Koehn, U., 89
Krashen, S., 17
Kreiner, G., 91-92
Krumboltz, J. D., 97
Krupnick, J. L., 89
Kuehner, K. M., 52
Kugler, J. F., 20-21, 33, 39, 41-42

LaDue, R., 37
LaFromboise, T. D., 2-3, 9-10, 50-52, 56,
    60, 62-64, 69-70, 77-79, 82, 100, 124,
    127, 131
Lame Deer, 111
Lang, P. J., 45
Lashley, K. H., 17, 69
Lauver, P. J., 97
Lawson, A. W., 93
Lawson, G. W., 93
Lazarus, A. A., 44
Lazarus, P., 44, 56
Lee, C. C., 44, 96
Leighton, D. C., 79
Lent, R. W., 95-96
Lessner, J., 115
Leung, S. A., 98
Lewis, J., 46-47
Lieberman, L., 13
Lieblich, A., 46
Linn, R. L., 29
Linton, R. W., 11
Littlefield, A., 13
Littrell, J. M., 55
Littrell, M. A., 55
Liu, W. T., 89
Lochner, B. T., 94
Locust, C. L., 57, 64, 69, 73
Lofgren, D., 106
Lonner, W. J., 26, 43
Lowe, P. A., 21, 32
Lum, D., 78
Lyon, W. S., 25-26, 111-113

Mackey, D., 50

Mahoney, F. E., 98

Mails, T. E., 108

Malgady, R. G., 46

Malone, T. E., 93

Maloney, S., 80

Manaster, G. J., 98

Manning, M. L., 54, 62, 68, 73, 77

Manson, S. M., 31, 42, 64, 70-71, 73, 78, 100

Marsh, F. E., 20

Marshall, C. A., 125, 128

Martin, J., 129

Martin, W. E., 98

Maruyama, M., 88

Maxwell, J. A., 5, 6

McClam, T., 50

McCloud, J., 81

McFee, M., 54

McGoldrick, M., 79

McGrath, P., 11

McLenore, S. D., 15

McLeod, J., 47, 97

McShane, D. A., 35, 123

Medicine, B., 73, 129

Meggert, S., 118

Meier, S. T., 105

Mercer, J., 33

Metcalf, A., 57

Middleton-Moz, J., 82

Miller, N. B., 22, 100

Minor, C. W., 98

Miramontez, A., 79

Mitchell-Kernan, C., 52

Mohatt, G. V., 9

Moody, A. H., 98

Moran, J. R., 31

Morgan, J., 134

Morris, W., 13

Morrow, C. A., 88-90, 94

Morten, G., 8-9, 100

Mulhern, B., 51

Murphy, R., 94

Murray, H. A., 42

Mussell, K., 117

Myers, H. F., 89

Nagel, J., 14

Nason, J. D., 131-132

National Geographic Society, 109

Neisser, U., 35

Nelight, G., 70-71

Nelson, J. R., 125

Neukrug, E., 17-18

O'Brien, S., 22, 24, 37

O'Connell, J. C., 134

Oetting, E. R., 93

Okun, B. F., 81

Olmedo, E. L., 17, 21

Opler, M. E., 111, 116

Ostwald, S. W., 125

Ozer, E., 71

Pancheri, P., 32

Paniagua, F. A., 21, 23-25, 30-31, 37, 45

Parham, T. A., 13

Parker, A. C., 113

Patton, W., 47, 95

Pedersen, P. B., 57-58, 96-97

Peregoy, J. J., 4, 9, 61-62, 64, 70, 83

Peterson, G. W., 84-87

Pewewardy, C., 18

Phinney, J. S., 92, 94

Plas, J. M., 35

Polacca, M., 80

Porter, J., 34

Pringle, G. D., 92

Quintero, G. A., 71, 81

Radloff, L. S., 47

Ramsey, G. A., 46

Reardon, R. C., 84

Red Horse, J., 114

Reed, C. F., 92

Rehab Brief, 51

Reikowski, D. J., 97
Reinolds, C., 89
Reschly, D., 39
Reyhner, J., 69
Reynolds, C. R., 21, 23, 46, 128, 135
Reynolds, L. T., 13
Rice, F. P., 86, 91
Richards, G. E., 64
Richardson, E. H., 56-57, 63, 76
Richmond, L. J., 91
Ritchie, M. R., 17
Rivers, R. Y., 88-90, 94
Robbins, R. R., 127
Roberts, S., 72
Rogers, M. R., 33, 34
Rogler, L. H., 46
Rohner, R. P., 89
Rorschach, H., 42
Rotter, J., 86
Rowe, W., 61, 63
Rudolph, L. B., 54
Rueveni, U., 82
Ruhf, L., 82
Rushton, J. P., 13
Russo, N. F., 21
Ryan, C. W., 101-102
Rye, D. A., 17

Sabers, D., 39
Sadongei, M., 62
Saenz, A. L., 21, 32
Safady, R., 98
Sage, G. P., 67, 69, 73
Sampson, J. P., Jr., 84
Samuda, R. J., 21, 33-35
Sanders, D., 62
Saravanabhavan, R. C., 125, 128
Sattler, J. M., 38-39
Schaefer, R. T., 13-14
Schafer, C., 4
Schinke, S., 129
Schoenfeld, P., 82
Seymour-Smith, C., 3
Shore, J., 70-71
Silk-Walker, P., 31, 37

Simek-Morgan, L., 43
Simmons, B. J., 27
Simons, R. C., 24
Skinner, B. F., 112
Slaney, R. B., 92
Smolkin, L. B., 62
Snipp, C. M., 8
Sohi, B. K., 70, 127
Somervell, P., 31
Sorenson, G. P., 34
Speck, J. L., 82
Speck, R. V., 82
Spitzer, R. L., 47
Stapp, J., 21
Steward, R. J., 96
Stiggins, R., 27
Stone, W. O., 85
Stubben, J., 129
Sue, D., 8, 9, 72, 98
Sue, D. W., 72, 86, 98, 100
Suina, J. H., 62
Suinn, R. M., 30
Summer, L., 105
Super, D. E., 95
Sussman, L., 105, 116-117, 120
Sutton, C. T., 76-77
Suzuki, L. A., 20-21, 33, 39, 41-42, 79
Swaim, R. C., 93
Swartz, J. L., 84

Tafoya, T., 54
Talmon, M., 77
Telles, C. A., 14, 69
Thomas, K. R., 64
Thomason, T. C., 60, 62, 77, 129
Thompson, C. E., 2, 17
Thompson, C. L., 54
Thompson, J. W., 31, 37
Thorndike, R. L., 38
Thurman, P. J., 93
Tierney, W. G., 132
Trimble, J. E., 2, 4, 8-9, 17, 22, 50, 52, 54,
    56, 63, 70, 73, 75-76, 100, 124
Tucker, M. B., 52
Turbak, G., 16

Tuval-Mashiach, R., 46

U. S. Bureau of the Census, 8-10, 51, 72, 86, 89, 91, 127
U.S. Congress, 94
U.S. Department of Commerce, 49
U.S. Department of Education, 85
U.S. Department of Health and Human Services, 49, 70
U.S. Department of Justice, 94

Valle, R., 51
Vance, H. B., 33-37, 39-40, 134

Walker, R. D., 31, 37, 78
Walker, S. S., 84, 101
Wall, S., 136
Walsh, W. B., 41
Ward, C. J., 70
Warren, B., 120
Wax, M., 4
Wax, R., 4
Wayman, J., 93
Wechsler, D., 39
Wehrly, B., 15-16, 58
Weinbach, R. W., 52

Weizmann, F., 13
Westermeyer, J. J., 23, 25
Whitfield, W., 11
Wiggins, J. D., 98
Williams, C. L., 41
Wilson, T. P., 14
Winer, J. L., 92
Winthrop, R. H., 3
Wise, F., 22
Wise, P. S., 135
Witt, S. H., 69
Wolf, F. A., 26
Wolpe, J., 45
Woodside, M., 50
Wright, B., 108
Wyatt, G. E., 113

Yamamoto, J., 49
Yee, A. H., 13, 90
Youngman, G., 62
Yu, E. S. H., 89

Zilber, T., 46
Zitow, D., 55
Zuckerman, M., 12-13
Zunker, V. G., 84, 102

Subject Index

Abuse, 71, 79

Acculturation Rating Scale for Mexican Americans, 30

Adolescents, 59, 60, 62

Aging, 128

Ahtena, 3

Alaska, 9, 133

Alaska population, 3

Alcohol, 118

Alcoholism, 9, 37, 70, 93

Aleuts, 2, 3, 6, 7

Algonquian Indians, 5

American Indian Depression Schedule, 70

American Indian Religious Freedom Act of 1978, 69

American Psychological Association's Board of Ethnic Minority Affairs, 26

Anxiety disorders, 131

Apaches, 118

Arawak, 2

Arizona, 8, 30

Arkansas, 34

Assessment, 20, 27, 30, 32, 39, 44-45, 46, 47, 48, 123, 133, 134, 135

achievement testing, 29

and diagnosis, 23

and treatment, 23

authentic, 27, 28, 29

bias, 21, 23, 31, 35, 45, 46, 47

complexities of, 20

conducted in the child's native language, 35

counseling assessments, 21

cross-cultural, 46

culturally appropriate norms, 23

culture-free tests, 23

diverse techniques, 43

ethnic appropriate, 27

for linguistically diverse children, 35

intellectual, 35, 36, 48, 122, 135

legal influences and changes, 34

model, 45

multidisciplinary, 35

multiple intelligences, 27

objectives, 20

performance, 27, 28, 29

personality, 35, 41, 48, 122, 135

polemic debate, 21

portfolio, 29

problems, 47
procedure, 32
process, 20
qualitative information, 20
quantitative information, 20
recommended tests, 47
selected instruments, 21
synergetic, 43, 46
systemic group differences, 21
translation of tests, 23
Assimilation:
cultural, 15-16
structural, 15
Assiniboin, 111
Association of Aboriginal Post-Secondary
Institutions, 132
Athabascan linguistic group, 3
Attneave, Carolyn, 82
Attrition, 34-35, 48
Average income, 10
"BASIC-ID" paradigm, 45
Bateson, Mary Catherine, x
Behavior, 55, 63
Bender-Gestalt, 135
Bicultural, 55, 56
Biethnic youth, 99
Bighorn, Tiana, 80
Bilingualism:
education, 16
effects on intelligence test performance, 33
Bureau of Indian Affairs, 3, 60, 123

California, 8
California Personality Inventory, 41
Canada, 115
Career development program, 86
Catawba, 73
Cherokee, 106, 114
Cherokee Indian Hospital, 61
Cherokee Nation, 8, 48
Cheyenne, 116
Chippewa, 73
Chiricahua Apache, 22
Circle of Life, 114
Clowns, 108-111

College, 84
Contemporary Alaska Natives, 7
Contemporary Native American Indian, 9
"Contract with America," 123
Council of Energy Resource Tribes, 83
Counseling, 49-83
adults, 68-83
assessments, 21
characteristics, 54, 60
children, 49-67
cultural validity, 31
presenting problems for Native adolescents, 59
presenting problems for Native children, 59
synergetic, 55, 58, 63
Creative art mediums, 104-105
blankets, 106
clown motifs, 107
dolls, 107
masks, 107, 112-114
pottery, 106
sandpainting, 114
storytelling, 114, 115
Cree, 115, 116
Crow, 116
Cultural-bound syndromes, 24
Cultural-related syndromes, 24
ataque de nervios, 25
ghost sickness, 24, 25, 48
mal puesto, 25
wacinko, 24
wind/cold, 25
Culture, 11-12, 14, 18, 50, 51, 54, 55, 56,
58, 62-66, 69, 72-84, 87
culturally deprived, 12
culturally disadvantaged, 12

Dakota Sioux Indians, 33, 111
Degree of culturation, 14-18
acculturation, 14-15, 16-17, 30, 126, 129,
130
assimilation, 15-16, 129
enculturation, 14-15
from fully traditional to fully acculturated, 14

Delinquency, 10
Demographics on the development of Native peoples, 18
Department of Education, 3
Depression, 37, 70, 107
Diagnostic instruments, 131
Differences within Native cultures, 11
Disadvantages, 88-103
Distance learning, 133
Diversity, 8, 9
Draw-A-Person, 135
Dreams, 116
Dropout rates, 10
Drugs, 71, 93

EC-ER, 86
EC-IR, 86
Education, 70
Educational attainment, 10
Emic, 11
Employment, 84-103
Eskimo, 3, 4, 5
Ethnicity, 14, 18, 11
    ethnic group, 14, 49
    ethnic identity, 30, 92
    ethnic stereotypes, 3
    nationality or cultural characteristics of, 14
    physical characteristics of, 14
    within racial categories, 14
Etic, 11-12, 130
Exclusion, 125
Eyak, 3

Family therapy, 79
Fetishes, 106
Four ages of humans, 106

Games, 116
Gottfredson's concept, 95
Great Spirit, 108
Group therapy, 77, 78

History, 68, 79, 72, 75
Hopi, 40, 108-109, 110
Hunkpapa, 2, 48

IC-ER, 86
IC-IR, 86
Idioemic perspective, 12
Inclusion, 125
Indian Health Service, 31, 65, 70, 72, 123
Indian Law Center at the University of New Mexico, 3
Indigenous peoples, 2, 5, 16
Individuals with disabilities, 128
Infant mortality, 10
Ingallik, 3
International Test Commission, 46
Intertribal and interethnic marriages, 8
Inuits, 2, 3, 4, 5, 6, 48, 116
Iroquois, 113

Jacob's family, 80
Jennes, Diamond, 6

Kachinas, 108-110
Kaufman Assessment Battery for Children, 36, 38, 47
Koyukon, 3

Lakota, 2, 57, 111
Lame Deer, John Fire, 112
"Legalistic genetics," 4
Lester, David, 83
Lifestyle, 52
Limited-English-proficient, 32-33, 38, 40
Lummie, 48

Mandalas, 105
Mandan-Hidasta, 7
Marriages, 52, 55, 56
    intermarriages, 52
    mixed ancestry, 52, 55, 56
Medicine wheels, 105, 106
Medicine Man, 26
    See also Shaman

Menominee, 116
Mental disorders, 31
Mental illness, 10, 52, 94
Mental Processing Composite, 36
Mescalero Apache, 22
Metropolitan Achievement Test, 39
Miller's strategies, 100
Minnesota Multiphasic Personality Inventory, 41
Minnesota-Percepto-Diagnostic Test-Revised, 40
Misinformation and myths, 4
Mohawks, 73

"Nation," 3
Nation affiliation, 2
Native adults, 68-83
Native American Acculturation Scale, 30
Native American Church, 80, 81
Native American Indian Child Welfare Act, 23, 24
Native Center for American Indian and Alaska Native Mental Health, 31
Native groups, 60
Native societies today, 3
Native women, 70, 71, 78, 127
Native youth, 49-67
Navajo, 8, 38, 40, 105, 106, 110, 114
Network therapy, 82
New Mexico, 30

Office of Indian Education, 123
Oglala Sioux, 10
Oklahoma, 8
Onondaga, 113
Oral history, 47
    storytelling, 47
Oral literature, 22
    folklore, 22
Outward Bound Schools, 64

Papagos, 39, 40
Plains-Cree, 111
Plains-Ojibwa, 111

Polar Eskimos, 4
Political forces, 75
Ponca, 111
Population, 8, 9, 31, 124, 125, 126, 129, 130, 136
Positive self-concept, 4
Post-traumatic stress disorder, 131
Poverty, 10, 88
Power differentials, 18
    discrimination, 19
    position in the tribal hierarchy, 18
    prejudice, 19
Proactive counseling interventions, 1
Projective techniques, 42
Psychosocial obstacles, 92
Public Law 280, 24
Pueblo, 107

Q-sorts, 42

Race, 11, 12, 13, 14, 18, 19
    as a biological concept, 13
    biological and social components of, 13
    biological and social perspective of, 13
    ethnic groups within racial categories, 14
    physical or biological characteristics of, 12
    stereotypes of, 14
Racism, 18, 88
Relationships, 49-83
    counselors and counselees, 49-83
    marriage, 52, 69
Reservations, 51, 52, 69, 70, 83, 84, 86, 96
Rorschach, 42
Rosebud Personal Opinion Survey, 30

School psychology, 128
Schools, 50, 52, 66, 98
Seneca, 113
Shaman, 6, 25, 54, 111, 112, 113
    Anquakoq, 25
    medicine man, 26
    Native ethnobotany, 25
    Native healing practices, 25
    Native religious beliefs, 25
    professional study of, 26

shamanic treatments, 26
state of consciousness, 26
Sioux, 4, 116
Sioux Nation, 2, 11, 14
Social class, 17, 18
Sociocultural diversity, 17
Standard English, 32, 33, 40, 48
Standardized test scores, 34
Stanford Achievement Test, 34
Stanford-Binet Intelligence Scale-Fourth
    Edition, 38
Stereotypes, 14, 91, 126
Suicide, 37
Suicide rates, 10
Suinn-Lew Asian Self-Identity Acculturation
    Scale, 30
Sun Dance, 117
Synergetic counseling, 120
System of Multicultural Pluralistic Intelli-
    gence Assessment, 46

Tanaina, 3
Tanana, 3
Tell-Me-A-Story Test, 46, 47
Terminal liver cirrhosis, 10
Thematic Apperception Test, 42
Theories, 86
Toyons, 6
Tradition, 52, 55, 60, 61, 64, 68, 69, 72, 73
    beliefs, 52, 60, 61, 62, 68, 69
    helpers, 54, 60, 61, 62, 64, 65, 66, 78, 82
    values, 52, 61, 69

Training:
    ethnic-appropriate, 125
    of mental health counselors and thera-
        pists, 124
    programs, 124-125
"Tribe," 3, 63, 68, 69, 71, 79

Unemployment, 10
U.S. citizenship, 69

Violence, 37
Vision quest, 116
Vocational rehabilitation services, 125, 134

Washington, 33
Weschler Adult Intelligence Scale-Revised, 39
Weschler Intelligence Scale for Children-III,
    39, 40
Weschler Primary Preschool Scale of
    Intelligence-Revised, 39, 40
Winnebago, 116
Work, 84
Worldview, 55, 58, 75
Wyoming, 133

Yakima reservation, 33

Zuni, 106

About the Author

Roger D. Herring, Ed.D., NCC, NCSC, is Professor of Counselor Education at the University of Arkansas–Little Rock. His background includes 20 years of experience in public school teaching, administration, and counseling. He has received numerous awards for his research, including the 1999 American Counseling Association's Research Award. He has authored more than 50 articles and 3 texts, which emphasize multicultural counseling efforts. He is a leader in the field of the Synergetic Model of Counseling.